T5-DIH-529

FLORIDA STATE
UNIVERSITY LIBRARIES

JUN   4 1997

TALLAHASSEE, FLORIDA

Lessons from the Recession

SUNY Series in International Management

Andrezj Kozminski, Patricia Sanders,
and Sarah Sanderson King, editors

Lessons from the Recession

A Management and Communication Perspective

edited by

Sarah Sanderson King
and
Donald P. Cushman

STATE UNIVERSITY OF NEW YORK PRESS

HD
70
U5
L46
1997

Published by
State University of New York Press, Albany

© 1997 State University of New York

All rights reserved

Printed in the United States of America

No part of this book may be used or reproduced in any manner whatsoever
without written permission. No part of this book may be stored in a retrieval
system or transmitted in any form or by any means including electronic,
electrostatic, magnetic tape, mechanical, photocopying, recording, or
otherwise without the prior permission in writing of the publisher.

For information, address the State University of New York Press,
State University Plaza, Albany, NY 12246

Production by Marilyn Semerad
Marketing by Dana Yanulavich

Library of Congress Cataloging-in-Publication Data

Lessons from the recession : a management and communication
    perspective / edited by Sarah Sanderson King and Donald P. Cushman.
        p.   cm. — (SUNY series in international management)
    Includes bibliographical references and index.
    ISBN 0-7914-3291-2 (hc : alk. paper). — ISBN 0-7914-3292-0 (pbk.
: alk. paper)
    1. Management—United States.   2. United States—Economic
policy—1981-1993.   3. Recessions—United States.   4. Management-
-Europe.   5. Europe—Economic policy.   6. Recessions—United States.
7. Management—Asia.   8. Asia—Economic policy.   9. Recessions-
-Asia.   I. King, Sarah Sanderson, 1932-   .   I. Cushman, Donald P.
III. Series.
HD70.U5L46   1997
658—dc21   96-48281
                                                                   CIP

10 9 8 7 6 5 4 3 2 1

To Dr. Vittorio Torrisi, an outstanding communicator, consummate father, wise leader, global businessman, fellow world traveler, and quintessential friend for his vision and actions toward improving management communication in the world.

Contents

Preface

We had been invited by IRP-Immuno Pharmacology Research, a small Italian in vitro diagnostic firm, to hold our conference of world renowned scholars and researchers in Sicily, Italy. Through the efforts of Dr. Vittorio Torrisi, president, and Giuseppe Raimondi, vice president, we were hosted by government, civic, small and large business groups for three days of hospitality and graciousness. Twenty scholars and practitioners from the United States, Hong Kong, Australia, England, Poland, and the People's Republic of China participated.

It was the ideal setting for thinking and discussing theoretical and practical problems of "Communication and Management: Lessons from the Recession," the focus of this book. Sicily, Italy, is an absolutely gorgeous place which combines the ruggedness of the black lava cliffs of Hawaii, the vivid lushness of the foliage of the tropics and of colder climes, and the beauty of the blue-green waters which surround it.

꿹꿺

We want to thank the following for helping to make the 1995 conference a memorable occasion:

Katja, Nicco, Giovanni, and Vittorio Torrisi, the family who took us into their hearts and home and daily offered us warmth, care, and thoughtfulness in ways too numerous to mention

Giuseppe Raimondi whose organizational skills provided all of us not only with an excellent conference difficult for any other group to surpass but also with a view of another part of the world

and our other patrons—

Presidente della Regione Siciliana, On, Matteo Graziano Palazzo d'Orleans, Piazza Indipendenza, Palmero, Italy

Signor Sindaco della Citta' di Catania, Dott. Enzo Bianco Piazza
Duomo, Catania, Italy

Direttore Generale Banca Agricola Popolare di Ragusa, Dott.
Giovanni Cartia
via Matteotti, 84, Ragusa, Italy

Associazione dei Giovani Industrali della Provincia di Catanaia,
Ing. Giuseppe Brancatelli
viale Vittorio Veneto, 109, Catania, Italy

DONALD P. CUSHMAN
SARAH SANDERSON KING

June 31, 1996

1

Introduction: What Lessons Can Be Learned from Recession?

Sarah S. King and Donald P. Cushman

Technically, whenever the economy has two consecutive quarters or six months of negative growth in GNP/GDP, economists classify such an economic downturn as a recession. January through June 1991 met this criteria in the United States. Both Europe (1992–1993) and Asia (1993–1995) also experienced such a downturn. Recessions normally motivate both private corporations and governments to undertake unusual steps to halt the economic decline and to protect their assets from continued deterioration. It is significant that some recessions are only local, involving a single government's economy; others are regional, involving a group of economies; while still others may be global, thus affecting all the major economies of the world. Most recent recessions have been regional, but may shift slowly around the world, affecting only one region at a time. Such was the case from 1991 to 1995.

The major lessons learned from recession in each region of the world—the Americas, Europe, and Asia—have been very different. *First,* in the United States firms have restructured in order to significantly lower their break-even points. This has been accomplished by (a) streamlining productive efficiency, (b) continuous cuts in supplier costs, and (c) downsizing a firm's workforce and benefits while increasing quality and productivity. *Second,* in the European community it has brought into focus the relationships between high production costs, national distribution and sales restrictions, and national and corporate employer benefit programs. These forces have led to the shifting of production offshore to countries outside the European Community in order to lower production and wage costs. By early 1996 European manufacturers, including Mercedes Benz, BMW, Asea Brown and Boveri, Siemens, and so on, had moved

1

a portion of their production to the United States or to the former Eastern bloc countries to capitalize on lower production and wage costs. German unemployment, which is usually relatively stable, went from 5 to 11 percent. Economists were predicting that Europe was entering a new recession. *Third,* in Japan the rise in the yen relative to other world currencies and recession has led to (a) shifting production offshore to low-cost production areas such as the Americas, Asia, and Europe; (b) the closing of plants and the downsizing of the workforce and a reduction in *Keiratsu* strength; and (c) the government investing 500 million yen in jumpstarting the economy. By early 1996 the Japanese coalition government had lost the confidence of the people, its minister of economy was forced to resign, Japan's banking system was in deep trouble, and unemployment had doubled. The net result of all of this is that Japan also appears to be entering a new recession.

What has become increasingly apparent to the various regions of the world is that recessions are no longer the result of economic forces within the markets that can be influenced by the region itself. Instead, if for any reason your region is not globally competitive, that alone can trigger a recession within the region while the areas of the world which are globally competitive continue to grow at a very rapid rate and may be experiencing a period of long, rapid expansion.

This book is about how several corporations and governments responded to recession and the lessons they have learned. We have focused our attention on the management and communication lessons learned from these experiences. Some lessons were new, and some were old, suggesting that recessions were met both with continuous and with discontinuous strategies for change. Some worked well in mediating the effects of recessions, and some did not work at all, while still others appeared to work well. The lessons learned here are many, varied, and specific both for private and for public sector managers.

Lessons from America is the first section of the book which includes five essays, each with an important and unique insight into the management and communication process. In **chapter two, Lessons in Mass Media Depiction of Economic Conditions during a Recession, Ted J. Smith III and S. Robert Lichter** provide an in-depth analysis of how ABC, NBC, and CBS cover the issues involved in economic recession. In their analysis, Smith and Lichter suggest that the media systematically distort the real events involved in recession by making them seem longer, deeper, and more disastrous than they are. The authors then trace the effects of these distortions on political elections, attempts to mount an economic recovery, and resultant public pessimism. The lessons from recession provided by this analysis are clear and significant in their negative effect on the nations, the leaders, and economic recovery.

In **chapter three, Lessons from Benchmarking Downsizing in IBM, Sarah S. King and Donald P. Cushman** explore IBM's attempt to locate critical success factors for benchmarking organizational downsizing and their effective use in cutting overhead during and immediately after a recession. Much to the authors' surprise, the critical success factors were located and quite systematically employed, and yet problems remained due to specific failures in IBM's overall strategy for responding to recession. This inquiry raises some serious issues regarding the use of benchmarking in a single domain without maintaining high performance standards in other areas. The case study is stimulating and the implications powerful for all organizations using benchmarking, particularly in times of recession.

Chapter four, Lessons from Leading Organizational Turnaround at IBM by Cushman and King, explores the problem of leadership aimed at turning a firm such as IBM around in times of recession and recovery from recession. The leadership strategies of Lou Gerstner, aimed at turning IBM around during recession, all failed. Yet the firm's recovery from recession in an area Gerstner was attempting to downsize and render less significant to the overall business was so profitable that it made IBM appear to have recovered. However, the circumstances which led to this recovery in one division appear not to be repeatable, leaving IBM susceptible to large losses in another major downturn. The lessons involved in this case study are powerful and at times disquieting.

Chapter five, Lessons in Governmental Budgeting during Recession in the United States, by Susanne Morris, explores various governmental techniques for dealing with a tax shortfall in meeting budget demands during a recession. Since governments at all levels have become creative in resolving this issue, it is instructive to look at the long- and short-range effects of various solutions to this problem. Raising taxes, short-term borrowing, topping the funds, using capital outlays, substitution, enlarging time frames, paper adjustments, and spending ceilings are all evaluated. The political, economic, and social consequences of these decisions are discussed in this creative assessment of governmental budgeting techniques for responding to recession.

In **chapter six, Lessons from Entirement: Strategies and Skills for Self-Managed, Lifelong Development, Randall Harrison** addresses the issue of "entirement" and the strategies and skills for self-managed, lifelong development of managers and workers. A framework is provided to guide the development of individuals as creative learning and self-motivated actors.

Lessons from Europe is a section of the book containing four essays with unique and important insights. **Chapter seven, Lessons from Rethinking High-Speed Management: Successful Adaptation of American Theory to an European Company, by Giuseppe Raimondi,** is a case study of an application of the theories of high-speed management to the transformation of an in vitro diagnostic firm—Immuno Pharmacology Research, S.P.A. (IPR). Raimondi discusses the ways in which the integration, coordination, and control tools of high-speed management were utilized by a small Italian firm during the recession to predict and take advantage of the recession's effects rather than have them take advantage of the organization. He discusses the ways in which the small organization can utilize the HSM tools to advantage and contrasts their use in a small firm with that found in the large organizations such as multinationals. The individual worker is described by the author as the "basic functional cell" around whom the focus of change in a small firm must take place. The utilization of integration and coordination through teamwork and continuous improvement as the working operandi of every single individual within the organization's network is what produces the change or transformation, thus furthering the success of the firm.

In **chapter eight, Lessons in Communicating Change in Transition: Some Dilemmas and Strategic Choices, Artur Czynczyk, Robert MacDougall, and Krzysztof Obloj** explore how a multinational firm's training center can serve as a catalyst for organizational change. They look at the emergence of strategies designed to cope with the newly competitive, continuously changing economic environment which continues to develop in Poland after the last vestiges of Communist rule were finally dissolved in 1989. The first section includes a very brief discussion of the fall of communism, the rapid transformation into a market economy/democratic state, a recession which might be conceived of as partially "induced," and the openness which subsequently developed with respect to foreign investors. The second section deals with organizational communication dynamics and examines the agents of change, the shift to market economy principles and the effect these have on corporate culture. The chapter concludes with a discussion of the ways in which a management development center, established by a large multinational company in Poland, has developed and has implemented strategies which aim for clearly definable, consensually ascertainable ends for the individual as well as for the organization.

In **chapter nine, Lessons from Recession in Central and Eastern Europe, Andrzej K. Kozminski** counters the general public belief that former Socialist countries cannot teach the world important lessons regarding management success. He traces the fight for survival, functional restructuring, process restructuring, and continuous improvement programs and their effects on some of the best run small and midsized firms in the world. He concludes by listing four lessons from recession which emerged from this long, involved transition from socialism to capitalism during a recession. These are an ambition to succeed, the effective use of limited human resources, extreme caution in the use of credit and financial leverage, and the power of personal ownership as more important than more privatization through noninvolved stockholders buying a firm's stock.

In **chapter ten, Lessons in How Recession Taught Organizations to Communicate, Bill Quirke** argues that the major communication, management, and leadership skills employed by firms are not suited to dealing with problems during a recession. He then demonstrates how the demands of a recession require rapid responses in crisis situations where organizational problems fragment the normal management relationship. This new recession environment needs to be explored carefully and new rules developed to confront the issues encountered.

Lessons from Asia, the third section of our book, contains four essays with focused insights from the fastest growing region of the world. In **chapter eleven, Lessons from Japanese Multinationals and Japan's Government, Donald Cushman and Sarah S. King** argue that Japan's first recession in over forty years has called into question the effectiveness of the Japanese management system and the Japanese government's economic policies. The high value of the yen, the use of Japan as a platform for exporting private-sector goods to the rest of the world, lifelong employment, and the Japanese government's industrial policy are all being called into question. This chapter outlines Japan's new answers to these questions.

Chapter twelve, Lessons in Marketing Strategies during Recession from High-Speed Management to Sun Tzu's *Art of War*, by Ernest F. Martin, Jr., follows upon the themes of chapter twelve by exploring how marketing rules change in times of recession. The author argues that high-speed management tools and Sun Tzu's *Art of War* provide the broad outline of a constructive response to this problem. High-speed management upgrades information and communication systems to improve environmental scanning, speed-to-market, corporate benchmarking, value-chain analysis, transformational leadership, corporate climate, and teamwork in responding to rapid change. He then focuses on deception in dealing with competitors, protecting the security of plans, employing a flexible approach, speed, and timing in implementation as the essence of war. Examples are then provided of the combination of high-speed management and the principles of war in resolving marketing problems during recession.

In **chapter thirteen, Lessons in Managing Government Competitiveness, Ron Cullen** explores the central issues which governments confront in managing a nation, state, or local competitiveness during recession. Cullen argues that four global trends are reshaping governmental competitiveness. These include globalization of economies and of knowledge regarding government's effectiveness in responding to economic issues; the role governments play in private sector competitiveness; the role governments play in technology diffusion; and, finally, how governments handle diversity and its impact upon a nation's, state's, or local government's economic performance. These new challenges to government have led to the benchmarking of national competitiveness, the emergence of performance management in the public sector, and the need of governments to manage "comfort zones" between diverse constituencies or to suffer gridlock. A series of models are then put forward to guide governmental strategy and processes in responding to the demands of greater competitiveness during recession. The first model demonstrates how centrally planned and democratic governments can respond effectively to the demand for greater global competitiveness. The second model indicates how to manage comfort zones in diverse cultures to prevent governmental gridlock. The third model indicates how implementation corrections can be made during change. This insightful paper sketches the broad outline for a new theory of government responsiveness to shifting global economic forces.

In **chapter fourteen, Lessons in Government Communication: Strategies of Best Practices in Australia, Robyn Johnston** explores the lessons governments can learn from benchmarking an organization's best practices in successful handling of recession. Here the best-practices benchmarking program of the Australian government is investigated in the area of labor-management relations. The demonstration program was aimed at reducing labor unrest in

Australia while increasing labor productivity. The results are dramatic. Ten best practices are identified and studied in over 40 organizations. Outcomes are assessed and problems identified. Training programs, benchmarking, and enterprise agreements top the list of most commonly used programs and their effects on increased competitiveness. Finally, the communication problems are explored and appropriate solutions to each problem are identified. This paper is a landmark study in labor-management solutions to competitiveness issues during recession.

This then is the road map of our book **Lessons from Recession: A Management and Communication Perspective.** Enjoy the views expressed in each chapter.

Section One

Lessons from America

2

Lessons in Mass Media Depiction of Economic Conditions during a Recession

Ted J. Smith III and S. Robert Lichter

It is commonplace to note that any attempt to understand the nature and effects of a large-scale social event in a technologically advanced society must encompass two somewhat different bodies of knowledge: the factual reality of the event and its depiction in the mass media. Implicit in this view is the belief that social events are the products of human thought and action which, in turn, are a complex function of the individual's direct personal experiences and information received from the mass media and other individuals (who themselves are often dependent on the media for much of their information).

In the case of the American economic recession of 1990 and 1991, there are at least two reasons to believe that knowledge of its depiction in the media is especially important for an accurate understanding of the event itself. First, as an enormously complex, long-term phenomenon of truly national scope, a recession (like other large-scale economic phenomena) lies outside the range of direct personal experience. That is, while an individual may experience or observe certain specific aspects of a recession, knowledge of the recession as a whole (like knowledge of other large-scale economic phenomena) must come from other sources of information, especially the news media. Further, there is substantial evidence that a great many individuals do, in fact, seek out such economic information. *The Times Mirror News Interest Index,* based on periodic surveys of the adult population sponsored by the Times Mirror Center for the People and the Press, has consistently found that the economy is one of the few most closely followed topics covered by the news media. For example, the January 1993 survey found that 81 percent of the respondents claimed to follow reports about the economy

11

very (42 percent) or fairly (39 percent) closely, which placed interest in economic news second at that time only to news about the deployment of U.S. forces in Somalia (followed very or fairly closely by 89 percent of respondents). This followed a rating of 84 percent for economic news in the 1992 poll (Gersh, 1993). Additional evidence comes from recent newspaper readership studies, which have found that "business sections have climbed to the same level as hard and soft news and sports sections" (Winship, 1992).

Second, there is strong reason to believe that the difference between factual reality and its depiction in the media is especially great in the case of economic news. Following the seminal work of Epstein (1973) and Tuchman (esp. 1978), it is now widely accepted that news is a social construction which is perhaps best described as a commercial product. It is a product in the sense that it is crafted by journalists who must continuously select from an enormous variety of available materials in an effort to achieve a number of different and sometimes conflicting goals. It is commercial in the obvious sense that the product must generate sufficient revenues to defray the cost of production. This means that the news must attract an audience large enough to produce the necessary amount of paid advertising.

Although reporting is never an easy task, the production of economic news presents exceptional difficulties. Unlike an event such as a fire, a space launch, or a news conference, a journalist cannot directly observe, or show, the economy. The economy is known only through a vast and constantly changing body of economic information, much of it in the form of complex descriptive statistics of widely varying levels of reliability, and an even larger body of economic interpretations offered by sources of widely varying levels of insight and honesty. From these materials, and others of their own making, journalists must select a tiny subset to use in creating stories that will meet the interests, needs, and abilities of an audience of thousands or millions of disparate individuals.

Several factors influence those selections, not least of which is the character of the people who make them. Most news about economic affairs at the national level is reported initially in the national news media, defined as those media capable of reaching a substantial fraction of the entire American population or of the American policy-making elite. Included in this category are the major wire services, network television, CNN/HNN, network radio, the three largest weekly news magazines, and at least four daily newspapers: The *New York Times,* The *Wall Street Journal,* The *Washington Post,* and

USA Today. As shown by Lichter, Rothman, and Lichter (1986) and others, the journalists who work for the national media constitute a tiny, powerful, and remarkably homogeneous elite. Drawn largely from middle-class and upper middle-class families, they tend to be well educated and well paid, and their outlook is typically liberal, secular, and cosmopolitan. All of these characteristics can influence the way economic news is constructed.

In addition, of course, all journalists are members of a small, closed, and unitary profession and therefore must operate within a set of norms which define both the nature and the purpose of their craft. Those norms have undergone a quiet but profound transformation over the past 30 years (Smith, 1988a; 1988b; 1990). Under the older model, which is still the "official" view of the profession, journalists were assigned an essentially passive role in which their principal duty was to provide a factual account, governed by stringent standards of objectivity and fairness, of the flow of events and the conflict of ideas. But this view has gradually been replaced by a new "social responsibility" model in which journalists, no longer content to serve as mere conduits of information, have adopted the more active and exciting role of "champions of the people," whose principal duty is to assist in perfecting society by searching out problems, inequities, and abuses and demanding that they be resolved. At a minimum, the social responsibility model encourages journalists to supplement factual reports with evaluative interpretations; some argue it has led to reporting that is pervasively adversarial, tendentious, perfectionistic, and unrealistic (Smith, 1990; see also Patterson, 1993).

Other factors influence the selection of materials more directly. Like nearly all journalists, economic reporters must deal with strict limitations of time and space, and many, especially at the local level, lack any significant education in business or economics (Fasbinder, 1987, reporting on a study of business and economic journalists funded by the Ford Foundation and conducted by the Foundation for American Communications). These constraints all encourage coverage that is brief and relatively simple. In the case of television news, the pressures for brevity and simplicity are acute, as is the need to include materials that are concrete and therefore visual. Finally, the need to attract and hold a large general audience means that economic news should be timely, clear, and interesting. Unfortunately, in contrast to these constraints, the real economy is inherently complex and abstract, and the statistical information that gives the most accurate and complete account of the status of the economy is essentially historical, often ambiguous, and usually quite prosaic.

In short, economic coverage, especially at the national level, is the product of efforts by a small, homogeneous, and societally atypical group of journalists, guided by shared professional norms that increasingly stress social impact over mere factuality, to resolve the fundamental conflict between the needs and constraints of the commercial news media and the nature of economic reality and the information that best describes it. In this situation, it would not be surprising to discover substantial differences between the factual reality of economic events and their depiction in the news media. Several bodies of evidence suggest that such differences often exist.

First, numerous surveys (e.g., Sethi, 1977; *Business Week,* 1982; Evans, 1984; *Public Relations Journal,* 1989; Case, 1994) have revealed a widespread belief among members of the business community that business and economic reporting is often biased, simplistic, inaccurate, and distorted. Of the various media, television news (both network and local) is consistently ranked as the least accurate and fair. For example, a 1982 Harris survey of 600 high-level executives found that 73 percent of the respondents characterized "most business and financial news" on television as "antibusiness" (*Business Week,* 1982:26).

Additional evidence can be found in the numerous anecdotal reports of errors and distortions in economic news that are a mainstay of discussion in journals of opinion (e.g., Easterbrook, 1989) and the business and consumer press (e.g., Price, 1994; Bodnar, 1989). Since 1990, many of these have focused on deficiencies in coverage of the 1990 through 1991 recession and its aftermath, including the specific claims that excessively negative and sensationalistic reporting stifled the recovery (e.g., Gergen, 1992; Koretz, 1992; Labate, 1992) and misled voters in the 1992 elections (e.g., Bethell, 1992; Ladd, 1993; Lipset, 1993). To these should be added the findings of the more thorough and sophisticated studies of various aspects of economic coverage conducted on an ongoing basis by conservative "media watchdog" groups such as the Media Research Center (see especially Pines with Lamer, 1994) and the detailed examples included in the many extended critiques of the press that have appeared over the last 25 years (for a useful summary of earlier criticisms of economic reporting in these sources see Wood, 1985:28; for more recent examples see especially Crossen, 1994; Weaver, 1994).

Finally, several researchers have focused specifically on the relationship between economic reality and its depiction in the news media. In a highly sophisticated study of print coverage, Sanders, et al., examined coverage of six economic issues in seven national British newspapers from 1979 through 1987. They found substantial and systematic differences among the seven newspapers in the valence of economic coverage, which is indicative of a certain amount of interpretive bias in reporting, and "moderate" but consistently positive correlations between variations in the valence of economic reports and variations in the valence of various measures of the "objective economy." Thus, while the depictions offered did not generally contradict economic reality, there is evidence that "some newspapers tend to be more accurate in their coverage than others" (1993:175).

Studies of television economic news have focused primarily on the question of whether economic coverage tends to overemphasize negative economic news. Thus Weaver (1984) reported the results of an unpublished study conducted by the Institute of Applied Economics of all economic news on network television early evening newscasts for the last six months of 1983. It found that while 95 percent of the typically brief and factual "news items" reporting economic statistics were positive, 85 percent of the longer, more interpretive "news analyses" were predominantly negative and thus distorted the reality of economic conditions. These findings were challenged by Behr and Iyengar (1985) in a study of economic coverage on CBS, but their interpretation of their results appears to be fundamentally flawed (Harrington, 1989:19–20). Harrington conducted a study of all reports of the unemployment rate, the Consumer Price Index and economic growth as measured by real GNP on network television early evening newscasts from 1973 through 1984. He concluded (1989:17) that "the networks do give greater coverage to bad economic news during nonelection years, but the pattern disappears during election years."

However, the most detailed evidence comes from a very large-scale study (Smith, 1988c) of all business, economic, and financial news (a total of 13,915 stories) on network television early evening newscasts for three one-year periods: July 1 through June 30 of 1982 through 1983, 1984 through 1985, and 1986 through 1987. These periods include the recession of 1982 and 1983 and the 1982, 1984, and 1986 federal elections. By most traditional standards (1988c:6–14), the economy improved in each of the three years of study, moving from recession and early recovery in 1982 through 1983 to strong but slowing growth in 1984 through 1985 to renewed expansion in 1986 through 1987. But as shown by the selected findings in Table 2.1, television news presented a substantially different view of economic conditions.

Table 2.1   SELECTED CHARACTERISTICS OF TELEVISION ECONOMIC
NEWS, ALL NETWORKS, 1982–87

	1982–83	1984–85	1986–87
Economic focus stories—number	5191	4357	3709
Economic focus stories—hours	119.3	116.7	95.1
Reports of economic statistics	1022	543	373
Monthly unemployment/employment stories—number	48	32	35
Monthly unemployment/employment stories—minutes	138.8	51.2	28.8
Monthly unemployment/employment stories—leads	15	2	0
Valence of economic stories—% positive	6.0	6.0	5.0
Valence of economic stories—% negative	29.4	33.8	35.0
Valence of economic stories—% mixed	21.4	27.5	25.6
Valence of economic stories—% neutral	43.2	32.7	34.4

The first two rows of Table 2.1 report the number and cumulative length of all "economic focus" stories, defined as stories that devote at least 15 percent of their time to economic information. They show that, by both measures, the amount of coverage decreased substantially over the period of study. As indicated by rows 3 through 6, this decrease was especially notable in coverage of economic statistics. Row 3 shows the total number of reports of economic statistics (excluding daily stock market reports). These declined from 1,022 in 1982 and 1983 to 373 in 1986 and 1987, a reduction of 64 percent. Rows 4 through 6 show the number and length of stories reporting monthly unemployment and employment data and the number of times those stories were used as the lead item on a newscast. In 1982 and 1983, civilian unemployment rose from 9.5 percent to a post-depression high of 10.8 percent before dropping to 10.1 percent, and civilian employment registered a net loss of 200,000 jobs. In 1984 and 1985, unemployment jumped from 7.1 percent to 7.5 percent before falling slowly to 7.3 percent, but the economy added 1.7 million new jobs. In 1986 and 1987, unemployment dropped steadily from 7.1 percent to 6.3 percent, while employment rose by 3.3 million. However, network coverage followed an opposite course, dropping from 138.8 minutes and 15 leads in 1982 and 1983 to 28.8 minutes and no leads in 1986 and 1987. Finally, rows 7 through 10 show changes in the valence of coverage over the period of study. For this analysis, a story was coded as "positive" or "negative" if the ratio of valenced material in the story was 4:1 or greater, "mixed" if the ratio was less than 4:1, and "neutral" if it contained no valenced material. All simple reports of economic statistics were coded as "neutral." As shown by Table 2.1, the ratio of negative to positive stories increased over the course of the study, from less than 5:1 in 1982 and 1983 to 7:1 in 1986 and 1987. Thus, in general, the study found that as the economy improved over the course of the study period, it received less coverage on network television news and the coverage it did receive became substantially more negative in tone. As the more detailed findings of the study show, this pattern of coverage was achieved by progressively reducing or eliminating coverage of positive economic information (especially economic statistics) and focusing attention on those sectors or aspects of the economy (e.g., the trade and budget deficits) that were relatively weak.

Considered as a whole, the available evidence shows that the depiction of economic affairs in economic news (at least in the major national media) has often diverged substantially from the factual reality of economic events. This divergence seems to be especially marked in the coverage provided by network television, which has consistently overemphasized negative economic events and interpretations. This finding is particularly significant given the fact that network television newscasts have been listed since the mid-1960s as the principal source of news for most Americans. The remainder of this chapter reports partial results of a large-scale content analysis of all economic news on network television early evening newscasts in the 34-month period of August 1990 through May 1993. This period encompasses the entirety of the 1990 and 1991 economic recession and the first two years of the subsequent recovery, as well as the entire 1992 federal election campaign. The principal purpose of this part of the study was to establish in general terms how the 1990 and 1991 recession and subsequent recovery were depicted in network television news.

Methods

The study reported here was conducted by the Center for Media and Public Affairs (CMPA), a nonprofit, nonpartisan research institute located in Washington, D.C. As its primary focus of effort, the center has recorded and analyzed all network television early evening newscasts on a continuous basis since 1987. The analysis includes coding of certain baseline variables such as the number, length, topic, and sources of network news stories on a continuous basis, as well as more detailed analyses of coverage of selected topics of interest over more limited periods of time. Summary results of the various analyses are published in the center's bimonthly newsletter *Media Monitor,* and more detailed findings are published in academic and popular books, monographs, and articles.

In all of its research, the Center follows the standard procedures of scientific content analysis. Individual studies such as the one reported here proceed in two phases. First, a qualitative or emergent analysis of a relevant sample of network coverage is used to identify the topics, themes, symbols, and stylistic devices that make up the form and substance of the news stories. These categories form the basis of the second, quantitative analysis. In this second phase, paid coders are recruited and trained using detailed written instructions that define all relevant categories and coding rules and procedures. In order to minimize the chance of systematic errors, stories are assigned to coders on a random basis. Reliability scores are computed for all variables based on recoding of samples of completed work. Only those variables with a reliability of .80 or higher are retained for further study.

The study of economic news on which this chapter is based was initiated in August 1990 and expanded in April 1991, after which it ran continuously until its termination in May 1993. Conducted in conjunction with a detailed analysis of coverage of the 1992 federal election campaign (Lichter and Noyes, 1995), it identified and analyzed all economic stories on early evening network television newscasts from August 1, 1990, through May 31, 1993. Its variables and coding categories were derived in part from an earlier CMPA study of television economic news in 1987 and 1988, which was informed, in turn, by the analytical structure of the 1988 Smith study described above (1988c).

The full study of economic news in 1990 through 1993 includes detailed information on the topics, issues, economic and geographic sectors, anecdotes, statistics, characterizations, and sources found in television coverage of the economy and the recession. This chapter reports the findings for all major variables in the study that were designed to show how the networks depicted the condition and prospects of the American economy. These variables are the amount of economic coverage, opinions about the current status of the economy, opinions about the future prospects of the economy, opinions about the strength of the recovery, incidence of the word *recession,* valence of economic anecdotes, and opinions about who should fix the economy. The findings are crosstabulated by time period, network, and, in two instances, source.

Before turning to the results of the study, it may be useful to provide some context for their interpretation. Accordingly, Table 2.2 reports monthly data for the entire period of study on civilian unemployment, real growth, and inflation as measured by the Consumer Price Index. It should be stressed that the data in Table 2.2 (which were taken from the monthly publication *Economic Indicators* prepared for the Joint Economic Committee of Congress by the Council of Economic Advisers) are the figures released in the month indicated. Thus, while nearly all have been revised since their initial appearance, they represent the best information about the economy that was available to journalists at the time. Note also that the figures for unemployment and inflation describe the preceding month, while the figures for GNP/GDP describe the preceding quarter. These particular indicators were chosen for Table 2.2 both because of their intrinsic significance and because they are the only economic statistics that tend to be reported on a monthly basis by all three networks (Smith, 1988c:48).

As shown by the first column of Table 2.2, estimates of civilian unemployment rose almost without interruption from a low of 5.5 percent in August 1990 to 7.0 percent in July 1991, declined briefly, then rose continuously from 6.7 percent in October 1991 to a high of 7.8 percent in July 1992, before declining slowly to 7.0 percent in April and May 1993. Thus, in general, unemployment increased throughout most of the first 24 months of the study period and decreased throughout most of the last ten months. The second column of Table 2.2 reports monthly advanced (a) or revised (r) estimates of Gross National Product through November 1991 and, because of a change in the statistic preferred by the federal government, of Gross Domestic Product thereafter. It shows relatively slow growth for the second and third quarters of 1990, followed by three consecutive quarters of negative growth (which constitute the recession of 1990 and 1991), followed by moderate growth in the third quarter of 1992, marginal growth in the fourth quarter of 1992 (the source of extensive speculation about an impending "double-dip" recession) and moderate to strong growth thereafter. (It should be noted that revisions after September 1991 showed positive growth in the second quarter of that year. The recession therefore covered

Table 2.2   **ECONOMIC INDICATORS, NEGATIVE COVERAGE AND CONSUMER CONFIDENCE, 8/90–5/93**

	Civilian Unemployment	GNP: <D91 GDP: D91+	Consumer Price Index	% Negative Evaulations	CB consumer confidence
A90	5.5%	+1.2% (r)	+0.4%	97	85
S90	5.6%	+0.4% (r)	+0.8%	100	86
O90	5.7%	+1.8% (a)	+0.8%	81	63
N90	5.7%	+1.7% (r)	+0.6%	92	62
D90	5.8%	+1.4% (r)	+0.3%	90	61
J91	6.1%	−2.1% (a)	+0.3%	98	55
F91	6.2%	−2.0% (r)	+0.4%	88	59
M91	6.4%	−1.6% (r)	+0.2%	93	81
A91	6.8%	−2.8% (a)	−0.1%	100	79
M91	6.6%	−2.6% (r)	+0.2%	86	76
J91	6.9%	−2.8% (r)	+0.3%	89	78
J91	7.0%	+0.4% (a)	+0.2%	95	78
A91	6.7%	−0.1% (r)	+0.2%	90	76
S91	6.8%	−0.5% (r)	+0.2%	87	73
O91	6.7%	+2.4% (a)	+0.4%	85	60
N91	6.8%	+2.4% (a)	+0.1%	95	53
D91	6.8%	+1.8% (r)	+0.4%	97	53
J92	7.1%	+0.3% (a)	+0.3%	95	51
F92	7.1%	+0.8% (r)	+0.1%	93	47
M92	7.3%	+0.4% (r)	+0.3%	87	57
A92	7.3%	+2.0% (a)	+0.5%	78	65
M92	7.2%	+2.4% (r)	+0.2%	66	72
J92	7.5%	+2.7% (r)	+0.1%	71	73
J92	7.8%	+1.4% (a)	+0.3%	94	61
A92	7.7%	+1.4% (r)	+0.1%	97	58
S92	7.6%	+1.5% (r)	+0.3%	98	56
O92	7.5%	+2.7% (a)	+0.2%	62	53
N92	7.4%	+3.9% (r)	+0.4%	42	66
D92	7.2%	+3.4% (r)	+0.2%	34	78
J93	7.3%	+3.8% (a)	+0.1%	50	77
F93	7.1%	+4.8% (r)	+0.5%	66	69
M93	7.0%	+4.7% (r)	+0.3%	50	63
A93	7.0%	+1.8% (a)	+0.1%	100	68
M93	7.0%	+0.9% (r)	+0.4%	90	62

only the fourth quarter of 1990 and the first quarter of 1991, which is the minimum period—two consecutive quarters of negative real growth—required for an economic downturn to be officially classified as a "recession.") The third column of Table 2.2 shows that the rate of inflation was unacceptably high only for the first four months of the study, after which it declined to a consistently moderate level. Finally, the fifth column of Table 2.2 lists the initial (i.e., unrevised) announcement of the Consumer Board's consumer confidence index for the current month. Historically, this index has dropped below 80 during periods of recession, then risen above that level in periods of recovery. In 1990 through 1993, this pattern was broken. Confidence fell sharply in October 1990, rebounded to 81 in March 1991, hovered near that level until August 1991, then remained at low levels throughout most of the remainder of the period, rising above 70 only in May and June and December 1992 and January 1993.

Opinions about the reality of economic conditions during the period of study vary widely. As Lichter and Smith (1993) have noted, interpretations on network television were often near-apocalyptic in tone. For example, in December 1990 an economist told ABC, "The economy... almost looks as if it's sliding off a cliff." Four months later a union worker told CBS, "We're in a depression; we're not in a recession. There's no work. There's no jobs." And in January 1992 ABC's Jim Wooten told viewers, "The economy is a wreck." But more optimistic views were also common, especially in the more sophisticated print media. For example, a number of analysts (e.g., Ladd, 1992; Reynolds, 1993) pointed to the strengths of the American economy, especially in comparison with the rest of the industrialized world, a view that even some journalists eventually discovered (e.g., Kaplan, 1993). And as an October 1992 article in *The Economist* noted (1992:13):

> Slow growth is not a slump. America's recent slowdown has been so mild that it barely qualifies as a recession. In one way, therefore, comparisons with the 1930s are just bizarre. In the Depression America's output fell 30%; between 1990 and 1991 it fell 1%, and has been growing, though jerkily, since. What is surprising in America is not that the recovery remains slow and hesitant (after a mild recession, a mild recovery is to be expected) but that a big budget deficit and the lowest short-term interest rates for decades have failed to boost demand.

Obviously, this is not the place to attempt to adjudicate among these views. However, it should be noted that the recession of 1990 and 1991 was both brief and relatively shallow, that the American economy did expand continuously from the second quarter of 1991 through the end of the period of study, and that, while employment grew only slowly at best throughout most of the period, unemployment peaked at a modest 7.8 percent. In comparison, unemployment rose to 10.8 percent in the 1982 and 1983 recession, and the average yearly unemployment rate remained at 7.0 percent or above for the entire period of 1980 through 1986; over the four years of first Reagan administration, average yearly unemployment ranged from 7.5 percent to 9.7 percent.

Results

The results of the study are reported in Tables 2.3 through 2.12. Each shows the findings for a single variable, crosstabulated by time, network, and, in one instance, source.

Amount of Economic Coverage

For purposes of the study, a story was categorized as an economic story if at least 20 seconds of its content (or one-third of the content of stories of less than one minute in length) were devoted exclusively to economic issues. Routine daily stock market reports and stories focusing on noneconomic aspects of business corporations were excluded from the analysis.

Table 2.3 reports the number of economic stories on each network for each month of the study period. At least four aspects of the findings are noteworthy. First, it is clear that all three networks devoted substantial coverage to economic news, an average of more than one story per day throughout the course of the study.

Second, although the total number of economic stories on ABC and NBC was almost identical, the total for CBS was about one-fourth lower (1062 versus 1379 and 1392 for the other two networks). This could reflect a lesser emphasis on economic news by CBS. However, because this pattern is not clearly reflected in the frequency distributions of other variables in the study, it could mean only that CBS aired fewer but longer stories.

Third, the results show a wide variation in the total number of economic stories broadcast by the three networks each month, with the figures ranging from a low of 41 stories in October 1990 to a high

Table 2.3   NUMBER OF ECONOMIC STORIES, BY NETWORK, 8/90–5/93

	ABC	CBS	NBC	All
Aug 1990	26	29	25	80
Sep 1990	17	37	24	78
Oct 1990	11	22	8	41
Nov 1990	15	14	21	50
Dec 1990	31	19	34	84
Jan 1991	22	18	26	66
Feb 1991	15	13	20	48
Mar 1991	16	16	16	48
Apr 1991	15	18	15	48
May 1991	23	14	17	54
Jun 1991	17	15	19	51
Jul 1991	44	21	38	103
Aug 1991	20	15	41	76
Sep 1991	34	14	41	89
Oct 1991	53	33	35	121
Nov 1991	55	53	61	169
Dec 1991	72	58	62	192
Jan 1992	98	80	99	277
Feb 1992	61	50	66	177
Mar 1992	44	32	55	131
Apr 1992	40	34	49	123
May 1992	45	23	37	105
Jun 1992	47	30	32	109
Jul 1992	48	29	55	132
Aug 1992	48	24	45	117
Sep 1992	42	29	48	119
Oct 1992	37	26	38	101
Nov 1992	41	27	42	110
Dec 1992	45	23	35	103
Jan 1993	41	44	48	133
Feb 1993	90	81	87	258
Mar 1993	60	42	42	144
Apr 1993	41	35	48	124
May 1993	65	44	63	172
All	1379	1062	1392	3833

of 277 stories in January 1992. More specifically, there were three clear peaks in the amount of coverage: November 1991 through February 1992, a period of intense primary campaigning and widespread media speculation about a "double-dip" recession (which never materialized); January through March 1993, when there was extensive discussion of the new Clinton administration's economic policies and first budget; and May 1993, the last month of the study, when a sharp drop in the GDP estimate (from +1.8 percent to +0.9 percent) and lagging consumer confidence sparked renewed discussion about the strength of the economy.

Fourth, and potentially most significant, is the marked *increase* in the number of economic stories beginning in October 1991. Specifically, in the first 14 months of the study, a period which encompasses the entire 1990 through 1991 recession, the number of economic stories rose above 100 in only one month, July 1991; in contrast, in the second 20 months of the study, a period which encompasses nearly all of the economic recovery, the number of stories never dropped below 100. Taken at face value, these findings would appear to directly contradict the results of the Smith study (1988c). But the first 14 months of the study also encompassed the crisis and war with Iraq, a story which dominated coverage and almost certainly suppressed the amount of coverage of the recession. In addition, the highest sustained level of economic coverage (November 1991 through February 1992) occurred during a period when a great many network journalists reported that the American economy was in or nearing another recession. Thus no clear conclusion can be drawn from these results.

Evaluations of the Current Health or Stability of the Economy

This variable provides the most direct evidence of the evaluative tone of television coverage of the economy. Coders were instructed to record every instance in which a reporter or source offered an evaluation of the health or stability of the American economy or any of its sectors, regions, or states. Statements claiming that the economy (or one of its components) is healthy, stable, in good shape, or improving were coded as positive; those claiming that the economy (or one of its components) is unhealthy, unstable, in bad shape, or deteriorating were coded as negative; unclear assessments and those including both positive and negative aspects were coded as "mixed." Coders also recorded the component that had been evaluated and the source of the evaluation.

Results for this variable are summarized by quarter across all networks in Table 2.4 and reported by network and month in Table 2.5. For convenience of analysis, Table 2.5 is divided into two parts, with part "a" covering the first 17 months of the study period and part "b" covering the last 17 months.

The most obvious feature of these results is the almost uniformly negative character of evaluations of the current economy provided on network news. As shown in Table 2.4, 79.6 percent of all evaluations for the entire period of study were negative. As shown in Table 2.5, evaluations changed only from 85.3 percent negative in the first half of the study period, which encompasses the recession of 1990 and 1991, to 72.6 percent negative in the second half of the study period, which was entirely a time of recovery. Closer inspection of Table 2.4 shows that only in the fourth quarter of 1992 did positive evaluations outweigh negative, and then only by a slim margin of 103 to 93. Inspection of the summary columns of Table 2.5 shows that in only two of the 34 months of the study period, November and December 1992, were there more positive than negative evaluations across all networks. Table 2.5 also shows that positive evaluations outnumbered negative in only seven months on ABC (May, June, November, and December 1992 and January, February,

Table 2.4 **EVALUATIONS OF CURRENT ECONOMY, ALL NETWORKS, 8/90–5/93**

	Positive	**Negative**	**Mixed**
Aug–Sep 90	1	77	9
Oct–Dec 90	17	125	7
Jan–Mar 91	10	119	6
Apr–Jun 91	17	179	24
Jul–Sep 91	13	121	27
Oct–Dec 91	34	505	29
Jan–Mar 92	29	376	17
Apr–Jun 92	34	87	28
Jul–Sep 92	5	139	11
Oct–Dec 92	103	93	36
Jan–Mar 93	20	29	3
Apr–May 93	4	43	0
All	287	1893	197
%	12.1	79.6	8.9

Table 2.5a EVALUATIONS OF CURRENT ECONOMY, ALL SOURCES, BY NETWORK, 8/90–12/91

	ABC			CBS			NBC			All		
	Pos	Neg	Mix	Pos	Neg	Mix	Pos	Neg	Mix	Pos	Neg	Mix
A90	1	6	0	0	17	1	0	8	3	1	31	4
S90	0	10	0	0	20	2	0	16	3	0	46	5
O90	2	10	0	1	11	0	4	8	0	7	29	0
N90	1	11	0	1	13	1	1	12	4	3	36	5
D90	1	24	1	0	11	0	6	25	2	7	60	2
J91	0	10	0	1	8	0	0	21	0	1	39	1
F91	1	15	1	0	13	2	5	15	1	6	43	1
M91	1	8	2	2	10	0	0	19	1	3	37	4
A91	0	8	3	0	27	5	0	27	0	0	62	2
M91	2	17	7	1	10	1	7	34	6	10	61	14
J91	4	16	1	3	23	1	0	17	0	7	56	8
J91	0	12	0	1	9	2	1	16	0	2	37	2
A91	2	12	0	0	8	4	2	17	9	4	37	11
S91	2	14	0	3	13	1	2	20	10	7	47	14
O91	7	36	6	8	21	6	1	31	4	16	88	11
N91	4	61	3	7	56	3	0	75	1	11	192	10
D91	2	75	2	1	70	0	4	80	3	7	225	8
All	30	345	26	29	340	29	33	441	47	92	1126	102
%	7.5	86.0	6.5	7.3	85.4	7.3	6.3	84.6	9.0	7.0	85.3	7.7

Table 2.5b EVALUATIONS OF CURRENT ECONOMY, ALL SOURCES, BY NETWORK, 1/92–5/93

	ABC			CBS			NBC			All		
	Pos	Neg	Mix	Pos	Neg	Mix	Pos	Neg	Mix	Pos	Neg	Mix
J92	2	71	4	1	50	0	6	59	0	9	180	4
F92	4	33	2	1	48	1	5	46	1	10	127	4
M92	3	17	3	2	23	2	5	29	4	10	69	9
A92	5	7	2	2	11	4	4	20	2	11	38	8
M92	8	5	11	2	13	2	5	11	2	15	29	15
J92	3	2	1	0	9	3	5	9	1	8	20	5
J92	0	16	3	1	18	1	2	15	1	3	49	5
A92	0	6	1	1	15	1	0	12	2	1	36	4
S92	0	25	1	0	15	0	1	14	1	1	54	2
O92	10	12	1	9	10	2	11	26	3	30	48	6
N92	17	9	6	5	9	3	11	6	3	33	24	12
D92	14	8	4	12	7	5	14	6	9	40	21	18
J93	3	0	1	5	5	1	0	3	0	8	8	2
F93	3	2	0	1	12	1	6	5	0	10	19	1
M93	1	0	0	0	0	0	1	2	0	2	2	0
A93	0	1	0	0	2	0	0	4	0	0	7	0
M93	1	14	0	0	7	0	2	15	0	4	36	0
All	75	228	40	42	257	26	78	282	29	195	767	95
%	21.9	66.5	11.7	12.9	79.1	8.0	20.1	72.5	7.5	18.4	72.6	9.0

and March 1993) and one month on CBS (December 1992) and three months on NBC (November and December 1992 and February 1993).

Three factors appear to account for the predominance of positive evaluations in the fourth quarter of 1992. First, the total of 30 positive evaluations in October 1992—by far the largest number recorded in the study to that date—is largely a result of coverage of the 1992 election campaign: of the 30 positive evaluations, 18 came from President Bush or other members of his administration. Second, as shown by Table 2.2, all GDP estimates announced in the fourth quarter of 1992 indicated strong growth. A preliminary estimate of +2.7 percent real growth released in October 1992, which was met with great skepticism on all three networks, was followed by revised estimates of +3.9 percent in November and +3.4 percent in December. Coverage of these revised estimates accounts for many of the positive evaluations in those two months. Third, on December 22, 1992, the Business Cycle Dating Committee officially declared that the recession was over and that it had ended in March 1991.

As the above discussion suggests, and inspection of Table 2.5 confirms, evaluations of the economy were remarkably similar across the three networks. For the first half of the study period, evaluations ranged only from 84.6 percent negative on NBC to 86.0 percent negative on ABC; for the second half of the period they ranged only from 66.5 percent negative on ABC to 79.1 percent negative on CBS. In terms of numbers, however, NBC coverage included substantially more evaluations of the economy (910) than either ABC (744) or CBS (723).

Tables 2.4 and 2.5 also show that the most negative evaluations of the economy did not occur during the recession itself (January through October 1991, based on the information available at the time) but in three other periods. These are August and September 1990, when the impending recession was widely predicted; November 1991 through January 1992, when speculation about a "double-dip" recession was rife and the networks aired an average of 199 negative evaluations a month; and July through September 1992, a key period of the 1992 election when the announcement in July of an increase in unemployment to 7.8 percent produced widespread skepticism on network newscasts about the health of the economy (despite the fact that the July unemployment figure was primarily the result of new workers entering the labor force). This pattern can also be seen quite clearly in the fourth column of Table 2.2, which reports the percentage of negative evaluations each month, with the percentage computed as the ratio of negative evaluations to positive and negative evaluations (i.e., excluding mixed evaluations).

Finally, it is important to note the pattern of evaluations that emerged from January through April 1993. After two months of predominantly positive evaluations and the official announcement of the end of the recession, and with consistently positive growth figures (see Table 2.2), the networks responded by drastically reducing the number of evaluations of the economy they offered in their newscasts. Specifically, over the first 29 months of the study period (August 1990 through December 1992) the networks offered an average of 67 evaluations each month. From January through April 1993, when virtually all of the major economic indicators were relatively positive, the average number of evaluations dropped to 14.8 per month, a decrease of 78 percent. But with new evidence of slowing growth, beginning with the announcement in the last week of April of an initial estimate of only +1.8 percent growth in the first quarter of 1993, the number of evaluations jumped to 40 in May, 90 percent of them negative. In short, given clearly positive economic information, the response of the networks was to greatly reduce the number of evaluations reported.

Predictions of the Future Direction of the Economy

This variable was designed to show the economic outlook presented on network television news. Coders were instructed to record every instance in which a reporter or source offered a prediction or assessment of the future state of the American economy or any of its sectors, regions, or states. Claims that the outlook for the economy (or one of its components) is positive or negative were categorized as such. Claims that the outlook is uncertain, unclear, or mixed were categorized as "uncertain." Coders also recorded the component that had been evaluated and the source of the evaluation.

Results for this variable are summarized by quarter across all networks in Table 2.6 and reported by network and month in Table 2.7. Once again, for convenience of analysis, Table 2.7 is divided into two parts, with part "a" covering the first 17 months of the study period and part "b" covering the last 17 months.

Turning first to Table 2.6, the generally pessimistic tone of television economic news is again apparent. Across the entire period of study, only 26.2 percent of the economic predictions were positive, compared to 38.7 percent negative and 35.1 percent uncertain. However, it should be noted that predictions about the future of the economy were substantially more positive than evaluations of its current health as described above. Further, the networks offered

Table 2.6　ECONOMIC PREDICTIONS, ALL NETWORKS, 8/90–5/93

	Positive	Negative	Uncertain
Aug–Sep 90	1	14	14
Oct–Dec 90	5	26	4
Jan–Mar 91	19	9	15
Apr–Jun 91	2	0	5
Jul–Sep 91	1	6	2
Oct–Dec 91	12	23	21
Jan–Mar 92	19	17	40
Apr–Jun 92	12	8	6
Jul–Sep 92	4	20	6
Oct–Dec 92	11	13	12
Jan–Mar 93	8	3	2
Apr–May 93	1	1	0
All	95	140	127
%	26.2	38.7	35.1

only 362 predictions about the future of the economy, compared to 2,377 evaluations of its current health.

Predictions about the future of the economy were also much more variable than evaluations of its current health. This can be seen most clearly by examining the monthly data in Table 2.7. From August through December 1990, with the recession impending, predictions were both numerous (a total of 64, for an average of 12.8 per month) and largely negative (63.5 percent). From January through September 1991, when the available evidence indicated the economy was in a recession, predictions moved from relatively optimistic (44.1 percent positive, 34.9 percent uncertain, 20.9 percent negative) from January through March, to predominantly uncertain (71.4 percent) from April through June, to predominantly negative (66.7 percent) from July through September. Further, the number of predictions dropped dramatically, from an average of 12.8 per month from August through December 1990 and 14.3 per month from January through March 1991 to 2.7 per month from April through September. Thus, as the recession drew to a close, predictions became both more negative and less numerous. From October 1991 through January 1992, when there was extensive speculation about a double-dip recession, predictions were predominantly uncertain (39.8 percent) or negative (37.9 percent) and increased in number to an average of

Table 2.7a ECONOMIC PREDICTIONS, ALL SOURCES, BY NETWORK, 8/90–12/91

	ABC			CBS			NBC			All		
	Pos	Neg	Unc	Pos	Neg	Unc	Pos	Neg	Unc	Pos	Neg	Unc
A90	0	1	3	0	2	4	1	5	2	1	8	9
S90	0	1	1	0	4	3	0	1	1	0	6	5
O90	1	1	0	1	4	1	0	2	1	2	7	2
N90	0	1	1	0	3	0	1	2	0	1	6	1
D90	0	0	3	0	5	1	2	8	0	2	13	1
J91	3	1	0	3	0	0	1	2	6	4	3	9
F91	0	1	3	1	2	0	4	1	0	7	4	0
M91	2	0	0	0	0	3	5	2	0	8	2	6
A91	0	0	0	0	0	1	0	0	0	0	0	1
M91	0	0	0	1	0	0	1	0	1	1	0	1
J91	1	0	0	0	0	2	0	0	1	1	0	3
J91	0	0	1	0	0	0	0	2	1	1	2	1
A91	0	0	0	0	0	1	0	2	0	0	2	1
S91	0	0	1	0	1	0	0	1	0	0	2	0
O91	1	1	0	0	0	1	1	5	2	2	6	4
N91	3	3	9	0	0	0	4	5	3	7	8	13
D91	1	2	0	0	3	3	2	4	1	3	9	4
All	12	12	22	6	24	20	22	42	19	40	78	61
%	26.1	26.1	47.8	12.0	48.0	40.0	26.5	50.6	22.9	22.3	43.6	34.1

Table 2.7b EVALUATIONS OF CURRENT ECONOMY, ALL SOURCES, BY NETWORK, 1/92–5/93

	ABC			CBS			NBC			All		
	Pos	Neg	Unc	Pos	Neg	Unc	Pos	Neg	Unc	Pos	Neg	Unc
J92	4	5	10	4	10	6	1	1	4	9	16	20
F92	2	0	2	1	0	3	2	0	2	5	0	7
M92	2	0	3	0	1	8	3	0	2	5	1	13
A92	0	2	1	2	1	0	2	3	1	4	6	2
M92	4	1	0	2	1	4	0	0	0	6	2	4
J92	0	0	0	1	0	0	1	0	0	2	0	0
J92	1	2	1	0	2	0	0	2	1	1	6	2
A92	2	4	2	0	2	1	0	1	0	2	7	3
S92	0	0	0	1	3	1	0	4	0	1	7	1
O92	0	4	1	0	2	3	1	3	1	1	9	5
N92	4	0	1	0	0	1	2	1	2	6	1	4
D92	2	0	0	1	3	2	1	0	1	4	3	3
J93	0	0	1	3	1	0	0	1	1	3	2	2
F93	0	0	0	0	0	0	2	1	0	2	1	0
M93	3	0	0	0	0	0	3	0	0	3	0	0
A93	0	0	0	0	0	0	0	0	0	0	0	0
M93	1	1	0	0	0	0	1	0	0	1	1	0
All	25	19	22	15	26	29	15	17	15	55	62	66
%	37.9	28.8	33.3	21.4	37.1	41.4	31.9	36.2	31.9	30.1	33.9	36.1

25.8 per month. From February through June 1992, when it became apparent that the economy had not slipped back into a recession, predictions became relatively positive (38.6 percent positive, 45.6 percent uncertain, 15.8 percent negative) and much less numerous at 11.4 per month. From July through October 1992, after the announcement of an increase to 7.8 percent unemployment on July 2 and during the most crucial months of the 1992 campaign, predictions continued at a rate of 11.3 per month but became overwhelmingly negative (64.4 percent) in valence. Finally, from November 1992 through May 1993, when evidence that the recession was over became overwhelming and the economy recorded two consecutive quarters of strong growth, predictions became predominantly positive (52.8 percent) but dropped in frequency to 5.1 per month. Thus, in general, as prospects for the economy improved, predictions usually became more positive but always less numerous.

Table 2.7 also shows some interesting variations by network. The number of predictions was fairly similar for all of the networks, ranging from a low of 112 on ABC to a high of 130 on NBC. But the valence of the predictions varied systematically. Throughout the course of the study, ABC was clearly the most optimistic of the networks (33.0 percent positive, 27.7 percent negative, 39.3 percent uncertain) and CBS was clearly the most pessimistic (17.5 percent positive, 41.7 percent negative, 40.8 percent uncertain). NBC (28.5 percent positive, 45.4 percent negative, 26.2 percent uncertain) occupied the middle ground.

Source of Evaluations and Predictions

As noted above, coders recorded the source of each evaluation or prediction. In all CMPA research, source coding is based on a continuously updated list of over 2,000 individual and institutional sources, which includes all current members of Congress, senior administration officials, and on-camera network journalists. A comment is attributed to a nonjournalist source if it is uttered by that source or quoted or paraphrased by a journalist and directly attributed to that source. All other comments are attributed to the journalist who utters them. Thus comments attributed to a journalist include those made wholly on the journalist's own authority and those attributed solely to unnamed individuals or groups. For purposes of the present study, specific source attributions were collapsed into the seven source categories shown in Table 2.8: reporters,

Table 2.8   EVALUATIONS OF CURRENT AND FUTURE ECONOMY, BY
SOURCE, 8/90–5/93

		Current			Future		
		Pos	**Neg**	**Mixed**	**Pos**	**Neg**	**Uncrtn**
Reporters	ABC	49	375	29	6	14	21
	CBS	21	332	25	3	21	26
	NBC	70	519	42	4	11	14
	All	**140**	**1226**	**96**	**13**	**46**	**61**
Administration	ABC	32	50	20	13	3	7
	CBS	26	50	11	18	4	3
	NBC	16	42	17	13	5	2
	All	**74**	**142**	**48**	**44**	**12**	**12**
Congress	ABC	0	20	0	0	0	3
	CBS	0	28	1	0	1	1
	NBC	2	14	1	0	0	0
	All	**2**	**62**	**2**	**0**	**1**	**4**
Other governmental	ABC	0	7	2	0	1	0
	CBS	3	18	5	1	1	3
	NBC	0	12	1	1	1	3
	All	**3**	**37**	**8**	**2**	**3**	**6**
Analysts	ABC	8	37	9	0	10	6
	CBS	5	65	6	4	18	4
	NBC	6	33	5	2	5	6
	All	**19**	**135**	**20**	**6**	**33**	**16**
Industry personnel	ABC	13	47	5	8	13	3
	CBS	10	64	6	7	11	8
	NBC	15	67	5	5	6	11
	All	**38**	**178**	**16**	**20**	**30**	**22**
Other individuals	ABC	3	37	1	4	2	2
	CBS	6	40	1	4	12	3
	NBC	12	36	5	2	1	1
	All	**21**	**113**	**7**	**10**	**15**	**6**

administration officials (including the sitting President), Congress, other governmental figures (including Bill Clinton when he was campaigning for the presidency), economic analysts (defined as those nongovernmental individuals and groups whose principal job or purpose is to analyze some aspect of the economy), industry personnel (including trade associations and their representatives as well as most business people), and others (a residual category for all other nonjournalist sources, including ordinary citizens and polls).

Table 2.8 provides summary data on evaluations of the current economy and predictions about the future of the economy crosstabulated by source and network. The most obvious feature of Table 2.8 is the extent to which journalists dominate the economic evaluations and predictions on network television news. Of 2,377 evaluations of the current health or stability of the economy, 1,462 (61.5 percent) were offered by journalists on their own authority or the authority of unspecified sources, and of 362 predictions about the future status of the economy, 120 (33.1 percent) were offered by journalists.

A second striking feature of the data reported in Table 2.8 is the pattern of comments across sources. In the case of evaluations of the current health of the economy, only administration sources offered a substantial proportion (28.0 percent) of positive evaluations; all other sources were overwhelmingly negative in their evaluations. Similarly, in the case of predictions about the economy's future, only administration sources offered a predominantly positive outlook (64.7 percent); among the other six groups of sources, positive predictions ranged only from 0 percent to 32.2 percent.

Finally, it should be noted that the distribution of opinions across the various categories of sources is remarkably consistent across the three television networks. Not only did the three networks tend to use very similar numbers of each category of sources, but they also provided very similar distributions of opinion within each of those source categories.

Characterizations of the Size of the Recovery

This variable focused specifically on descriptions of any actual or impending economic recovery. It was added to the study in April 1991. Coders were instructed to record every instance in which a reporter or source offered any explicit characterization of the size or strength of the recovery. Explicit claims that the recovery is or is likely to be great, large, fast, or strong were coded as "positive," while explicit claims that the recovery is or is likely to be short, small, mild, or in some way weaker than hoped were coded as "negative." Claims that included both positive and negative characterizations or asserted that the size of the actual or impending recovery is unclear were coded as "mixed."

Data for this variable are reported in Table 2.9, which displays an extremely simple and consistent pattern of results. Across all time periods and all networks, characterizations of the size of the recovery were invariably and overwhelmingly negative. This is true

Table 2.9 CHARACTERIZATIONS OF THE RECOVERY, ALL SOURCES, 4/91–5/93

	ABC			CBS			NBC			All		
	Pos	Neg	Mix	Pos	Neg	Mix	Pos	Neg	Mix	Pos	Neg	Mix
Apr–Jun 91	0	7	1	0	5	2	0	5	0	0	17	3
Jul–Sep 91	0	8	3	0	2	1	0	9	1	0	19	5
Oct–Dec 91	0	3	2	0	8	6	1	11	1	1	22	9
Jan–Mar 92	0	5	4	0	4	2	0	4	4	0	13	10
Apr–Jun 92	1	9	2	1	8	5	0	9	0	1	26	7
Jul–Sep 92	1	6	1	0	5	1	0	3	1	2	14	3
Oct–Dec 92	0	2	0	0	4	3	0	8	1	0	14	4
Jan–Mar 93	0	3	3	0	2	2	0	1	1	0	6	6
Apr–May 93	0	2	0	0	0	0	0	0	0	0	2	0
All	2	45	16	1	38	22	1	50	9	4	133	47
%	3.1	71.4	25.4	1.6	62.3	36.1	1.7	83.3	15.0	2.2	72.3	25.5

even in the period from October 1992 through March 1993, when (as shown in Table 2.2) monthly estimates of real growth ranged from +2.7 percent to +4.8 percent and averaged +3.8 percent. Of the 30 characterizations of the size of the recovery during this period, none was positive and 20 (66.7 percent) were negative.

References to the "Recession"

This variable was intended to provide a global measure of the way network news depicted the overall performance of the economy. Coders were instructed to record every instance in which a reporter or source uttered the word *recession* in the course of a story. In this instance, coding of the variable was terminated at the end of September 1992. Thus data are available only from August 1990 through September 1992.

Table 2.10 reports the total number of times the word *recession* was used on network newscasts during the 26 months of the study period, crosstabulated by month and network. The most obvious finding displayed in Table 2.10 is that the word *recession* was used with some frequency throughout the period of study, especially on NBC. Beyond that, no especially remarkable pattern is evident. Use of the word was especially frequent from April through June 1991, which coincides with the release of the most negative growth figures, and most frequent from November 1991 through February 1992, when there was widespread speculation on network news about a double-dip recession. Use of the word was least frequent from August 1990 through March 1991, which may simply reflect the displacement of economic stories by coverage of the crisis and war with Iraq, and from May through July 1992, when the available economic data indicated moderate growth coupled with rising unemployment.

Valence of Economic Anecdotes

This variable was designed to provide an indication of the kind of "spin" imparted to stories by network journalists. In part because of the perceived need to find concrete, personal, and therefore visual materials, television journalists often illustrate their coverage with anecdotes. The CMPA codebook defines an anecdote as follows:

> An anecdote is a type of news coverage that seeks to give insight into an issue by showing everyday individuals doing everyday things. It can focus on a person, a family unit, a company,

Table 2.10   REFERENCES TO *RECESSION*, ALL SOURCES, 8/90–9/92

	ABC	CBS	NBC	All
Aug 1990	17	6	27	50
Sep 1990	9	24	36	69
Oct 1990	13	7	2	22
Nov 1990	3	5	10	18
Dec 1990	19	15	39	73
Jan 1991	14	14	28	56
Feb 1991	7	12	9	28
Mar 1991	17	11	24	52
Apr 1991	18	67	67	152
May 1991	48	24	93	165
Jun 1991	33	48	45	126
Jul 1991	45	21	33	99
Aug 1991	15	9	48	72
Sep 1991	33	30	39	102
Oct 1991	30	24	42	96
Nov 1991	54	54	30	138
Dec 1991	117	96	99	323
Jan 1992	72	36	90	198
Feb 1992	87	42	39	168
Mar 1992	24	33	42	99
Apr 1992	21	12	36	69
May 1992	3	18	12	33
Jun 1992	18	3	15	36
Jul 1992	18	3	15	36
Aug 1992	15	33	15	63
Sep 1992	18	24	9	51
All	753	683	945	2381

or an institutional program. To be considered an anecdote, the coverage must profile the subject for a substantial amount of time (at least 10 seconds). An anecdote must also give background information (for example, names, age, situation, etc.).

Anecdotes are particularly significant because, unlike naturally occurring public events or hard data such as economic statistics, their content is almost completely under the control of the journalist. They therefore provide an especially clear indication of the way journalists choose to depict reality, although in this as in all other cases, journalistic choice is constrained by a number of factors (including time, resources, and news values).

Beginning in April 1991, coders were instructed to record every anecdote encountered in network coverage of the economy and categorize it by subject, economic issue, and valence. Valence was defined as the response to the question: How is the subject faring? Anecdotes in which the subject was depicted as doing well were coded as "positive," those in which the subject was shown as doing poorly were coded "negative," and those which gave a mixed portrayal of how well the subject is faring were coded "mixed."

Table 2.11 reports the valence of all anecdotes used in network coverage of the economy crosstabulated by quarter and network. Because of the time-consuming nature of the task and the demands of a concurrent detailed analysis of the 1992 election campaign, this variable was dropped from the study from September through December 1992.

Three findings in Table 2.11 are noteworthy. First, as might be expected, a plurality (46.8 percent) of all of the economic anecdotes used on network television were negative, and in only two periods of study (April through June 1992 and April through May 1993) did positive anecdotes outweigh negative. However, second, it is important to note that a substantial fraction (31.6 percent) of all anecdotes were positive, and, on NBC, positive and negative anecdotes were almost equal in number. In contrast, negative anecdotes outnumbered positive by a ratio of more than 2:1 on CBS. Finally, nearly half of all of the anecdotes (290 of 602, or 48.2 percent) were broadcast from October 1991 through March 1992. This finding can be explained in part by the greater number of stories in that period. As shown in Table 2.11, of the 3,024 economic stories carried on network television from April 1991 through May 1993 (excluding October through December 1992), 1,067 (or 35.3 percent) were broadcast from October 1991 through March 1992. But as the disparity between the number of anecdotes used (48.2 percent) and the number of stories broadcast (35.3 percent) indicates, coverage during this period, which included extensive speculation about a double-dip recession, was marked by an unusually heavy reliance on anecdotal (i.e., "soft") information.

Opinions of Who Should Fix the Economy

The final variable in the study sought to determine where television news placed the responsibility for improving or "fixing" the economy.

Table 2.11   VALENCE OF ECONOMIC ANECDOTES, BY NETWORK, 4/91–5/93

	ABC			CBS			NBC			All		
	Pos	Neg	Mix	Pos	Neg	Mix	Pos	Neg	Mix	Pos	Neg	Mix
Apr–Jun 91	3	8	2	1	16	3	4	7	4	8	31	9
Jul–Sep 91	3	4	3	2	7	0	9	10	3	14	21	6
Oct–Dec 91	10	28	9	7	28	5	12	9	8	29	65	22
Jan–Mar 92	20	17	11	13	22	8	28	42	13	61	81	32
Apr–Jun 92	4	4	3	10	9	2	17	11	9	31	24	14
Jul–Sep 92	1	10	6	5	9	3	17	11	8	23	30	17
Oct–Dec 92	na	na	na	na	na	na	na	na	na	na	na	na
Jan–Mar 93	7	9	12	5	6	9	4	10	4	16	25	25
Apr–May 93	6	1	2	1	2	1	1	2	2	8	5	5
All	54	81	48	44	99	31	92	102	51	190	282	130
%	29.5	44.3	26.2	25.3	56.9	17.8	37.6	41.6	20.8	31.6	46.8	21.6

Accordingly, coders were instructed to record every instance in which a reporter or source assigned responsibility for changing or improving the American economy or one of its sectors, regions, or states to a particular party, using the 19 categories listed in Table 2.12. This variable was added to the study in April 1991.

Data for this variable are reported by network in Table 2.12. Although opinions about who should fix the economy were expressed on network television only 71 times during the period of study, they formed a highly consistent pattern. Responsibility was placed most often (19 times) on the President, followed closely by the government or politicians (16 times) and Congress (10 times). In all, 49 of the 71 attributions (69.0 percent) placed responsibility on some

Table 2.12   OPINIONS OF WHO SHOULD FIX THE ECONOMY, ALL
SOURCES, 4/91–5/93

	ABC	CBS	NBC	All
George Bush/Bill Clinton	5	7	7	19
The White House	0	0	0	0
Congress	3	3	4	10
Republicans	0	0	0	0
Democrats	1	0	1	2
The government/politicians	6	3	7	16
Consumers	0	1	0	1
Unions/workers	0	0	2	2
Media	0	0	0	0
Japan	0	0	0	0
Other countries	0	0	0	0
World economy	0	0	0	0
Banking	2	1	0	3
The Federal Reserve	2	0	0	2
Inudstry/private companies	0	1	3	4
Wall Street	0	0	0	0
America/all of us/everyone/etc.	3	1	4	8
Do not fix (let market forces fix)	1	0	1	2
Other	0	0	2	2
All	23	17	31	71

political agent. Further, in only two of the 71 cases (2.8 percent) did a source suggest that the economy should be allowed to fix itself (i.e., through the normal operation of market forces). Thus the view expressed on television news can be accurately described as both statist and interventionist.

Discussion

Considered as a whole, the findings of this study are highly consistent with those of earlier studies of network television economic coverage, especially the large-scale analysis reported by Smith (1988c). The one major area in which the findings of the two studies do not coincide concerns the amount of economic coverage. As shown in Table 2.1, Smith (1988c) found that, in general, as the economy improved, the amount of coverage decreased. As shown in Table 2.3, that pattern was not confirmed by the results of the present study. Two factors may account for this disparity. First, as noted above, the 1990 and 1991 recession coincided with the crisis and war with Iraq, which may well have reduced the amount of economic coverage. Second, the recoveries from the 1982 and 1983 and 1990 and 1991 recessions followed somewhat different courses. The severe 1982–83 recession was followed by a classical recovery: clear, robust, and generally consistent. In contrast, the relatively mild 1990–91 recession was followed by a comparatively weak and hesitant recovery marked by stagnant employment and, through July, slowly rising unemployment. This led to continuing concerns among at least some qualified observers that the economy could slip into another recession, and these concerns sparked massive amounts of coverage, especially from November 1991 through February 1992.

Significantly, this pattern coincides with a similar finding in the Smith study. In July and August 1986, weak GNP estimates produced similar fears of an imminent recession among some observers and a corresponding spike in the amount of economic coverage. Specifically, the amount of coverage (measured by number of stories) was 41 percent higher in July and August 1986 than in the succeeding ten months (Smith, 1988c:26). These and other findings from the two studies suggest that network coverage may be greatest when an economic downturn is anticipated (regardless of whether the downturn actually occurs, and therefore to some degree regardless of its actual likelihood), somewhat lower during the downturn itself, and lowest during periods of economic growth and stability.

Other findings of the two studies coincide quite closely. Like the earlier study, the present analysis found that network coverage from 1990 through 1993 was consistently and often overwhelmingly negative, across all measures of evaluative content. Further, the valence of coverage corresponded only very roughly to the major indicators of economic performance, especially from November 1991 through February 1992 and July through October 1992. The study also shows that when those economic indicators were clearly positive (e.g., from January through April 1993) network journalists responded by dramatically reducing the number of economic evaluations they broadcast. Finally, the study provides limited but clear corroboration of the claim that network news tends to be predominantly statist and interventionist in perspective.

Given these findings, the question then arises of their possible effects. As noted above, the extraordinary outburst of generally negative economic coverage from November 1991 through February 1992 sparked an intense debate about whether media negativism was having an adverse effect on the economy by depressing consumer confidence. In support of this view, advocates generally pointed to the unprecedented and otherwise inexplicable behavior of indicators such as the Conference Board's consumer confidence index. As even a casual inspection of the data reported in Table 2.2 will show, there is very little correlation between any of the three indicators of actual economic performance and variations in the consumer confidence index, especially in the second half of the study period. In contrast, there is a fairly close relationship between the percentage of negative evaluations of the current economy on network news (computed as the ratio of negative evaluations to the total of negative and positive evaluations) and consumer confidence, especially when confidence is lagged by one month and especially in the second half of the study period. This relationship is now the subject of further study.

There is also reason to believe that network economic coverage influenced the outcome of the 1992 presidential election, as observers such as Everett Carll Ladd (1993) and Seymour Martin Lipset (1993) have argued. The 1992 election was closely contested and, thanks in part to the efforts of journalists in the national news media (Smith, 1992), dominated by economic issues. In this situation, it is difficult to believe that the unduly negative economic coverage on network television, especially from July through October 1992, did not have some negative effect on support for George Bush. As Mutz (1992:20) has argued:

>An accumulation of evidence across a wide variety of topics shows that people's personal experiences (including economic experiences) rarely influence their political judgments. . . . Instead, people's perceptions of national economic conditions have an important influence on their political attitudes. As a result, mass media play an extremely important role. Citizens typically rely on media coverage to form perceptions of what economic conditions are like outside the realm of their own personal experiences. People exposed to media coverage of the economy typically do not generalize from their own life experiences in forming impressions of national economic conditions; they rely instead on media-derived impressions of the nation as a whole.

These issues, which may never be fully resolved, are addressed in greater detail elsewhere (Lichter and Noyes, 1995). For now it must suffice to close with two observations. First, it is generally agreed that Ronald Reagan won re-election by a landslide in 1984 largely because the economy was performing so well, while George Bush lost his re-election bid in 1992 largely because the economy was performing so poorly. It is therefore instructive to note that in October 1984, the latest estimate of real GNP growth was +2.7 percent, down from +3.6 percent in September, and unemployment stood at 7.4 percent, down from 7.5 percent the month before; in October 1992, the latest estimate of real GDP growth was +2.7 percent, up from +1.5 percent in September, and unemployment stood at 7.5 percent, down from 7.6 percent the month before. Of course, the economy in October 1992 differed in important ways from the economy in October 1984. But presumably one of the most important differences was the fact that in October 1992, civilian employment stood at 117.7 million, compared to 105.2 million in October 1984. In short, it is difficult to avoid the conclusion that the highly negative view of the economy in 1992 was due in large part to widespread misperceptions about its performance and prospects, and that unduly negative coverage on network television played some major role in forming those misperceptions. However, second, in 1994 with Bill Clinton in the White House and the economy continuing to perform quite strongly, the Democrats lost control of both houses of Congress for the first time in 40 years. It is therefore interesting to note that in a *Newsweek* (1992) poll of adult Americans released on the eve of the election, 72 percent of respondents listed television as "a very important source of . . . information about

President Clinton and his administration," 51 percent expressed disapproval of "the way he is handling the nation's economy," and 59 percent agreed that "the United States economy is still in recession." Thus there is some reason to believe that television coverage of the economy is at least a nonpartisan despoiler.

3

Lessons from Benchmarking Downsizing in IBM

Sarah S. King and Donald P. Cushman

Benchmarking involves more than simple emulation. It is a mechanism to search for best practices to improve strategic and operational performance. Emulation will not always be successful because firms do not have the same resources, technological expertise, distinctive skills, and corporate culture.
(Y. K. Shetty, 1993:40)

In this chapter we are going to examine an example of organizational benchmarking which raises some important issues regarding how benchmarking must fit within broader organizational activities to be effective. In so doing we hope to shed light on some larger organizational communication processes which, if not properly treated, can undermine the benchmarking of downsizing communication activities.

Organizational benchmarking is a widely employed tool for continuously improving an organization's performance. In a survey of 580 multinational firms in four major industries—computers, automobiles, hospitals, and banks—the American Quality Foundation and Ernst and Young (Port, Cary, Kelley, and Forest, 1992) found that 93 percent of the firms surveyed had employed some form of benchmarking and that 31 percent of the firms benchmarked business processes and products on a regular basis. IBM, for example, had undertaken 500 such studies in a two-year period; ATT had undertaken 150 studies in the same time frame (Jacob, 1992:102).

However, most firms who attempt benchmarking report that their efforts failed to achieve their objectives. Studies undertaken by Arthur D. Little, A. T. Kearney, Rath and Strong, and Ernst and Young, involving over 1,200 firms across industries in America,

47

Europe, and Asia, report that between 60 and 70 percent of all such efforts fail to meet management's expectations for success (*Fortune,* May 18, 1992:12; *Wall Street Journal,* May 14, 1991: B1; and *The Economist,* April 18, 1992:67).

It is the purpose of this chapter to explore in some detail one firm's attempt to benchmark and then implement that benchmark in a high-profile communication process—organizational downsizing. Our task will be to examine why so many firms find successful benchmarking so difficult. Such a task divides itself into three parts: (1) an exploration of the research literature both on the inappropriate and on the appropriate use of communication in organizational downsizing, (2) an inquiry into IBM's use of benchmarking communication in downsizing in order to enhance organizational performance, and (3) the drawing of some conclusions regarding the appropriate use of communication in organizational downsizing efforts. Let us explore each of these in turn.

An Inquiry into the Research on the Inappropriate and Appropriate Use of Communication in Organizational Downsizing

Downsizing refers to the planned elimination of positions or jobs . . . Downsizing may occur by reducing work, as well as by eliminating functions, hierarchial levels, or units. It may also occur by implementing cost containment strategies that streamline activities such as transaction processing, information systems, or sign-off policies. (Cascio, 1993:95)

Organizational downsizing normally takes place following a business downturn, a major acquisition, and/or a major loss of market shares. In such cases a firm must either downsize or absorb the cost of maintaining its workforce by shrinking margins, reducing profits, or incurring a loss. However, in recent years, downsizing has become a way of life for firms as they continuously push to improve organizational performance, improve productivity and quality, and reduce costs through outsourcing and joint ventures. Cascio (1994:8–13) reports that between 1985 and 1993, 98 percent of Canadian firms, 94 percent of British firms, 90 percent of German firms, 85 percent of U.S. firms, and 69 percent of Japanese firms reported some form of downsizing. In addition, 50 percent said downsizing had nothing to do with recession and 66 percent of all firms reported downsizing again the following year. Before downsizing, only 6 percent tried cutting pay, 9 percent cut paid holidays, 9 percent tried reducing the workweek, and 14 percent tried job sharing. Downsizing is therefore not the strategy of last but of first resort in cutting costs. In addition, 57 percent of the firms reported that they had to replace some downsized workers. Finally, after downsizing, only 34 percent reported productivity increases, 22 percent reported productivity decreases, and 38 percent reported no change. Results like these lead many observers to suggest that the primary use of downsizing is to buy time for management to recover from its own errors in decision making (Cascio, 1994, 8–13).

Since 1980, U.S. manufacturing firms alone have cut over 2 million workers. In the most recent recession downsizing has focused primarily on middle managers (Camron, Freeman, and Mishra, 1991). Downsizing during recession most often takes place in order to (1) lower overhead, (2) speed up response time, (3) eliminate bureaucracy, (4) eliminate bottlenecks in communication, (5) create entrepreneurship, and (6) increase productivity (Murray, 1995). However, several studies aimed at measuring the effects of downsizing on a firm's performance yielded mixed results.

Studies undertaken by the American Management Association of 1,142 firms and the Society of Human Resource Management of 1,468 firms found harmful outcomes. More than half of the firms said downsizing was badly or not well handled and had the same or lower levels of productivity. However, research conducted by the University of Michigan of 2,500 managers and Schweiger and Denisi employing a control and an experimental plant revealed positive results. The Michigan study (1994) determined that the way in which communiction was handled during downsizing was more important in determining organizational effectiveness than the size of the workforce reduction and/or the cost savings that occurred. The Schweiger and Denisi experimental study (1994), employing a control manufacturing unit where communication was normal before and during the downsizing and in an experimental manufacturing unit where communication was more frequent and involving, found that the experimental plant yielded dramatically superior results (see Table 3.1).

We need to explore in some detail (a) the negative impact of downsizing on organizational performance and (b) the critical success factors for successful communication during downsizing. Let us explore each of these in turn.

Table 3.1 DOWNSIZING EFFECTS OF EARLY AND FREQUENT
COMMUNICATION

Employee Attitude	Control Plant (communication in the normal way)	Experimental Plant (early and frequent communication)
stress	90% increase	no change
uncertainty	24% increase	2% increase
job satisfaction	21% increase	7% increase
commitment	11% decrease	no change
company trustworthy honest, caring	25% decrease	14% increase
intentions to remain	12% decrease	6% decrease
performance	20% decrease	no change

Source: Schweiger and Denisi, 1991: 110–135.

The Negative Impact of Downsizing on Organizational Performance

Numerous studies document the significant attributes involved in organizational decline.

Several other studies document how the negative attributes of downsizing can contribute to organizational decline (Cameron, Freeman, and Mishra, 1991; Cameron, 1994; Baumohl, 1993). These include (1) implementing voluntary early retirement programs, (2) making across-the-board layoffs, (3) eliminating training and development programs, (4) making quick and deep reductions in personnel, (5) placing survivors in challenging jobs without training, (6) emphasizing employee accountability in place of employee involvement, (7) expecting survivors to work harder, (8) implementing layoffs too slowly, and (9) promising high monetary rewards rather than career advancement (Hitt, Keats, Harback, and Nixon, 1994:25).

Still other studies indicate how downsizing can be undertaken so as to inhibit organizational decline. These include (1) systematic analysis in advance of where to downsize, (2) gradual implementation of downsizing, (3) increased employee involvement in targeting areas for downsizing, (4) increased communication, (5) employee participation in the decision-making regarding downsizing, (6) coordination of downsizing efforts with outside organizations, (7) increased hourly and salaried teamwork, (8) increasing market adaptation (Cameron, 1994:201; Buck, 1988; Henkoff, 1990).

Collectively these studies argue for carefully locating the critical success factors in communication during downsizing so as to improve organizational performance.

Table 3.2 NEGATIVE ATTRIBUTES ASSOCIATED WITH
ORGANIZATIONAL DECLINE (THE "DIRTY DOZEN")

Attribute	Explanation
Centralization	Decision-making is pulled toward the top of the organization. Less power is shared.
Short-term, crisis mentality	Long-term planning is neglected. The focus is on immediacy.
Loss of innovativeness	Trial-and-error learning is curtailed. Less tolerance for risk and failure associated with creative activity.
Resistance to change	Conservatism and threat-rigidity response lead to "hunkering-down" and a protectionist stance.
Decreasing morale	Infighting and a "mean mood" permeate the organization.
Politicized special interest	Special interest groups recognize groups and become more vocal. The climate becomes politicized.
Nonprioritized cutbacks	Across-the-board cutbacks are used to ameliorate conflict. Priorities are not obvious.
Loss of trust	Leaders lose the confidence of subordinates, and distrust among organization members increases.
Increasing conflict	Fewer resources result in internal competition and fighting for a smaller pie.
Lack of teamwork	Individualism and disconnectedness make teamwork difficult. Individuals are not inclined to form teams.
Lack of leadership	Leadership anemia occurs as leaders are scapegoated, priorities unclear, and a siege mentality prevails.

Source: Cameron, 1994:190.

Locating the Critical Success Factors for Communication in Organizational Downsizing

Careful research on the critical success factors involved in communication in organizational downsizing divides itself into two areas, (a) the communication involved in decision making to downsize and (b) the communication of these downsizing decisions to all employees. Both areas are well researched, and the critical success factors are clearly delineated.

The Communication Involved in Decision Making

Cameron (1994) explored the communication factors involved in decision making to downsize at thirty assembly plants, fabricating plants, suppliers, and independent market units in the U.S. auto industry between 1987 and 1990. The five most successful units in terms of reduced costs and productivity gains were examined in detail and contrasted with the other 25 units examined. This contrast yielded thirty critical success factors in nine areas of decision making.

Prescriptions for Best Practices

Approach
1. Approach downsizing as a long-term strategy and a way of life rather than as a single program or target to be completed and abandoned.
2. Approach the human resources in the organization as assets rather than as liabilities and plan to invest in their development and ideas.
3. Approach downsizing as an opportunity for improvement rather than as merely a reaction to a threat or crisis.

Preparation
4. Prepare for downsizing before it is mandated or crucial for survival rather than waiting until time for advanced analysis is gone and a "ready-fire-aim" approach is required.
5. Identify the future mission of the organization, its core competencies, and an organizational structure that will most effectively accomplish the mission via the core competencies as the way to develop downsizing strategies, as opposed to formulating strategy based merely on headcount targets.
6. Establish targets, deadlines, and objectives for downsizing independent of the mandated downsizing goals from parent organizations in order to prepare the organization to view downsizing as an improvement strategy rather than as the cause of a loss of discretion.

Involvement
7. Involve employees in identifying what needs to change through downsizing and in implementing those changes rather than driving downsizing from the top down.
8. Hold everyone accountable for downsizing goals rather than treating it as only top management's responsibility.

9. Involve customers and suppliers in designing and suggesting improvements in downsizing strategies rather than focusing entirely internally.

Leadership

10. Ensure that the leader(s) is(are) visible, accessible, and interacting frequently with those affected by the downsizing instead of succumbing to the temptation to avoid confrontation, pain, and discomfort associated with managing downsizing.

11. Associate downsizing with a clearly articulated vision of a desired future for the organization, not merely as an escape from the past.

12. Project positive energy and initiative from the leader(s) in order to motivate the workforce in a downsizing organization instead of adopting a defensive or paranoid perspective.

Communication

13. Ensure that everyone is fully informed of the purposes of downsizing, the strategies to be pursued, the costs involved, the time frame, and so on, rather than revealing only "need to know" information and keeping sensitive information at the top.

14. Over-communicate as the downsizing process unfolds so that information is provided frequently, consistently, and honestly to all employees on the progress and processes in downsizing rather than reporting only decisions and results or allowing rumors and ambiguity to flourish.

15. Generate ongoing analyses and feedback from participants in the downsizing process rather than completing the process before an evaluation is done.

Support

16. Provide equal attention to and support for those who stay in the organization and those who leave the organization rather than focusing all benefits on casualties.

17. Provide safety nets (adequate lead time, financial benefits, counseling, retraining, outplacement services, etc.) for those who leave the organization so as to smooth the transition to another position, rather than letting people go with only the required severance pay and advance notice.

18. Provide training, cross-training, and retraining in advance of downsizing in order to help individuals know how to

adapt to downsizing rather than relying merely on post hoc on-the-job training.

Cost Cutting

19. Institute a variety of cost-cutting activities (such as restricting overtime, providing leave without pay, eliminating redundancies) rather than limiting downsizing to headcount reductions.
20. Focus on attacking sources of organizational fat which often go unnoticed and unmeasured, such as data fat (excess information), procedure fat (excess meetings), time fat (excess response time), and launch fat (excess new programs), rather than concentrating on cutting only the noticeable and measured features of the organization.
21. Map and analyze all processes in the organization to eliminate inefficiencies, redundancies, non-value-added steps and resources, and to redesign work, rather than assuming that old processes must be maintained.

Measurement

22. Measure speed and time used in the organization, not merely headcount, in looking for ways to downsize.
23. Develop specific measures of all activities and processes that directly relate to the key products and services provided by the organization in order to determine how improvements can be made rather than measuring only outputs.
24. Assess the skills, experience, and relevant attributes of all human resources so as to help improve decision making, regarding personnel and assignments, when downsizing and restructuring occur.

Implementation

25. Implement a broad array of downsizing strategies including redesign strategies and system strategies (e.g., culture change) instead of relying narrowly on headcount reduction strategies.
26. Administer downsizing equitably and fairly by ensuring that adverse impacts are not experienced unevenly by unempowered people (e.g., minorities, certain age groups) rather than implementing strategies based on power.

27. Provide opportunities for personal growth and development for individuals in the midst of downsizing rather than ignoring everything except profits and the financial bottom line.

28. Form cross-level and cross-functional teams to plan and implement downsizing with no required handoffs, rather than implementing downsizing using only a chain of command.

29. Change the appraisal, reward, selection, development, and communication systems to reflect the new goals and objectives of the downsized organization rather than keeping these systems the same as in the old, larger organizational form.

30. Implement downsizing by beginning with small wins—i.e., changing things that can be changed quickly and easily—which, when celebrated, create impetus toward desired results rather than attacking downsizing as a large, complex, indivisible task. (Cameron, 1994:207–210)

The Critical Success Factors Involved in Communicating Downsizing to Employees

Larkin and Larkin (1994:69–74) clearly delineate five critical success factors across all industries for successfully communicating downsizing to employees. These five criteria turn on who, what, and when (Larkin and Larkin, 1994:61–74).

WHO

31. The top management should communicate face-to-face and at the same time in writing to first-line supervisors on the downsizing and a test should be administered to check their accurate understanding of the information.

32. Then frontline supervisors should communicate face-to-face the materials to employees and a test administered to check their accurate understanding of the materials.

WHAT

33. The information communicated should be only—how many people are going? what are the criteria for selection? when do the terminations happen? and how much is the severance package?

34. This material should be presented simply in face-to-face interaction and written materials with examples only.

WHEN
35. The information should be presented within a short-time span, first to supervisors and then to employees. (Larkin and Larkin, 1995:61–74)

Having located several critical success factors in effective organizational downsizing, we are now in a position to see the effects of one firm's attempt to employ them.

A Case Study of One Firm's Use of Critical Success Factors in Downsizing to Improve Organizational Performance

The late Thomas Watson Jr. of IBM liked to tell Kierkegaard's tale about a man who relished watching the annual flight of wild ducks.

Each year he sowed a nearby lake with feed so the ducks would stop to eat. Some of the ducks gave up flying south and wintered at the lake instead. In time they grew fat and lazy. Why bother to fly when you have everything laid out for you right here?

The moral: You can make a wild duck tame, but you can never make a tame duck wild again.

In spite of this caution, IBM became a tame duck company in a wild duck industry. It is paying the price. So are the employees worldwide. Since 1986 185,000 have been let go. (McMenamin, 1994:126)

We have selected IBM as the basis for our case study for four reasons. *First,* IBM has downsized 185,000 employees between 1986 and 1994, more than any other U.S. firm. *Second,* IBM lost $18 billion between 1991 and 1993 but rebounded by earning $2.9 billion profit in 1994 at the height of its downsizing effort. *Third,* by 1993 IBM had achieved some success in implementing the previously outlined 35 critical success factors. *Fourth,* IBM's $2.9 billion recovery was not primarily the result of its downsizing efforts. The question is Why not? (Sherman, 1994:82)

In order to understand this downsizing effort and the reasons for its mixed results, we will (1) explore IBM's 1993 market position, strategy for change, and organizational targets; (2) explore its 1993 and 1994 downsizing effort in light of the previously outlined critical success factors, market positions, strategies for change, and organizational targets; and (3) investigate why IBM's 1994 and 1995 turnaround was not tied to its massive downsizing efforts.

IBM's Market Position and Strategy for Change

By early 1993, the International Business Machine Corporation (IBM) was a wounded giant. Between 1987 and 1993, IBM had "vaporized $60 billion in market value" (Sherman, 1994:78). Between 1991 and 1993, IBM had reported losses of $16 billion and its product lines profit margins had dropped from 50 percent to 32 percent in spite of shedding 100,000 workers. IBM was continuing to lose market shares in all five of its computer segments (Sagar and Cortese, 1995: 43). While IBM was clearly in trouble, it led the world in total computer and software sales. In the United States, IBM's $60 billion in sales was greater than the combined sales of the next six largest firms—Apple, Compaq, DEC, Hewlett-Packard, SUN, and Packard-Bell. IBM led the world in market shares in three of the five segments of the computer market mainframes, midrange, and PCs while remaining a top player in the other two—super computers and workstations (Robothan, 1994:25).

In spring 1993, IBM's Board of Directors appointed Lou Gerstner, a former senior executive of RJR/Nabisco, American Express, and McKinsey's Consulting as CEO to lead a turnaround of the firm. After carefully auditing IBM's operations, IBM's consultants noted,

> The problem is simple. Despite efforts to diversify, too much of IBM's revenue—49 percent—comes from computer hardware. And virtually every IBM hardware market is marked by eroding prices and profits. Between 1990 and 1993, a total of $14 billion in hardware profits evaporated . . . In fact, there is an alarming slide underway in IBM's large computer business—the product that delivers the highest profits and, equally important, secures IBM's hold on corporate customers. (Sagar and Cortese, 1994:97)

In late 1993 Gerstner came up with a final "bloodletting"—so he says—that resulted in an $8.9 billion loss. "To be blunt," Gerstner says, "the failure to capitalize on the sea of change in our industry is the single most important mistake that IBM has made in the last decade" (Sagar and Cortese, 1994:98). Gerstner thus began IBM's turnaround by trying to shift its reliance on mainframes and midsized computers to a balanced product mix by investing in PC, software, and improved marketing and sales. This was to be accomplished by reengineering IBM's management integration, coordination, and control processes. Gerstner attempted to focus IBM's *integration system on the development and use* of several core technologies across all its computer lines from handheld to mini. Gerstner's plan was to sell and/or lease these core technologies to other firms. This would allow IBM, the largest computer maker in the world, and its partners to leverage the cost and superiority of these technologies to set a worldwide standard that would replace the current Intel/Microsoft standard which employs the pentium chip and Windows software (Sherman, 1994:85).

First, Gerstner would employ IBM's power chip as the competitor for Intel's pentium chip. The power chip employs RISC technology (technospeak for Reduced Instructor-Set Computing). This technology allows IBM to provide 25 percent more information and speed per chip than Intel's pentium or 486 chips.

Second, Gerstner would employ IBM's workplace micro-kernals technology in linking IBM's hardware to its software application systems. The workplace micro-kernal can take on the personality of any operating system—OS2 warp, Windows 95, and so on. This would allow all IBM computers to work on any software operation system, thus making IBM computers more compatible and more flexible than any other system.

Third, IBM planned to upgrade OS2 warp, IBM's current operating system for PC computers so it would be better, quicker, and easier to use than any other competitor and get it to market faster than comparable operating systems.

Fourth, IBM would continue to fund Taligent, a joint venture with Apple to develop the workplace micro-kernal needed for a better flexible hardware/software linking system.

Fifth, IBM would attempt to involve all software application developers in a collective effort to expand IBM's portfolio of applications for IBM's computer systems.

Sixth, Gerstner would use the profits earned in its highly successful mainframe computers and software businesses to fund the development and sale of these new core technologies (Cortese, 1994:111–112).

Seventh, Gerstner's $8.9 billion charge against earning in 1993 included $2 billion in capital to be used in the next two years to create room for the new management team to maneuver. In addition, $2 billion was to come from property sales both of buildings and of IBM's famed art collection, and $8 billion from intended overhead cuts creating a battle chest of $12 billion to mount IBM's turnaround (Sagar, 1995:116–126).

In an attempt to investigate how to improve IBM's coordination systems, Gerstner began several benchmarking projects with competitors and several internal evaluation projects with consultants. These projects focused on evaluating and recommending improvements in several IBM business processes, namely updating and improving the (a) computer information systems, (b) hardward development, (c) production processes, (d) customer services, (e) marketing, (f) software development, (g) applications development, and (h) IBM management structure (Sagar and Cortese, 1994:96).

Finally, in an attempt to improve IBM's control systems, Gerstner established a 37-person executive council with seven new outside managers, to put in place a new management pay system in which 75 percent of all salary beyond base pay would be tied to unit profits and to begin setting strict and challenging performance targets. Next he asked Jerome York, IBM's new VP for finance, to study IBM's major competitors and estimate how much IBM would have to cut its overhead to remain competitive. Next, he asked his human relations vice president to carefully undertake a series of benchmark scenarios for IBM's downsizing based on the best available information. Finally, he asked York to prepare a description of market performance and projections for the next two years (Sherman, 1994:78–90).

IBM's Effectiveness in Downsizing and Its Strategy for Change

Between 1986 and 1995, IBM downsized its 420,000 workforce to 210,000 workers. Each year IBM's human resource management division came closer and closer to employing successfully all the critical success factors for effective downsizing listed in the first section of this chapter. In fact, between 1993 and 1995 when IBM downsized about 80,000 employees, the critical success factors involved in (a) approach, (b) preparation, (c) involvement, (d) leadership, (e) communication, (f) support, (g) costcutting, (h) measurement, and (i) information were systematically employed and carefully monitored. However, because of the interaction effects of IBM's downsizing efforts with the firm's strategic, leadership, and coordination decisions, some of the negative attributes associated with organizational decline still emerged, namely those regarding (a) resistance to change, (b) decreasing morale, and (c) loss of trust in organized management (Cushman and King, 1995; Merlo, 1995; Tadjbachsh, 1991; Tungate, 1990).

The effect of these negative attributes on IBM was lessened by April 1995 due to several noteworthy reversals in IBM's overall performance. *First,* IBM's sales, profits, and stock value advanced in 1994. In 1994, sales increased from $62 to $64 billion, profits increased from $-

8.9 to $3 billion, and stock price rose from $45 to $60 per share. By the first quarter of 1995, sales had reached $15.7 billion, profits $1.5 billion, and stock prices, $90 per share. *Second* and more important, IBM's growth both in sales and in profits cut across all product lines as gross profit margins rose from 39 to 42 percent. This reversed a three-year decline in gross profit margin from 55.9 to 39 percent (Hardy, 1995:209; Ziegler, 1995:A3). Let us explore more specifically these increases and their effects upon organizational downsizing.

First, market shares, profits, and margins were dramatically up in the *mainframe* and *midsize computer* markets. This area accounted for 68 percent of IBM's total profits in 1995, up from 65 percent in 1994. Here IBM had to supplement downsizing with hiring in order to meet the unexpected demand (Sagar, 1995:82; *The Economist,* 1995:56; Sagar and Cortese, 1995:42).

Second, market shares, profits, and margins went dramatically down in the PC market. Here a new top executive arrived from outside IBM. He was immediately confronted by the need to offload over $700 million in inventory to make room for a new PC, the Aptiva (Kirkpatrick, 1994:118). The new head of the PC division, Richard Thoman, was late in getting the product to market due to research and development and manufacturing problems and then substantially underestimated the demand for the product. When he attempted to increase production dramatically, he had major problems with suppliers (Ziegler, 95:1B). In the fourth quarter of 1993, IBM's share of the PC market rose from 15 to 18 percent in the United States and IBM led the market in shares. Then in 1994, when the troubles with the new PC set in, market shares dropped from 18 to 5 percent, while the PC market as a whole gained 27 percent. IBM watched as Compaq, Apple, and Packard Bell passed them in market shares. Several managerial and coordination problems associated with reengineering led to a $1 billion loss. This in turn evaporated all the financial gains made from downsizing (Sagar and Cortese, 1995:43; Kirkpatrick, 1994:10). These problems led to the departure of two of Thompson's associates—the general manager and the head of manufacturing. Such problems demonstrated how an ongoing downsizing effort can be undermined by leadership and coordination problems which evaporate the financial gains from downsizing and leave a division in disarray (Ziegler, 1995:B8; Ziegler, 1995:B1).

Third, between 1990 and 1994, IBM's sales staff was cut from 150,000 to 70,000. In 1995, under senior VP Robert LaBent, sales operating costs were to be cut by another third. A reengineering and downsizing program aimed at (1) cutting workers, (2) converting portions of the sales staff to computer consultants, (3) routing more sales through outlets, and (4) tieing the remaining sales and consultants' pay—60 percent to profitability and 40 percent to customer satisfaction—was undertaken. However, this downsizing was confronted by two problems—the failure of the PC and software divisions to bring products to market on time, and the lack of parts for PCs, leaving many customers very unsatisfied. This had a serious demoralizing impact on PC computer sales at a time when PC sales for most firms were up 27 percent (Sagar, McWilliams, and Hof, 1994:110; Sagar, 1994:126).

Fourth, in spring 1994, an internal review of IBM's software businesses concluded "that most units were uncompetitive, bloated, and inefficient" (Sagar and Cortese, 1995:43). All software workers were decentralized to their irrespective hardware platform units. This in turn led to infighting and gridlock. Similarly, IBM's joint venture with Apple to develop a key component for the workplace micro-kernal was long overdue. In addition, while IBM's OS2 warp operating systems sales had reached 9 million, their chief competitor, Microsoft Windows, had sold 60 million with a new upgraded system due out in April 1995. Several analysts pointed out that IBM had spent more on advertising and marketing OS2 warp than the system had taken in in revenues. Late in 1994, Gerstner combined all software units under senior VP John Thompson, and let two more of IBM's top software managers go. These moves along with organizational downsizing left the software unit in disarray, evaporating IBM's savings from downsizing in these units.

Several questions remain to be answered. What role did IBM's benchmarking play in its downsizing? What role did downsizing play in IBM's turnaround? What has our case study of IBM's downsizing taught us about the effective use of benchmark critical success factors? The answers to these questions appear both complex and important.

Conclusions Regarding the Appropriate Use of Communicating Benchmarking Organizational Downsizing

Benchmarking is a tool for assessing best practices and using the resulting stretch objectives as design criteria for changing the performance of an organization. (Jennings and Westfall, 1992:22)

The way the majority of companies downsize, the short-term quick fixes to productivity, competitiveness, and costs that result are paltry when placed against the measurable casualty long-term damage done. (Cascio, 1994:8)

We began this chapter by pointing out that most U.S. firms are involved in some type of benchmarking project, that most of the Fortune 500 corporations are involved in downsizing projects, and that 60 to 70 percent of all these efforts will not meet management's objectives for success. Next we located a detailed set of critical success factors for downsizing from firms which had met management's objectives for success. Then we noted that IBM had applied successfully these critical success factors to its most recent downsizing effort. Finally, we found that while IBM employed critical success factors, the downsizing met with mixed results. More specifically we found

First, that IBM's *corporate strategy* significantly altered the effectiveness of the downsizing outcomes in some units, irrespective of the benchmarking critical success factors.

Second, that IBM's *leadership decision-making* significantly altered the effectiveness of downsizing in some units, irrespective of benchmarking critical success factors.

Third, that IBM's *inter-unit coordination* significantly altered the effectiveness of downsizing in some units, irrespective of IBM's use of benchmarking critical success factors.

Fourth, that the *actions of IBM competitors* significantly altered the effectiveness of downsizing in some units, irrespective of IBM's use of benchmarking critical success factors.

Fifth, IBM's downsizing did significantly contribute to the $6.5 billion cuts in overhead which led to a $3 billion increase in 1994 profits. However, how much of this contribution carried over to their $3 billion profit in 1994 and $1.5 billion in profits for the first quarter of 1995 is unclear. Without an audit of IBM's $12 billion turnaround war chest, it is unclear exactly how much the downsizing contributed and how much evaporated in the $1 billion loss in PCs and the reduced sales in software.

In short, the effective benchmarking of any organizational communication activity is dependent upon the effective use of all communication and management activities. In high-performance firms, we can explore these activities, one at a time, and isolate critical success factors which work because all the other activities of the firm are performing well. However, in low-performance firms, numerous other factors can significantly alter the application of critical success factors and thus an understanding of their success or failure. This is what occurred in IBM with a negative synergistic mix of rearview mirror corporate strategies, hesitant leadership decision-making, lack of inter-unit coordination, and aggressive competitors. If you downsize enough, it may in some form lead to a reduced operating cost, all other things being held constant. It is not clear that this is what happened at IBM which, as a "tame duck," has not yet made the migratory leap from a traditional stance of continuous change to the demands of discontinuous change.

4

Lessons from Leading Organizational Turnaround at IBM

Donald P. Cushman and Sarah S. King

IBM is back on its feet and we're moving forward, gathering momentum. The firm's stock price has more than doubled, while sales, profits, and product margins are up. Most encouraging, we're winning again in the marketplace with customers.
Lou Gerstner, 1995 (reported in Hays, 1995)

Everyone loves a winner, and Lou Gerstner, CEO of IBM, appears to have a winner's credentials. Gerstner took over the reins of IBM in April 1992. At that time IBM had lost $60,000 in stockholder values, had registered $17 billion in losses, had laid off 100,000 workers, and was clearly a corporation in crises. After three years of reengineering and an additional $8.9 billion in changes against profits, Gerstner, in January 1995, reported to stockholders that in 1994 IBM's sales rose from $62 billion to $64 billion, profits rose from $-8.9 billion to $+3 billion with stock prices rising from $45 to $60 per share (Sagar and Cortese, 1995:42). In addition, three months later, Gerstner reported that in the first quarter of 1995, IBM had $15.7 billion in sales and $1.5 billion in profits, and stock prices rose to $90 per share (Ziegler, 1995:A3). Gerstner proclaimed that "IBM was back." (Hays, 1995:B6)

At the same time, several experts in the computer industry challenged this claim. Hays and Ziegler (1995:A1) argue that IBM is profiting handsomely from several factors that they believe will disappear between 1996 and 1998. *First,* a surging economy which led to a rapid increase in computer sales will turn down by 1996. *Second,* mainframe computer sales which account for 50 percent of IBM's current profits will drop dramatically in the next few years.

Third, one-third of IBM's profits are an artifact of translating foreign sales into weak U.S. dollars. *Fourth,* most of Gerstner's reengineering efforts have failed to reposition IBM for increased competitiveness and growth. In short, IBM's current performance is based on nonrepeatable, accidental factors and has little to do with Gerstner's leadership. Therefore, IBM may slide back into debt during the next recession (Hays and Ziegler, 1995).

It is the purpose of this chapter to explore IBM's attempt to recover from a recession and Gerstner's role in leading IBM's recovery. Our hope is to learn something about organizational turnaround from recession. Our inquiry will be divided into three stages: (1) an inquiry into Gerstner's analysis of IBM's market position, problems, and strategy for turnaround; (2) an exploration of Gerstner's successes and failures in implementing his strategy; and (3) drawing some conclusions regarding lessons which can be learned from leading organizational turnaround following a recession. Let us address each of these issues in turn.

Gerstner's Turnaround Strategy for IBM

[Turnaround leaders] face two fundamental tasks: first, to develop and articulate exactly what the company is trying to accomplish, and second, to create an environment in which employees can figure out what needs to be done and then do it well.
(Huey, 1994:44)

Between 1986 and 1992, IBM had vaporized $60 billion in stockholder value, taken a $17 billion charge against profits, laid off 100,000 workers, watched its market shares across its five major computer markets shrink, and stood by as its profit margins shrunk from 60 to 39 percent (Sherman, 1994:82). However, IBM remained the largest computer and software maker in the world. In addition, IBM still was number one in market shares in three of the world's top five computer markets with 20.6 market shares in mainframes, 19.2 percent in midrange computers, and 13 percent market shares in PC computers. In addition, IBM remained a major player in supercomputers with 1.8 percent market shares, and in workstations with 8.4 percent market shares. In the U.S. computer market. IBM's $60 billion in sales was greater than the combined sales of the next six largest firms—Apple, Compaq, DEC, Hewlett Packard, SUN, and Packard Bell (Robotham, 1994:25; Sagar and Cortese, 1995:43).

By mid-April 1993, IBM's Board of Directors had appointed Lou Gerstner, a former senior executive at RJR Nabisco, American Express, and McKinsey's Consulting as CEO to lead IBM's recovery from recession. Gerstner began by talking with several nationally known CEOs—Jack Welch of GE, Bill Gates of Microsoft, Lawrence Bossidy of Allied Signal, Andy Grove of Intel, and so on. Then he commissioned several external and internal consultants to audit, benchmark, and evaluate IBM's various units performances.

Next, Gerstner evaluated IBM's gross profits and margins in each of its five market segments between 1990 and 1993. *First,* in *hardware,* IBM's profits dropped from *24.5 billion* in 1990 to *10 billion* in 1993 and its margins dropped from 55.9 percent to 32.3 percent. The $14.6 billion in losses during the 1990 through 1993 recession suggested the need to increase IBM's revenues and profits from other divisions. *Second,* in *software,* profits remained flat at *$6.5 billion* with margins slipping from *68.4 percent to 60.7 percent.* *Third,* in *computer maintenance,* profits also remained flat at *$3.5 billion* with margins falling from 54.1 to 51.4 percent. *Fourth,* in *computer leasing,* profits remained flat at $2.7 billion with margins flat at 58.3 percent. *Fifth,* in *computer services,* profits rose from $.8 billion to $1.5 billion as margins dropped from 19.6 percent to 14.7 percent. The major problems confronting Gerstner are to decrease IBM's reliance on hardware profits by increasing the profits and margins in IBM's other businesses (Sagar and Cortese, 1994:97).

By mid-1993, Gerstner had concluded that IBM's core technologies in computer chips (the power chip) and software operating systems (OS2 warp) and micro-kernal technology (Workplace) were the best in the industry. The problems at IBM were primarily attributable to a poor management structure, corporate attitude, and management behaviors. By year's end, Gerstner took an $8.9 billion charge against profits in what he termed IBM's "last bloodletting" and announced his plans for an IBM turnaround (Sagar and Cortese, 1994:96).

First, at *a strategic level,* IBM would attempt to employ its superiority in core technologies across all hardware lines (i.e., PCs, workstations, client servers, mini and mainframe computer systems) while at the same time expanding the sale of these core technologies to other computer makers. Gerstner hoped this strategy would have two effects: (1) increase IBM's profits from all its hardware platforms leading to a more balanced set of profits, and (2) allow IBM, the largest computer maker in the world, to leverage the cost and superiority of its technologies to set a new worldwide computer standard. This new standard would then replace the current Intel and Microsoft standard based on the Pentium chip and Windows software operating systems (Sagar and Cortese, 1994:96).

Second, at *an operational level* IBM would reengineer its organizational integration, coordination, and control processes. This, Gerstner hoped, would improve IBM's productivity, speed-to-market, and, in turn, market shares. It would also help make IBM more responsive to its customer needs while challenging its most effective competitors (Sagar, 1995:120).

Gerstner focused his reengineering of IBM's *integration processes* on the development and use of several core technologies across all computer lines. He hoped to employ *IBM's power chip* as the *competitor for Intel's pentium chip.* The power chip employs reduced instruction-set computing technology (RISC). This technology allows IBM to provide 25 percent more information and speed per chip than Intel's pentium or 486 chip. He wanted to employ *IBM's workplace micro-kernal technology* as a competitor to *Microsoft's Windows.* The micro-kernal technology would link IBM's hardware to its software operating system's OS2 warp. The workplace micro-kernal can take on the personality of any operating system—OS2 warp or Windows 95. This would allow IBM's computers to work on all operating and applications systems software. Gerstner would continue to fund Taligent, IBM's joint venture with Apple computer to develop the workplace micro-kernal. In addition, he would encourage all software firms to develop applications for all of IBM's hardware platforms, thus expanding IBM's portfolio of applications. IBM would use the profits from mainframes to fund the development and sales of these core technologies. Finally, Gerstner's $8.9 billion charge against earnings in 1993 included $3 billion in capital to be used in the next two years for reengineering. In addition, IBM sold $2 billion in buildings and property and $.5 billion in rare art from its collection and saved $8 billion in overhead from downsizing. He thus put $13.5 billion in IBM's war chest to mount its turnaround (Sagar, 1995:116–120).

In evaluating IBM's *coordination processes,* Gerstner decided to set up eight teams to reengineer IBM's business processes. These included IBM's (a) internal computer information systems, (b) hardware development, (c) production processes, (d) customer service, (e) marketing and sales processes, (f) software development, (g) applications development, and (h) management structures. These reengineering efforts were to be completed within 36 months (Sagar and Cortese, 1994:96).

In an attempt to improve IBM's *control processes*, Gerstner established a 37-person executive council with seven new outside managers, put in place a new management compensation system in which 75 percent of all salaries beyond base pay would be tied to unit profits, and began setting clear and challenging performance targets. Jerome York, IBM's new VP for finance, led a major study of competitors to determine how much IBM would need to cut in overhead to remain competitive. Gerstner then asked IBM's human relations VP to carefully undertake a series of benchmarking scenarios for IBM's downsizing. Finally, he asked York to prepare market projections on key competitors' performances (Sherman, 1994:78–90).

Gerstner's Effectiveness in Implementing His Turnaround Strategy

What I've found in IBM is that the very core strengths had always been there and were still there. The problem was more the attitudes, the kind of management structures, and the management behaviors that got built up in the face of success . . .

Then we did things relating to the compensation system and to breaking down the fiefdoms. And we had a few public hangings of people who didn't want to get on the new program. That told everybody we were serious.
Lou Gerstner 1995 (in Sagar, 1995:120)

On April 21, 1995, IBM's VP for finance, York, announced dramatic first quarter performance results—net income rose to $15.7 billion, profits to $1.2, margins from 29.2 to 42.4 percent, with profits up across all product lines, while expenses fell 3.4 percent. In addition, IBM spent $1.5 billion on a stock repurchase and retired $7.7 billion in debt while maintaining a $10.5 billion cash balance, raising the prospect of a major IBM acquisition. York cautioned that IBM still needed to cut $1.5 billion in operating costs, that the PC and disc drive units, while improving in performance, still had not turned the corner, and that while software sales were up 11 percent, two-thirds of the sales were in mainframes. In short, there was work that needed to be done (Ziegler, 1995:A3).

On April 26, 1995, at a stockholders' meeting, Gerstner announced that "IBM was back." Conceding that IBM still had much to do in better forecasting demand for products and in improving their PC business, Gerstner concluded that IBM would be the industrial leader again. Gerstner described 1994 as a "watershed year" in new product innovation with nearly half of all first quarter revenues coming from products introduced in the previous 18 months. This included a new high-end mainframe, a new midrange parallel power ranger, and the RS6000 workstation (Hays, 1995:B6). Let us explore IBM's progress in detail.

First, market shares, profits, and margins were up in most hardware areas (i.e., mainframes and midsize and workstation computer markets). IBM came out with important new products in each of these markets. These new products accounted for 50 percent of all sales. These hardware platforms accounted for 68 percent of IBM's total profits in the first quarter of 1995 up from 65 percent in 1994, with mainframe sales and software accounted for 50 percent of the profits. Adding the 68 percent of total profits from hardware to the 30 percent of growth in profits derived from converting foreign sales into weak U.S. dollars accounts for 98 percent of IBM's profits. This very high concentration of profits in the hardware area runs counter to Gerstner's stated strategy of relying less on hardware for sales and profits and more on IBM's four other profit areas—software, maintenance, leasing, and service (Hays and Ziegler, 1995:A1).

Three problems arose from IBM's over-reliance on hardware. Mainframe sales and software, which accounted for 50 percent of all profits, are sensitive to economic cycles. They tend to surge up during economic upturns and drop during economic downturns. The United States just came out of an upturn and in 1996 is predicted to hit a major downturn. In addition, several studies by mainframe vendors report that 80 percent of all customers intend to migrate their operations to cheaper midrange computers, workstations, and/ or customer server networks (Hays and Ziegler, 1995:A1). In all these areas, IBM faces stiff competition. In mainframe computers Hitachi is taking away IBM market shares. In workstations Hewlett Packard and IBM are locked in a battle for the top spot with 32 percent and 29 percent market shares. In customer servers Compaq and IBM are battling with 20 and 18 percent market shares (McCartney, 1995:B4).

Hitachi has developed a bipolar mainframe twice as powerful as IBM's. IBM had put off upgrading its bipolar mainframe to concentrate on developing its CMOS mainframe technology. However, its new CMOS mainframe accounted for only one-third of its new sales. Even IBM loyalists appear to be cutting back. Terry Jones, president of AMR Corporation's Saber reservation system and the poster boy on IBM's latest annual report has decided to shift to Hitachi mainframes. IBM lost a large mainframe contract to the Chinese government when Compaq computers convinced China to employ client servers and PCs in place of mainframes. In addition, Delaware North, Sygma Inc., Sprint, and Dupont are turning to IBM's competitors for midrange computers, and/or client servers (Hays and Ziegler, 1995:A1). Finally, IBM extended its OS2 software operating system across its lines of mini computers, client servers, and workstations. However, the new micro-kernal which was to allow all software operating and application systems to run on IBM's hardware has not been completed. So IBM's mini computers, client servers, and workstations are short on application systems that can run on these platforms (Hays and Ziegler, 1995:A1).

So with IBM's mainframe market shrinking and subject to cyclical swings, with competition from Hitachi's mainframes from above and Hewlett Packard workstations and Compaq's client servers from below, along with IBM's micro-kernal software problems, it may be difficult to sustain 50 percent profits in this area in the next few years.

Second, IBM's market shares, profits, and margins have dropped dramatically in the rapidly expanding PC market. Here a new top executive arrived from outside IBM. He was immediately confronted by the need to offload over $700 million in inventory to make room for a new PC, the Activa (Kirkpatrick, 1994:118). The new head of the PC division, Richard Thoman, was then late in getting the PC products to market due to research and development and manufacturing problems and substantially underestimating the demand for these PC products. When IBM attempted to increase production dramatically, it had major problems with suppliers (Ziegler, 1995:1B).

In the fourth quarter of 1993, IBM's share of the United States PC market rose from 13 to 18 percent and IBM led the world in PC market shares. Then in 1994, when the PC units' delivery problems began to emerge, United States market shares dropped from 18 to 5 percent, while the PC market as a whole gained 27 percent. IBM watched as Compaq, Apple, and Packard Bell passed them in U.S. market shares, with Compaq being number one in the world. IBM's PC division reported a $1 billion loss in 1994. This in turn evaporated all the gains from downsizing and left the division in disarray (Sagar and Cortese, 1995:45; Kirkpatrick, 1994:10). These problems led in turn to the departure of two of Thoman's assistants—the general manager and the head of manufacturing. IBM immediately set up teams to reengineer these processes (Ziegler, 1995:B8; Ziegler, 1995:B1).

By April 1995, Thoman had begun to make some deliveries of the Activa PC and Butterfly laptop computers (Ziegler, 1995:B8). However, finding a solution to IBM's supplier and manufacturing problems is probably one to two years away (Hill, 1995:R4). Gerstner believes that the PC division will make some real progress in 1995. He argues, "Let me tell you something. Thoman made a very very brave decision that I supported: to make a whole lot of fundamental changes simultaneously" (Sagar, 1995:117). This has left the PC division in disarray for the next 36 months. IBM's new products in the PC market, OS2 warp operating system, Activa and Butterfly, may be outdated by the time the PC division solves its supplier, manufacturing, and market analysis problems. The cost of developing these new products along with advertising them will not be regrouped, so this division will be unprofitable for the next two years unless creative bookkeeping is employed.

Third, in spring 1994, an internal review of IBM's software businesses concluded "that most units were uncompetitive, bloated, and inefficient" (Sagar and Cortese, 1995:43). Under IBM's former CEO, all software workers had been decentralized to their respective hardware platform units. This in turn led to infighting and gridlock. In addition, IBM's joint venture with Apple to develop a key component for the workplace micro-kernal was long overdue. While IBM's OS2 warp operating systems sales had reached 9 million, their chief competitor, Microsoft Windows, had sold 60 million with a new upgraded system due out in April 1995. Several analysts pointed out that IBM had spent more on advertising and marketing OS2 warp than the system had taken in in revenues. Late in 1994, Gerstner combined all software units under senior VP John Thompson and let two more of IBM's top software managers go.

In May 1995, the software unit got its Remote PC Networks software to market. However, it was late and had been brought out in such a piecemeal fashion that it severely limited the sales of IBM's client server system. In addition, this version works only on IBM's workstation (*Wall Street Journal* Staff, 1995:B4). Finally, in May 1995, Gerstner sent a memo to his top 100 executives requesting that each place a telephone call to at least 10 software vendors and ask them to write applications software for OS2 (Cortese, 1995:6). Thus IBM hardware operating on OS2 in the mini computer, workstation, client server, PC, and handheld markets was limited by software application problems pending outside help. These problems, along with organizational downsizing, have left the software unit in disarray again, evaporating all the savings gained from downsizing those units.

Fourth, IBM's three other businesses—computer maintenance, leasing, and service—account for less than 15 percent of IBM's sales and profits. They would all need to be expanded substantially by acquisitions if they are to take up the slack in balancing hardware sales and profits. The *computer maintenance division* received a boost on May 6, 1995, when IBM acquired GE Capital's computer maintenance unit for between $50 and $100 million. GE's unit employs 1,300 workers (Bloomberg, 1995:37). IBM's *service unit* revenues rose 33 percent in the first quarter of 1995 to $2.4 million. IBM has the funds available to make a major acquisition in this area, but as yet has failed to move.

Finally, IBM's strategy of leveraging the superiority of its core technologies across its computer lines to challenge Intel's pentium chip and Windows software appears to be a failure with both firms expanding dramatically their market shares just as they are ready to bring out upgraded chips and software (Hays and Ziegler, 1995:A1).

What can we conclude from this analysis and evaluation regarding the implementation of Gerstner's turnaround strategy?

Conclusions Regarding Lessons Learned from Gerstner's Turnaround Strategy

Management has to think like a fighter pilot. You can't always make the right decision. You have to learn to adjust.
(Steward, 1993:67)

Five conclusions are suggested by our analysis.

First, while IBM does appear to have some technological capability in parallel processing, workstations, and PCs, these advantages have been minimized, if not undermined, by poor product sales projections; weak coordination between suppliers, manufacturing, and sales; and major problems in software development.

Second, at IBM, "management improvement is job one," and it is not moving forward. Six key managers have been replaced in the past two years with little improvement showing at this time in the units from which they came. In addition, more integration, coordination, and control problems have surfaced than under Gerstner's predecessor.

Third, IBM's hardware division may be under siege from clean, lean, and mean competitors and may be the next area in which heads will roll.

Fourth, IBM's PC, software, and sales divisions are undergoing reengineering and will not be well soon.

Fifth, IBM, under Gerstner's leadership, may or may not be back. If (a) the global economy can stay out of recession; (b) IBM can quickly reengineer its mainframe, PC, software, supplier, manufacturing, and sales processes; (c) IBM can make several large acquisitions in the computer maintenance, leasing, and/or service area; (d) IBM can upgrade its core technologies; (e) IBM can build a strong management team, then IBM will indeed be back. Until now, little that Lou Gerstner has done can be directly traceable to IBM's turnaround. In the words of Lou Gerstner himself, "If mainframes weren't holding up the company, the sheet would come off the cadaver" (Sagar and Cortese, 1995:42).

5

Lessons in Governmental Budgeting during Recession in the United States

Susanne Morris

Introduction

In the late 1970s and early 1980s a combination of increasing expenditures and declining revenues created varying degrees of fiscal stress for many governments in the United States. Increasing expenditures were, in part, attributable to changes in federal programs and an unusual amount of inflation but also to the economic recession which produced substantial unemployment and thereby increased social services costs. The recession also contributed to loss of tax revenue and, in part, to the citizen tax revolts which also diminished government revenues. The result for some governments was a degree of fiscal stress unmatched since the depression of the 1930s.

The effects of this fiscal stress were thought to be reflected in three different types of governmental response (Nagel, 1980:8): changed output in many kinds of services, increased interest in efficiency and productivity, and substantial budgetary cutback. While all of these responses are interrelated in varying ways, it is the latter which interests us here.

In this analysis of budgetary behavior in a cutback situation, we will be essentially looking at organizational response to substantial environmental transformation and uncertainty in a particular functional area of government—budgeting.

In a cutback situation, the availability of resources becomes much more tenuous and problematic than is the case in "normal" times. The level of commitment to existing policies would seem inevitably to alter as attention to the budgetary emergency becomes more necessary. Under such conditions the interrelationships between budget constraints—particularly in political units which must

75

maintain parity between expenditures and revenues—and policy imperatives will change and such change calls for new analysis and interpretation.

This chapter addresses this issue focusing on two research questions: (1) to what extent do rules and other structural constraints shape budgetary decision making as financial instability and economic decline worsen? and (2) what is the response of budgetary decision makers under conditions of protracted fiscal stress? In addressing these questions the research provides a fuller understanding of budgetary behavior and the role of the budget under other than growth conditions. An end note looks at these implications in a broader way.

Budgets typically are viewed as means for planning, management, and control. But budgets are also powerful communication tools in the policy-making process (Wooldridge, 1984). They tell us a great deal about our policy preferences as well as our capacity to govern our affairs.

The Research Design

The study involved a two-stage analysis of the argument that incrementalism is an inadequate model to explain budgetary behavior in a cutback era. In stage one, tests are made of the linear, marginality, and fair-shares dimensions of incrementalist theory through quantitative analyses of budget appropriations based on the work of Davis, Dempster, and Wildavsky (1974): Natchez and Bupp (1973); and Hoole, Handley, and Ostrom (1979) among others. These results have been reported elsewhere (Morris and Brierly, 1990 and 1991).

The second stage explored in depth the response of budgetary decision makers to changing conditions of resource availability and uncertainty. Hypotheses were drawn in part from Schick's work (1980) which is a conceptual framework similar to Wildavsky's (1975) but which explicitly addresses and formulates hypotheses concerning behavioral response in adapting budgets to resource scarcity. Attention is focused in this stage on the dimensions of incrementalism which emphasize the annual cycle, budgetary roles and centralization issue in the budgetary process, and the role of the budget itself.

Data were drawn from the Michigan State government experience from 1963 through 1984. During this twenty-one-year period, state government had to recede from previous spending commitments thirteen times. And in three of those fiscal years—FY1980 through mid-1983—the state of Michigan reduced state spending by more than $2.6 billion. In constant dollars, spending in FY 1982 alone was the equivalent of a drop of 21.5 percent compared to FY 1979, in some respects the last "normal" year before that fiscal crisis began.

Although Michigan has not been alone among the states in facing fiscal crisis and is like 49 of the 50 states in needing to maintain a balanced budget (Yondorf and Summers, 1983:16), the state has been exceptional in having to manage such severe and continuing cuts. A 1981 survey of fiscal pressures in the fifty states found that Michigan had been the most seriously affected (*Comparative State Politics Newsletter*, 1981:1, 16).

The Michigan experience was selected, in part, because it represents an extreme case which is potentially a crucial test of the budget theory propositions. According to Lijphart (1971:692), this sort of theory-confirming or theory-infirming case study is enhanced if the case is extreme on one of the variables.

Michigan data were also selected because the level of professionalization within the legislative and executive branches is relatively high compared to that of other states. Therefore, we may assume that the quality of information developed and secured during the time period reflects state-of-the-art analysis within the states and that inability to forecast revenue falls was not a product of administrative or technical incompetence. In addition, Michigan data was also selected because, as the nation's tenth largest state, and as an industrialized, urbanized state, Michigan has developed the full range of programs customarily found in these more complex socioeconomic systems.

Finally, Michigan data was also chosen for accessibility to this researcher. Having been a legislative staff member in the mid-1970s and having maintained contact with many individuals in the Michigan legislative and executive branches through activities with professional associations increased the likelihood that information about budgetary decisions would be available to this researcher if such data were available to anyone outside the budgetary process.

The Research Setting: The Michigan Political Economic Environment

The research setting, the environment which spawned interest in this particular research problem, is state government in Michigan, the Great Lakes state, the union's eighth largest by population (Lane,

1984:642), and until recently, at least, home of the automobile capital of the world. Reported here are the events which shaped the budget process in the cutback periods: 1970 through 1974, 1974 through 1975, and 1980 through 1983.

As previously noted, public budgeting takes place in political and economic environments which may vary considerably in stability and resources. It has been argued that the combination of those variables tends to produce distinct budgetary outcomes. What follows is an examination of the environment which produced the exceptional budgetary outcomes which are the focus of this study.

The Cyclical Economy

Fundamental to Michigan's condition is its status as an industrial state with a highly cyclical economy. No one who studies the state can escape making that observation. For example, an analysis by Bryan and Howard (1979) of unemployment rates in the 50 states plus the District of Columbia from 1957 through 1977 showed that Michigan's unemployment ranged from a low of 3.5 to 13.8, making it number one in the nation.

At the center of Michigan industry is the automobile. Automobiles have dominated the Michigan economy for decades. A University of Michigan study in the early 1970s reported that 80 percent of the variance in the Michigan economy could be attributed to changes in the auto industry. Although the link began to weaken in the mid-70s, when a combination of increasing interest rates and fuel shortages brought about by the international oil crisis caused consumers to rethink their automobile preferences, motor vehicles and related products still are a significant part of Michigan's economy. As of 1983 (Rosen and Wang) one in six Michigan workers owed his or her living to the auto or related industries.

National economic cycles have traditionally been magnified in Michigan because of the dominance of high-wage durable-goods industries. As of 1980, although only 22 percent of the nation's workers were employed in manufacturing, that percentage was 7 percent higher in Michigan. According to a major study released in 1982 (Brazer and Laren), national industrial output which slumped three percent in 1969 and 1970, nine percent from 1973 through 1975, and an equal amount from 1979 through 1980, was magnified in Michigan to 16, 18, and 31 percent respectively.

Slumps in the national economy come to Michigan later, are deeper, and stay longer. For example, when leading economic indicators showed that the national economy was going into a period of stagnation in fall 1976, newspapers in the Michigan capital reported that the economy was good there (*The State Journal*, October 30, 1976). But when the national economy was showing a turnaround in 1982, and unemployment stood at 8.5 percent, joblessness in Michigan was 14.9 percent and going higher.

Michigan's Declining Share of the National Economic Pie

Because of the changing structure of the national economy, in which manufacturing and heavy industry is shrinking and services are expanding, Michigan's personal income has been steadily eroding. Once among the highest in the nation, Michigan's share of U.S. per capita income has tumbled during the last thirty years to a point just below the national average.

Yet Michigan continues to receive relatively less federal largesse because of disadvantageous federal policies. Among the states, Michigan is a net donor to the federal treasury and shares unequally in federal monies. Because it is a high-wage state, Michiganians send relatively large amounts of tax dollars to the federal government. For example, in 1980 Michigan ranked fifth among the states in contributing federal tax dollars and was last in receiving assistance. State policymakers say this inequity arises from several factors. Among them: matching formulas for federal spending programs are based on per capita wealth but do not take into account unemployment rates, cost differentials, tax effort, or relative welfare burden. The national defense build-up which has poured billions into some states has largely bypassed Michigan, along with other midwestern and northeastern states (Hollister, 1983a).

Other federal policies have also cost Michigan directly. For example, adoption of the Individual Retirement Act (IRA) income tax deduction reduced tax receipts in Michigan for a period just when they were needed most because the state's income tax is based on the federal system. Adoption of the federal Omnibus Reconciliation Act which took effect in October 1981 forced Michigan to reduce its state budget by $50 million. And, when federal assistance has been available (for example, to shore up the state's unemployment compensation fund), it has had to be repaid.

Michigan's financial market credibility is only partially controlled by state policymakers. Financial rating services external to the state play a crucial role in the state's ability to borrow money on the national market.

The Population Base: Its Shrinking Rate of Growth and Some Consequences

From 1960 to 1970, Michigan's population grew by 11.4 percent. In the decade that followed, growth slowed to 4.2 percent. And from 1980 through 1982, population actually shrank by almost two percent. Out migration increased, and, instead of consisting largely of retirees heading to Florida and other points south, record numbers of midcareer workers left looking for better opportunities elsewhere. Most of this loss was attributed to the state's stagnating economy (Gorwitz, 1982; 1983a; 1983b).

The consequences of this population decline meant not only an absolute loss in income and business tax revenue, but also contraction of federal aid which is based, in part, on population size. It also cost Michigan a seat in Congress (Gorwitz, 1982).

At the time that Michigan's population was shrinking, its distribution was also changing. Outmigration from the cities into suburban and exurban areas continued, bringing with it a redistribution of political preferences wherein suburban and exurban interests, traditionally more fiscally conservative, became more dominant (Gorwitz, 1982).

An Aging Liberal Political Establishment under Siege and a Disbelieving Electorate

In the post–World War II period, this industrialized, high-wage, relatively well educated population had begun to vote for fairly consistently liberal administrations in state government. As one veteran observer says,

> From 1948 on, it [was] impossible for the Republicans to be elected as mainstream . . . You either had to be (or act like) an independent or a Democrat. [Governor] Romney played the independent game and [Governor] Milliken made an accommodation with the Democrats and took the Republican Party to the left. There was an aspiration for programming beyond resource and unwillingness to raise the level of taxation to accommodate that resource . . . So we [did not] have . . . a balanced budget for more than a decade. Milliken made this political choice, hoping that things were going to improve.
>
> It's sort of like embezzlement. If you were to interview an embezzler, he's never going to tell you that he's going to steal

money. He says that he's going to borrow money, nobody will know, and that he's going to use this money to make money and then return it. So, in fact, I would say that the government policy from 1974 to 1982 was a policy of embezzlement.

Captured in this view are a configuration of forces:

- a constituency increasingly interested in expanding public services and unconvinced that funds are insufficient to cover everything.
- a legislative body eager to respond to that preference (for more information on the legislative process, see Morris, 1979) and
- a much-elected governor, also committed through accommodation to those preferences, but lodged in a political party traditionally opposed to raising taxes. This antipathy toward raising taxes was powerfully reinforced through recurrent (almost annual) exposure to various voter initiatives designed to limit government spending, one of which did succeed in 1978 and markedly changed the nature of state budgeting in Michigan.

However, hidden in this view are undercurrents arising from the natural competition between the legislature and the executive. For example, in spring 1976, although it was not an election year for the Senate, lawmakers there twice declined to give the governor's budget-year extension bill immediate effect, which meant that the law would not have been implemented until the following April, leaving the state seriously in arrears in that fiscal year. Only the governor's threats to unleash further budget slashes in social services finally persuaded the Senate to give him what he wanted (*The State Journal,* May 15, 1976).

Also hidden are contradictory views about the leadership role of the governor, especially of the governor whose term in office extended for the greatest share of the time period under study. There are those who argue that after years in office, the governor simply tired of being involved and left things to his underlings who lacked the power to carry through. There are those scholars (e.g., VerBurg and Press, 1982) who argue that the governor, enamored of professionalism, turned the budget process over to the technocrats who could make no political decisions. Then there is a management view that the governor, being a skilled executive, believed in delegation and let his budget officer take care of things. And there is a fifth view that the governor, a skilled politician, knew he was in an untenable position and let his underlings take the heat.

Add to this those demographic changes and the industrial and financial forces unleashed by a turbulent economy described above, and one has the setting for a budget under stress.

Findings: The State Response to Recession

As observed previously, a fiscal crisis consists of the following components: (1) inadequate resources to meet (2) spending obligations in (3) an uncertain environment. There are various options available to a state to deal with these components. They are interrelated. Exercising one often means doing something with another.

1. The problem of inadequate resources can be met by raising revenue through tax increases or short-term borrowing, using reserves such as equity in various state funds or capital outlay reserves, substitution, or enlarging the time period on which the revenue collection is based. Temporary "paper" adjustments can also be made in hopes that the crisis will go away.

2. Too many spending obligations can be handled by reducing expenditures. These can either be immediate cuts in spending commitments, mandated lapses wherein funds previously appropriated for a particular program are withdrawn and returned to the general account, wage reductions, or delayed payments. Here, paper adjustments can be made as well.

3. An uncertain environment can be stabilized through a) counter-cyclical economic measures such as various development or savings programs, b) political coalition building to sustain the state while the siege lasts and make needed changes, and c) tactical holding decisions such as adoption of a kind of budgetary "going rate."

A fourth option theoretically exists. That is to do nothing, but in Michigan's case, that was not available. The constitution required a balanced budget and certain obligations had to be honored.

Michigan exercised all of these options, some more enthusiastically, timely, and thoroughly than others. Let us review them.

The Revenue Dilemma

The Tax Issue

Although tax increases were least likely to be discussed openly as a remedy for the fiscal crisis, the state of Michigan did raise taxes several times during the period under study. In 1970 and 1971 the state income tax rate was increased from 2.6 to 3.9 percent in order to counter the revenue-depleting effects of a record-length autoworkers strike. Again, in November 1974, income taxes were increased from 3.9 to 4.6 percent to replace lost revenues when voters approved a sales tax ban on food and drugs. In August 1975 the Single Business Tax was adopted, partly to cover a looming deficit. And again in 1981 and 1982, a six-month, one-percent income tax increase was adopted together with an increase in the cigarette tax. When these taxes lapsed in September 1982, a 1.5 percent increase (from 4.6 to 6.35 percent) in income tax together with a .25 percent increase in cigarette tax was adopted in 1982 and 1983.

These taxes were raised at some cost. The third round of income tax increases was especially painful and cost the Democrats control of the Senate in 1984. Nevertheless, some thought the leaders acted too late. As one observer (Drake, September 25, 1986) noted,

> I do know that throughout the 1980–82 period [the Speaker] went repeatedly to [the governor] a number of times in my presence so I know it happened and said, "Look, don't you think we've cut all we can cut in the budget here? Isn't it time to go for the tax increase?" [The Governor] repeatedly said, "No, I don't think we can."
>
> [The Governor] took great pride in not raising taxes and the longer that period became [i.e., his tenure in office] the more committed he was to try to get out of office without doing it. If he truly had that as a goal, I think that was a major stumbling block to dealing with that situation earlier.
>
> Over that time period [the Speaker] repeatedly offered to do whatever was necessary to bring the Democrats in the legislature along if (the Governor) would consent to work with the Republicans in the legislature. It simply did not happen until 1982. Then, all [the Governor] proposed, I believe, even then was a temporary tax and that's what we ended up with, a temporary tax increase. I know [the Governor] proposed a half

percent for the calendar year and we ended up with a one percent for six months of the fiscal year.

Short-Term Borrowing

Michigan continuously shored up its leaky budgets with short-term borrowing during this period. This was something the state constitution allowed, but the framers did not have in mind anything other than contingency purposes when they permitted it because they also wrote in a proviso that any borrowing had to be repaid within the fiscal year. As resources became leaner with each passing year, short-term borrowing became critical to cover October 1 payments into the school aid fund, for example, when tax revenues were not receivable until October 15. Overuse of short-term borrowing together with the state's declining credit worthiness eventually caused Wall Street money lenders, the prime source of such funds, to cut the source of supply. As the state budget director said, "They have immense power over this state. If they drop my rating and I can't borrow, then we can't pay our bills in October, we have payless paydays, we have chaos" (*The Detroit News,* March 3, 1982).

Michigan reached its nadir in this respect in September 1982 when only a letter of credit issued by a consortia of five Japanese banks permitted the state to borrow $500 million. The banks charged a 12 percent fee.

Tapping the Funds

The state of Michigan used its equity in numerous funds to get additional revenue during this period. Budgeters borrowed $45 million from the Motor Vehicle Accident Claims Fund in 1970 and 1971 and $50 million from its Veterans' Trust Fund, $34.6 million from the teachers' pension fund contingency reserve, and other millions from the Uninsured Motorist Fund in FY 1975 and 1976.

In 1978 and 1979, the state took $25 million from the Liquor Control Commission revolving fund. In 1979 and 1980 the state borrowed $26 million from the Recreational (Kammer) Trust Fund and $46.2 million more in 1980 and 1981 (Heckman, 1981a). That same year the state also attempted to borrow $20.1 million from the Railroad Delinquent Tax Fund but gave up when it was found that some of the fund had already been committed elsewhere (*The State Jour-*

nal, September 30, 1981). The state also borrowed from the Budget Stabilization Fund, but as that fund was set up expressly for that purpose, it is discussed in a later section.

Using Capital Outlay Reserves

In addition to making outright cuts in capital outlay commitments through executive orders, on at least two occasions ($51 million in FY 1974 and 1975 and $46.2 million in FY 1980 and 1981) Michigan raised additional revenue by what some call nonfunding unencumbered capital outlay reserves (Heckman, 1981b). The procedure was this: normally, at the end of a fiscal year, all unspent (unencumbered) capital outlay appropriations balances would be carried over into the following fiscal year and marked for expenditure. A fund reserve is also carried over to cover appropriations. By diverting funds normally used to fund that reserve, the revenue can be used to cover deficits in other areas. The cost of that procedure was that it required consistent yearly capital outlay appropriations.

Substitution

Once a useful ploy for states in a federal system, substitution of federal for state funds has become much more difficult to do as federal lawmakers have tightened loopholes. Nevertheless, Michigan was able to generate $88 million in FY 1981 and 1982 by substituting federal funds in programs administered by the departments of Social Services and Mental Health and by a newer form of substitution, user fees (Citizens Research Council, 1982). According to Knott and Langley (1993), infusion of federal funds helped significantly to stabilize revenue during the recession.

Enlarging the Time Frame

Michigan extended its fiscal year by three months in 1975 and 1976 and considered extending it twelve months in 1979 and 1980 (Heckman, 1981b). At the time the first extension was approved in 1976, the intention was to bring the state back to a July 1 through June 30 fiscal year by mid-1979, having followed the original extension with a twelve-month fiscal year and then a 21-month fiscal year (*The State Journal,* May 15, 1976). However, subsequent events canceled those plans.

The Paper Adjustments

According to generally accepted accounting procedures, organizations account for monies received and spent either by the cash method or by accrual. The cash method counts monies only when they are actually received and spent. Accrual counts when they are earned and obligated. For an example, an item ordered in September is considered obligated in September by the accrual method, but if it is actually paid for in October, is not accounted for until October under the cash method. Accountants tend to recommend accrual accounting because it pictures financial activity closer to decision points and therefore gives less distorted data points to analyze for planning purposes. In some instances, some organizations use both methods for different accounts, but using both, that is, accruing revenue and not liabilities, for the same account is bad practice. However, it can be an attractive maneuver if budgets have to be in balance at the end of a fiscal year and bills for activities undertaken near the end of the year are unlikely to appear until several weeks into the new year.

From 1975 through 1982, Michigan steadily accrued revenues (but not liabilities) for assorted sources. Beginning with the marathon end-of-year adjustment on June 30, 1975, the state accrued revenues for sales, use, and withholding taxes. As one tax committee aide later said, "Suddenly we started to get into what has been popularly known in this state as 'Chinese bookkeeping.' "

The following fiscal year (1975–76), utility property taxes were added. In 1977 and 1978, in an attempt at reform, the entire Medicaid account was shifted to accrual accounting, but the liabilities were shifted back to a cash basis in 1980 and 1981. In 1979 and 1980, revenues from the single business tax and insurance premiums were put on an accrual basis, as were oil and gas taxes and beer and wine taxes in 1981 and 1982. That same fiscal year, two more shifts took place. Liabilities for utility bills of welfare recipients were returned to cash accounting, but the state also began to pay back the debt on property tax credits by starting to accrue liabilities.

Playing around with the Medicaid account was by far the most costly. It was a prime bone of contention in the October 1981 negotiations with Wall Street lenders and was partly to blame for Michigan's subsequent credit-rating drop to lowest in the nation the following December. The other cost was, of course, the tax reckoning. In 1981 and 1982, the state needed to pass a ten-cent increase in the cigarette tax, part of which was used to correct the bookkeeping manipulations.

Although fudging the books in an attempt to meet the constitutional requirements for a balanced budget received the most notoriety, at least one study (Citizens Research Council, 1982) indicated that this option had less fiscal impact—at least during the crisis years 1980 through 1982—than the other options of reducing expenditures or raising revenues. Although it was the leading variable in 1981, accounting for 37 percent of the adjustments made to eliminate General Fund/General Purpose imbalances, over the three-year period it accounted for about 25 percent.

Attempts to Reduce Expenditures

Spending Ceilings

In addition to the constitutional requirement for a balanced budget, state lawmakers made at least two other attempts to set spending limits. The first occurred in 1977 as part of the legislation establishing the Budget Stabilization Fund (BSF). In addition to its "saving for a rainy day" feature, the Budget Stabilization Fund served to limit the rate of growth in state spending.

Indeed, the governor pushed for adoption early in 1977 before the adoption of the budget for the ensuing fiscal year, because the BSF language established ceilings for the budget. At the time, budget officials saw it as similar to the federal process in which ceilings are set early in the process, before specific appropriations are approved (*The State Journal,* January 25, 1977). Michigan was the first state to adopt such a fund.

The second occurred in 1980 when the Senate adopted new budgeting procedures which required targets to be set before appropriations could be approved. Some saw this as reinforcing the target setting required by the prior BSF legislation; others saw it as redundant.

Spending Reductions

Even though spending ceilings may have been readjusted downward, sometimes it is necessary to back away from appropriations commitments. The most conspicuous efforts in this category are the spending reductions mandated through executive orders. However, in addition to these were other methods which were often taken before the heavy axe of the executive orders was swung.

These methods included freezes in hiring, travel, and equipment purchases.

Often regarded as first maneuvers, these options were exercised by the governor in November 1978 when the second recession seemed possible. As he said, "I must act now to anticipate an economic downturn in order to meet the constitutional obligations of a balanced budget" (*The Detroit News*, November 23, 1978).

Mandated Lapses

Another means used to withdraw from appropriations commitments, mandated lapses are "agreements between the Executive Office and the Legislature to transfer appropriations from various line item appropriations into the Executive or Administrative component appropriation line item, such as a retirement line item" (Heckman, 1981b).

Michigan policymakers resorted to mandated lapses on at least two occasions. In 1979 and 1980, $60.8 million was recaptured through this means and $31.8 million in 1981 and 1982 (Heckman, 1981b).

Wage Reductions

Personnel costs in many public organizations account for about 80 percent of operating costs. Therefore, it is not surprising that efforts to reduce spending would involve some sort of wage reductions. In Michigan, wage reductions took several forms. Some involved downsizing jobs in which full-time jobs were made into three-quarter or half-time positions. Others included voluntary wage reductions; voluntary wage deferrals; mandatory wage reductions, including cuts in total pay and total hours that could be worked and mandatory payless days. For example, in 1980 and 1981, Michigan attempted to cut a proposed nine percent pay increase for civil service workers to 4.5 percent, saving the GF/GP about $43 million. Later, the executive office required that executive branch employees work six days without pay, which saved another estimated $12 million. Some legislative employees had one day's pay deducted from their biweekly paycheck and were required to take off 16 days, some of which were discretionary, saving another $700,000 (Heckman, 1981b).

Another approach involved deferring pay increases. In a hotly contested decision in August 1982, the Michigan Civil Service Commission reversed its April 1982 decision to approve a five percent pay increase for 17,000 state workers and moved to delay the increase until the beginning of the new fiscal year in October. Three public employee unions filed court suits, claiming that the commission violated constitutionally set procedures for setting civil service wages. They won. The following year the courts ruled that the governor's need to reduce spending does not limit the civil service commission's power to set wages (*Michigan Association of Governmental Employees v. Michigan Civil Service Commission* (1983) 336 N.W.2d 463, 125 Mich. App. 180).

Of course, the ultimate tactic in wage reduction was layoffs. As mentioned previously, during this period the number of state employees was reduced by about 16,000. The cost of this in terms of employee morale has never been fully documented, but is described in terms of one department in Mowbray, Tableman, and Gould (1984).

One feature of the layoffs involved what came to be known as "bumping." A pink-slipped employee could save his or her job by identifying someone with less seniority and, in effect, commandeering that person's position. The state retained presumably more experienced and qualified employees that way, but the dislocations were enormous. People employed in one department such as Social Services might wind up in Treasury doing quite unrelated work. Although some found the changes energizing, the indirect net cost in terms of lost efficiency has yet to be studied comprehensively. However, House (1981), among others, has identified bumping as a questionable policy akin to penny wisdom and pound foolishness.

Delayed Payments

Another tactic used was deferred payments, which took several forms. The most controversial were the delays in installment payments to public institutions. Schools, colleges, universities, and local governments were all affected as in, for example, the February 1982 decision to defer $225 million in school aid, higher education, and local revenue-sharing payments and a similar decision in January 1983. The argument at the time was that the payments would be made up later, but as late as November 1986, some were still waiting for restitution.

The other form was delay in payments to contractors. In October 1980, faced with a cash crunch, this was one of the options chosen by the state of Michigan. That was the same month that banks cut off the state's short-term credit because lawmakers had been unable to formulate a budget.

Negative Appropriations

These were used to penalize agencies which had overspent funds. The overrun is built into the following year's appropriation, which, if stable, means that the agency has, in effect, reduced resources for the following year (Heckman, 1981b). But spending reductions were never easy. One reason why expenditures were so hard to cut had to do with the increasing demand for social services. One analysis (Heckman, 1981a) showed that Aid for Families with Dependent Children (AFDC) and General Assistance cases increased 50 percent between October 1979 and April 1981. From 1980 through 1982, more than $600 million went to supplemental spending, 80 percent of which went to the Department of Social Services which experienced unprecedented increases in welfare caseloads. The Citizens Research Council (1982) estimated that $100 million of that was actually never appropriated but simply runover in accounts, "indicative of a breakdown in legislative control of spending."

One of the reasons for the upsurge in welfare caseloads was the incapacity of unemployment insurance to meet demand. A few facts about the Unemployment Insurance Trust Fund will explain this. The Unemployment Insurance Trust Fund is a reserve against which insured unemployed workers may draw benefits up to a maximum of 39 weeks, almost 10 months, of which the first 26 weeks are funded by employers and the remaining 13 by state and federal government. These benefits are paid through the Michigan Employment Security Commission (MESC), a division of the state's Department of Labor. The devastation of the recessions both in 1974 and 1975 and in 1979 through 1982 were such that funds were rapidly exhausted. Workers who were without other benefits then sought welfare assistance. The other aspect of this incapacity, of course, derived from the fact that unemployment insurance was available only to about one-third of the state's unemployed workers (Blaustein, 1982). Again, those with no other recourse looked to welfare benefits from the state.

Although the state GF/GP budget was not directly affected by the fund exhaustion and consequent borrowing until March 1982, when a change in the law made states liable for interest on the debt (prior to that borrowing was interest free), the GF/SP was, and the consequent increase in employer taxes needed to repay the fund tended to depress other efforts to attract private industry to Michigan and, in any case, made existing employers wary of other kinds of tax increases.

Another reason why costs were so hard to contain was that some were never put into the equation. The cost of the debt, for example, was never budgeted. In order to meet obligations during the 1980 through 1982 crisis, Michigan engaged in a great deal of short-term borrowing to get working capital. Interest on these notes was estimated at $176 million, but it was never budgeted (Citizens Research Council, 1982).

Stabilizing an Uncertain Fiscal Environment

Countercyclical Economic Measures

The most direct effort in this area involved establishment of the Budget Stabilization Fund (BSF), described previously. As the name suggests, the BSF was primarily an attempt to stabilize revenue flows. The Stabilization Fund works by formula tied to the level of Michigan Personal Income (MPI). If real (i.e., deflated less transfer payments) growth is greater than two percent, then the state must pay into the fund. Payouts in the form of limited quarterly withdrawals for public works projects are allowed under two conditions: (1) if unemployment levels reach eight percent (larger withdrawals are allowed if it exceeds 12 percent) (House Taxation Committee, 1983) and (2) if there is negative growth in the adjusted MPI (Bryan and Howard, 1979).

The BSF was recommended by the Michigan Economic Action Council which was chaired by Michael Blumenthal, a prominent Michigan industrialist and later secretary of the treasury under President Carter. Adoption of the BSF was a joint effort of Speaker of the House Bobby Crim and Governor Milliken. As one observer said,

> My memory is that Crim took the idea to Milliken and said, "Look, we've got to take a look at some fundamental things that need to be done here." It was basically a recognition that we had a cyclical economy and that we needed to adopt something that would put us in a situation where in the good economic years we did two things: we controlled spending by adopting a formula that forced us to put some money aside and secondly, kept us from reducing the rate of taxation, i.e., kept a certain base level of taxation but controlled the growth of that base and allowed us to take it out on the low side. (Drake, September 25, 1986)

But the BSF, good as it was, was limited. As the same person went on to say,

> The concept of the BFS clearly is not one that would allow you to handle something like the 80–82 [crisis]. It could handle a 75–76 recession, which I guess you might characterize as more of a normal recession, but could not even begin to handle something like an 80–82 crisis, which for this state was a depression, not a recession.
>
> As we finally went into the recession of the early 80s, we might have had $450 million or $500 if we hadn't made that [previous cut in BSF funding]. But 1980, '81, '82 and '83 collectively were such horrendous years that the existence of another $200 million or so in the fund would not have made a material difference in the way we had to respond to that time—we blew through that money so fast. (Drake, September 25, 1986).

Welcome as the BSF was, however, it was only designed to deal with future spending. It was not designed to take care of already incurred debts which had been, in effect, rolled over since 1975 (Citizens Research Council, 1983).

Other counter-cyclical economic measures taken by the state of Michigan certainly include the numerous economic development programs endorsed annually but particularly in the governor's budget messages of 1977, the economic development package proposed by the governor in 1981, and the budget messages of 1982 and 1983.

Political Coalition Building

Although discussed more fully elsewhere, this was clearly a stabilizing tactic needed to sustain the political leadership through the state's fiscal crisis. It was most clearly seen in the procedures used in dealing with the executive orders mandating budget cuts.

Rationalization of the Budget Process

Some would not characterize budget reform as an attempt to reduce environmental uncertainty. However, it should certainly be included because these reforms typically have the effect, in part, of controlling uncertainty internal to the system by requiring enhanced planning.

During the period under study, the state of Michigan saw a progression of attempts at budget reform, even though not all of them were precipitated by fiscal crisis. Among them:

- in 1971, the House Fiscal Agency attempted to implement a program budgeting system and, although this system was not ultimately used, a variation was introduced by the executive office from 1972 through 1973.
- In 1975 there was attempted introduction of a legislatively sponsored program-evaluation zero-base budget system.
- In 1976 and 1977, the executive budget began to be developed according to target budget concepts in which each department submitted requests based on 95, 100, and 108 percent support of prior year appropriations. Programs were also ranked according to priority.
- The 1981 through 1982 budget was developed on a minimum-operating-level approach, and the Management and Budget Act of 1984 consolidated budget practice and tightened reporting requirements.

Tactical Holding Decisions

Sometimes the environment seems so unstable that the only known is the immediate past. When revenue and spending patterns seemed most inscrutable in mid-1980, Michigan lawmakers opted not to pass a full-year budget for 1980 and 1981, but passed an interim measure for October through December instead that, in effect, adopted going rates based on those of the previous fiscal year. The interim budget was ultimately repealed and folded into the full budget when it was passed (Heckman, 1981). However, this decision was not without cost. Michigan lost what little remained of its credit standing, and banks refused to issue the state loans because there was no plan—that is, budget—available on which repayment could be plotted.

The Attempt to Peer into the Future

The key to controlling the environment is prediction. The state of Michigan also attempted to do that. State officials signed a contract with the University of Michigan to fund development of the University of Michigan model for forecasting Michigan tax revenue and the Michigan economy. Need for such outside assistance was explained by one long-term observer in this way: "The principal reason was that legislative leadership simply did not trust what the governor's office, this [DMB] department, and this office [Revenue and Tax Analysis] was telling them and had every reason to believe that [the budget director] was not so much lying as withholding information. In fact, I know that to be the case."

Despite the availability of the model and the assistance of world-class economists, revenues in the crisis period (1980, 1981, and 1982) were overestimated by $1.3 billion, 92 percent of which was appropriated (Citizens Research Council, 1983).

Summary and a Post Script

Thus, there were many options available to state government to confront a fiscal crisis, and Michigan policymakers exercised them all. There were efforts to raise revenues, reduce spending, and reduce environmental uncertainty. All were done amid enormous controversy and with considerable pain to policymakers and citizens alike.

On November 8, 1985, the governor of Michigan declared "solvency day," having retired a $1.7 billion debt from the most volatile budgetary era in its history. This governor, elected in 1982 on a platform of fiscal reform and economic recovery, had ended the crisis at some political cost. Forced to push through a tax increase, he lost two supportive senators through recalls and, consequently, party control of the Senate. He had to issue an executive order mandating further budget cuts in 1983. He had to lead an angered, poorer citizenry and preside over a demoralized bureaucracy. He was faced with weakened educational systems and court challenges on lowered patient or inmate/staff ratios in state institutions. Infrastructure—highways, bridges, dams, and sewer and water lines—always vulnerable in a frost-zone state and neglected through maintenance cuts were in substantial need of attention. The governor was re-elected in 1986, vindicating some of these decisions, but lost a try for a third term in 1990, when he was swept aside by his opponent, one of the most fiscally conservative in the nation. These were part of the political, economic, and social fallout from the fiscal crisis. Some issues had been remedied rather quickly and some are still being addressed.

Most of the strategies and tactics just described, which were used in the state of Michigan, have been used by policy makers elsewhere when faced with recession. The District of Columbia in its current recession, for example, has become notorious for delayed payments to contractors. "Bumping" has also been used with obviously inefficient effects. Massive cuts in local aid through re-allocation of property tax revenue, as well as wage reductions and layoffs, have been used in California in response to economic decline brought about by reduced defense spending (Gold and Ritchie, 1993; Savage, 1992). Massachusetts launched a tax amnesty program which attracted national attention (and was also used in Michigan) because it attempted to recapture revenues due but never received.

Analysis of the strategies used in Michigan over time showed that policy makers fairly early attempted to deal with the consequences of recession in a constructive way, through implementation of a "rainy day fund." However, when the recession crisis became overwhelming, leaders resorted to stonewalling. The inventory of tactics just described includes most of those frequently used. A combination of force from outsiders (Wall Street creditors) and votes by the citizenry finally forced some of the most unpleasant decisions that had to be made to bring aspirations for the state budget in alignment with economic reality.

These are the negative aspects of the story. It would be unfair to suggest that this is all that was done. Crisis poses opportunity as well as threats. In Michigan, efforts turned to modernizing the industrial plant and work force. Substantial investment was made in the Michigan Strategic Fund in 1986 and the Michigan Modernization Service in 1987. The state surveyed its economic base and chose to target advanced manufacturing. The state also attempted to become more inviting to economic development through cutting taxes on small business and making changes in the workers compensation program (Osborne, 1990).

Massachusetts, also hurt by the recession of the late 1970s (here too caused in part by reductions in federal defense spending), targeted economic development in communities. New programs were designed to resuscitate mature industries. Using its strength in developing infrastructure, the state invested heavily in roads, waterworks, and educational institutions, and when industry decided to invest in these areas, the state provided additional incentives with tax breaks, investment, and worker training. A comprehensive and quite successful program was also begun to help people into jobs and off public income assistance programs. In addition, the state launched a job-training program that provided matching grants to businesses that wanted to set up new training programs. This ensured that the training was demand driven and that the supply would more effectively match demand (Bay State Skills Corporation, 1986).

Many of the economic development successes in Massachusetts were enabled through linkages with the science and technology innovators located in an area known as "Route 128." In coming to terms with its own recession experience in the 1970s, the state of New York also turned to investment in science and technology, specifically through a state-funded Science and Technology Foundation (New York State Assembly, 1986). It underwrote a broad span of technology development programs. It included a fund for seed capital, business incubator programs, and seven industry-university associations called "Centers for Advanced Technology." The foundation also funded regional technology development units which aided emerging technology firms. In addition, the concept of an agricultural extension service was adapted in an industrial extension service.

These examples suggest that in facing the effects of recession, states used some of the painful lessons to rethink traditional relationships. Although they would inevitably be subject to the larger national and international economic forces, they began to reach out and redefine, to the extent that they could, the environment in which they existed. In reaching out, states have sought to establish linkages with commerce and industry, small business, universities, community groups, and others. In the mid-1990s as politico-economic forces cause the federal government to shrink some of its commitments and turn them over to the states, it is apparent that the states will be needing to build on these linkages even more.

6

Lessons for Entirement: Strategies and Skills for Self-Management, Lifelong Development

Randall Harrison

Introduction

Entirement is a coined term, used here to indicate a state of lifelong development. In essence, it means living one's entire life wisely, from start to finish, in all its facets, in all the ways it touches other people. Obviously, living wisely is a challenge. And, in our modern age of rapidly accelerating change, living wisely is a growing challenge, perhaps more difficult now than ever before in history. We do, however, have an extensive literature on human development, achievement, and renewal. 'Entirement' explores this reservoir of knowledge for skills and strategies that would help the individual live more wisely. It is hoped that this knowledge could be put in the hands of individuals and made available to those who manage, coach, and mentor. In the emerging "learning organization" of the future, the quest for entirement is likely to grow. This chapter provides a first overview of what may be in store for the individual and for well-managed organizations of the future.

We appear to be at a unique hinge of history. The opportunities ahead are amazing. But so, too, are the perils. "Information Age" . . . "Knowledge Society" . . . "Wisdom World" . . . We are engulfed by major transformations. For the individual, this means more opportunity—and more demands—than ever before. In particular, lifelong learning will be crucial to success, perhaps even to survival. Similarly, for those aspiring to manage in this complex, fast-changing world, the challenges are daunting. As never before, the manager of the future will need to be alearning leader—a coach, mentor, and guide.

Entirement is one way to frame this challenge of lifelong development, achievement, and renewal. In brief, entirement draws attention to growth across the entire life span. It explores the entire range of individual potential, not just a few skills or talents. Also, it considers the entire impact of life choices, for the individual and for the wider world.

Challenges Ahead

We are now in a rapidly changing world. Ornstein and Ehrlich (1989) argue that we now see more change in a decade than we used to see in millennia. And, they suggest, the pace is quickening. More than a quarter of a century ago, Toffler (1970) called attention to this trend with his phrase *future shock*. A decade later, in *The Third Wave,* Toffler (1980) pointed to the global shift from agriculture to industry to high-tech information. This current era of tumultuous change creates new challenges at the individual, organizational, and global levels.

Until recently, in most industrial societies, the individual career followed a highly predictable and well-differentiated pattern: school, work, retirement. And within each sector, progression was predictable. In school, there was a steady advancement, K through 12, kindergarten through high school, perhaps topped off with a few years of college. Within the work sector, there was usually a well-identified corporate ladder to climb. Even for those who were not upwardly mobile, there was the assumption that the individual could stay in the same career, perhaps the same job, throughout the work life. And retirement, when it did come, was usually short and idle.

Fast-Changing Assumptions

All this is rapidly changing. Education is no longer restricted to the early years. It's not K through 12; it's K through 80+, i.e., lifelong. Work and learning are intertwined, with frequent periods of retraining, renewal, and redirection. Where the school and the employer once determined what was to be learned and when, the individual is increasingly responsible for those decisions.

A young person entering the work force today is likely to have at least three different careers—not just different jobs, but different careers. So the individual needs to develop quite different facets of ability. In particular, individuals may need to master skills that transfer from one problem domain to another. And the individual may want to emphasize "building-block" talents that can provide stepping stones to larger pyramids of achievement.

Retirement, when it comes, is likely to be long and potentially active (Carroll, 1994). In a sense, modern retirement may come early, either by choice or by ejection of the worker from the work force. Older workers may retire from one career, then re-enter the work force in a different capacity and retire again. And, while retirement age may be dropping for many, life expectancy is creeping upward. Until recently, 50 was considered old; 65 was ancient. Now, if a male reaches 50, and if he does not do anything foolish, he's likely to reach 75. A female, if she's fortunate enough to avoid cancer and heart disease, is likely to reach her nineties. In short, for many individuals, more than a third of their lives will be spent in what was once considered "the retirement years."

These changes for the individual, of course, reflect what is happening at the organizational and the global levels. As economies move up or down, employment increases or decreases. Some firms go out of business, and others prosper in new-found niches. Riding on top of these business cycles is like traveling across the landscape on an undulating highway. Such a road, in a dip, may reveal geologic substrata of a far different order than the apparent surface terrain. Similarly, an economic recession may expose underlying discontinuous change, trends which would be less obvious during prosperous times.

Recession or Redirection?

In the United States, for example, recent downturns in the economy sent shockwaves through the work force. For many, what seemed at first to be temporary dislocations have become a continuing way of life. *Downsizing* became the watchword of the day, in industry after industry, in state after state. Workers who always assumed they had a secure niche in the "American Dream" suddenly awoke to the economic nightmare of unemployment. Hardest hit were the least skilled, but, recently, workers at all levels have been shaken. Whole echelons of middle management were wiped out. With mergers and acquisitions, even top management experienced sudden "redundancy," and corporate boards became more assertive, easing out CEOs who did not downsize their organizations fast enough. As traditional, well-paying jobs disappear, we see growing anxiety and emerging groups, armies of unemployed and under-employed—individuals who can become a volatile political force. Intergroup hostilities increase, racial tensions rise, and anti-immigrant sentiment boils over. In one way or another, similar scenarios are unfolding in several European countries and around the world.

Public attention is drawn to these daily events and to the ups and downs of the current business cycle. But largely unnoticed—beneath these present economic waves—deep currents of social change are moving. Drucker (1994) argues that the sweeping transformations of the 20th century are unprecedented in human history. And, he suggests, these momentous shifts will extend well into the next century. The amazing flow of farm hands and domestics into factories, earlier in the 20th century, went surprisingly smoothly. Or perhaps, says Drucker, it is not so surprising; farm hands and domestics were more skilled and versatile than they needed to be for the factory jobs they took on the assembly line. However, this is not true today of industrial workers who are trying to move into the new high-tech, information jobs of the future. Competing for these jobs will require a major change in attitudes, values, learning, and mindset.

Knowledge-Value Revolutions

A driving force in this new era will be the emerging "knowledge society." Or, more precisely, "knowledges society," since it will involve the cumulative interaction of many sets of knowledge. Increasingly, knowledge will be an essential ingredient of products and services (Sakaiya, 1991). In fact, Aubrey and Cohen (1995) argue that the future key is "working wisdom."

The implications of this transformation are many. It may mean "the end of work," as we have known it down through recorded history (Rifkin, 1995). In any case, it will place unprecedented demands on our educational institutions, formal and informal (Drucker, 1994). There is no indication that this is a short-range challenge, one amenable to a quick fix. Quite the contrary. It appears that change will accelerate, and with it a fast-growing array of new demands. Concepts such as 'high-speed management' will become increasingly important in this global, information economy (Cushman and King, 1995). And, rather than quiet stability, the future promises "continuous revolution," in the words of Tichy and Sherman (1993). (In their book, *Control Your Destiny or Someone Else Will,* Tichy and Sherman provide a firsthand account of the continuing revolution installed by Jack Welsh at GE.)

For those who are prepared, this new world can mean exciting opportunities and enormous personal satisfaction. But continuous, rapid change can also lead to stress, frustration, and disappointment. At the personal level, it can cause mental and physical anguish. At the societal level, it can lead to major unrest and upheaval. Perhaps, as never before, individuals will have to find meaning for their lives; they will not be able simply to follow in the comfortable footsteps of their forebears.

New Assumptions

This brief survey of challenges leads to four basic assumptions about the future.

1. *Learning is essential.* To get on the playing field, and to stay on the field, the worker of the future will have to be a learner. Learning will be important for a full life, in or out of the workplace.
2. *Learning is lifelong.* In the future, the individual will need to learn continually and constantly improve. Even retirement will provide unprecedented challenges and opportunities.
3. *Development will be multifaceted.* To meet changing opportunities, the individual will need to develop a range of talents and abilities. It will be increasingly dangerous to rely on only one specialized skill.
4. *Development will be self-guided.* Increasingly, the individual will decide what to learn, when to learn it, and how to learn it. More and more of the educational decisions which were once in the hands of the school or the employer will be thrust upon the individual. And, for personal growth and achievement, the individual will need to become a sophisticated consumer of learning opportunities.

Entirement emphasizes the possibility—and the importance— of these individual developmental choices. A concept such as entirement obviously is not a panacea, a cure-all for the woes of modern society. It does not offer sure-fire salvation for someone hoping to survive and succeed. But it may be one small step in a helpful direction.

Entirement: The Concept

The coined word *entirement* is proposed as the label for this state of self-guided, lifelong development. The term seems felicitous in that it suggests the entire life-span, an entire range of developmental potential, and an entire spectrum of societal consequences.

The English words *retire* and *entire* sound similar. But, in fact, they come from quite different roots. The simple word *tire* comes from Old English, meaning "to become weary." But the *tire* in *retire* comes via Old French; it means "to pull back or withdraw." Add the suffix *-ment,* and the word becomes *retirement,* "the state or condition of having withdrawn."

Meanwhile, the *tire* in *entire* comes from a Latin root, *tangere,* meaning to touch or be involved. Add the prefix *en-* and the word means "to touch completely, to be involved in all aspects." Add *-ment* to this—entirement—and the word means "a state or condition of continual, complete involvement." This seems an appropriate term for what we hope to emphasize: the self-guided involvement in lifelong growth and development, the multifaceted exploration and expansion of individual potential.

Entirement Framework

Entirement builds along three basic dimensions: (1) a lifelong perspective; (2) a full-spectrum approach to potential; and (3) a careful consideration of impact.

THE LIFELONG PERSPECTIVE Choices and decisions are placed in the context of the complete lifespan. The assumption is that the individual is more likely to develop and achieve if there is a compelling personal vision—a set of long-range goals worth striving for. At the same time, in an era of rapid change, it is obviously important to be flexible and adaptable, to be able to take advantage of unforeseen opportunities and to recover quickly from unexpected setbacks. The lifespan perspective provides long-range direction which may help keep the individual moving forward whatever vicissitudes are encountered.

FULL-SPECTRUM POTENTIAL In an era of specialization and intense competition, it is easy to get locked into a single track of development. This works well for many, particularly if they are mining a rich vein which does not peter out. But in a turbulent, fast-changing world, it is also easy to end up in a cul-de-sac with no way out. In short, it may be increasingly important to keep one's options open, to develop all facets of potential. At the very least, one needs to be constantly scanning the environment for fertile niches where one's potential might have an opportunity to grow and prosper.

CONSIDERATION OF IMPACT The individual today has more choices—and more powerful choices—than ever before. At the same time, rapid change makes it increasingly difficult to predict the consequences of any given choice. Old assumptions may be suspect. And "new rules of the game" are still being formulated. In short, it may take extra effort and considerable thought to achieve what one really wants to accomplish—for the self and for the larger arenas of life.

Entirement Pathways

Individuals obviously differ enormously in their preparation and competence, in their motivation and determination. Ideally, entirement would provide a series of pathways for different individuals, at various life stages, in appropriate situations. Entirement would help individuals form learning alliances. And a variety of "intellectual toolkits" might provide specific skills and insights (Harrison, 1996). These, in turn, might be useful to individuals and to those who hope to mentor, coach and manage.

Among the topics that might be tackled are these:

- *Forming learning alliances:* networking; helping others learn; helping others help you learn.
- *Mentoring:* how to find a mentor; how to be a mentor; how to be your own mentor.
- *Profiles of potential:* knowing the self; identifying the areas of possible development which are most likely to be fruitful.
- *Environmental scanning:* how to read the tides of time; identifying ecological niches and fertile coves for future exploration.
- *Learning to learn:* how to cultivate an appetite for learning; adopting continuous improvement.
- *Learning to unlearn:* coping with change; pruning the habits that hobble.
- *Benchmarking personal progress:* finding learning models; celebrating success; learning from setbacks.
- *Higher-order thinking:* mastering skills necessary for solving complex, ambiguous problems. (Lifelong development, in fact, is such a problem.)
- *Cultivating wisdom:* exploring ways of knowing that will lead to socially desirable outcomes and inner serenity.

Each of these areas, in turn, could branch off into subskills which might be appropriate for particular individuals in given circumstances. In each of the above areas, there is now a rich research literature from which to draw. A few examples follow.

Implementing Entirement

Higher-Order Thinking

In a sense, entirement is a cluster of problems requiring "higher-order thinking." The literature on higher-order thinking may be useful in designing approaches to entirement. And, in turn, working on entirement seems likely to increase higher-order thinking skills, which could benefit the individual in other areas of work and life. In a report, "Education and Learning to Think," the National Research Council calls attention to the importance of higher-order thinking (Resnick, 1987). In brief, this is the kind required to solve complex, ambiguous problems, where there is no obvious "right answer." Higher-order thinking has the following characteristics:

- Higher-order thinking is "nonalgorithmic." In other words, there is no one rule that can be applied to ensure getting one right answer. The path of action is not fully specified in advance.
- Higher-order thinking tends to be complex. The total path is not "visible," mentally speaking, from any single vantage point.
- Higher-order thinking often yields multiple solutions, each with costs and benefits, rather than one unique solution— one "right" answer.
- Higher-order thinking involves nuanced judgment and interpretation. It is not an easy black or white, right or wrong situation. It is likely to mean dealing with fuzzy gray areas, which require subtle examination and thought.
- Higher-order thinking involves the application of multiple criteria, which sometimes conflict with one another. It is not possible to apply "one rule fits all." It is necessary to pick and choose and balance competing concerns.
- Higher-order thinking often involves uncertainty. Not everything that bears on the task at hand is known, and some aspects may be unknowable.

- Higher-order thinking involves self-regulation of the thinking process. It is not higher-order thinking if someone else "calls the plays" at every step.
- Higher-order thinking involves imposing meaning, finding structure in apparent disorder.
- Higher-order thinking is challenging. These elaborations and judgments take effort; they require mental work.

Parenthetically, the NRC report notes that, in the industrial age, the educational systems of most advanced nations provided two tracks, a high-literacy track and a low-literacy track. In the "low-lit," mass-education track, students were taught to read and write and "do sums." Basically, this prepared the workers required for an industrial society. They could read instructions, write reports, make change, and keep records. They were prepared to be the factory workers, the clerks, the secretaries. They were not expected to be creative problem solvers; they were expected to follow orders.

Meanwhile, the "hi-lit" track was for a relatively small elite. These students read the classics, debated issues, explored the sciences, appreciated the arts, and developed a broad perspective. They were expected to be creative, to solve complex problems, and to be leaders. However, as economies move from the industrial age to the new, high-tech, information age, a larger proportion of the work force is expected to be able to solve complex problems, to engage in higher-order thinking. This has placed enormous new demands on the educational systems of most economically advanced nations.

Self-Management

Given that higher-order thinking is self-regulated, it may be important to examine those situations in which the individual does "take charge." The extensive literature on human intelligence provides some leads. "Intelligence" traditionally was seen as a single dimension, which could be summed up in one number—the familiar IQ. Actually, "intelligence," as measured by an IQ score, seems to be a small part of what might be meant by intelligence.

In the first place, the IQ score usually encompasses only what can be measured on a paper-and-pencil test. In short, it measures, first, an individual's facility with particular symbols—verbal, numerical, or geometric. In addition, the IQ test taps a subset of all human problems. Usually, it examines (a) analytic skill, the ability to take a problem apart, and (b) synthesis, the ability to put things together. The ability to manipulate symbols is likely to be important for success in the modern world, as is analysis and synthesis. But not all people with high IQs succeed in life (Goleman, 1995).

Sternberg (1989) argues that the key to intelligence is "mental self-management." Rather than being analytically based, such a model of intelligence is strategy based. Sternberg sees three distinct aspects to intelligence: (1) analytic intelligence, which is useful in academic learning; (2) creative intelligence, which is useful for troubleshooting and for organizing ideas in new ways; and (3) practical intelligence, which is useful in managing the self and getting things done.

People who are especially successful in the real world are likely to be individuals who take full advantage of their intellectual potential and compensate for any weaknesses. They develop the talents they have, and they successfully skirt obstacles and interference.

Self-management also emerges as a theoretical construct in the work of Csikszentmihalyi (1993). He argues that the "self" naturally evolves toward integrated complexity. But he also sees the self as taking charge of its own development. Or at least that possibility exists. In summary, self-management appears to be an intriguing theoretical component of intelligence and of development.

The Human Development Literature

For the individual interested in entirement, one major area for exploration is what we do know about human development. We now have a vast body of knowledge in this area (Berger, 1991; Schaie and Willis, 1990). It is, in fact, difficult to do justice to this rich literature in one brief summary. But let us examine a few major dimensions.

Early views of development were basically "straight line": little people grew into big people. Then observers noted that, in most societies, there was at least one distinct discontinuity in the straight line. Usually, between childhood and adulthood was some "rite of passage," an acknowledgment that now the individual could and should take on new roles.

Early writers, such as Cooley (1902) and Mead (1934), pointed to the intricate interaction between society and the developing self-concept. Other researchers began to identify several specific stages of development. In this view, rather than being a straight line, development was more like a staircase, with periods of plateau, followed by sudden spurts of growth. In physical growth, stages of development are fairly obvious. But in social and cognitive areas, stage theories may be more problematic (Flavell, 1985).

Do all humans move through a set series of stages? Do they do so at certain ages? Is the order of such progress unchanging? These issues are still being debated. For one thing, the neat "staircase" model of steps may be too simple. Brazelton (1992) observes that just before any new growth spurt—physical, cognitive, or emotional—there is likely to be a period of regression, when older well-entrenched behavior "falls apart." Handy (1995) suggests that the growth of any individual—or organization—looks like a sigmoid curve, the frequently encountered S-curve. The key to successful change, he argues, is to launch a new growth curve while the old one is still climbing—not after the old curve has topped out. By then, the individual, or the organization, may not have the resources necessary to successfully launch a new upthrust.

Lifelong Development

The first-stage theorists, such as Freud (1905/1976) and Piaget (1977), emphasized development in the early years. But Erik Erikson (1950, 1987), having immigrated to the United States as an adult, was acutely aware of the challenges and crises that could arise in midlife. He eventually proposed an eight-stage theory of psychosocial development, across the entire life span.

To Erikson, life presented a succession of challenges. Each of these crises had to be successfully resolved before the individual could move on to the next "higher" problem. (If a crisis remained unresolved, it continued to haunt the individual, interfering with later development.)

Erikson's three adult stages were:

1. Intimacy vs. isolation. The successful resolution resulted in LOVE.
2. Generativity vs. stagnation. The successful resolution resulted in CARE.
3. Integrity vs. despair. The successful resolution resulted in WISDOM.

Erikson's theory is richer than sometimes portrayed in that he also allowed for extremes of the two competing forces; this identified "maladaptive tendencies" vs. "malignant tendencies." At any rate, Erikson succeeded in calling attention to the entire life span. And other theorists have drawn attention to different domains of development. Kohlberg (1984), for example, attempts to identify stages of moral development. And Kubler-Ross (1969) has plotted a series of stages as the individual approaches death.

Looking at the Life Course

A number of theorists have now dealt with the whole "life course." But let me mention especially the work of Levinson (1986). This theory figures prominently in the efforts of Tennant and Pogson (1995) to enrich adult education with an understanding of later life development. Levinson (1978) sees four major "eras" in life: (1) childhood and adolescence (birth to 20); (2) early adulthood (17–45); (3) middle adulthood (40–65); and (4) late adulthood (60 on). Between each era, there may be crucial, and perhaps difficult to negotiate, "transitions."

Levinson also emphasizes the "dream," an individual's vision of future accomplishment. This he sees as a crucial source of motivation; and, of course, the "dream" may change as the individual advances through different eras. Levinson also calls attention to "life structures," the person's cognitive frameworks concerning the nature and meaning of life. And he underscores the importance of "mentors," older and more experienced people who help the younger and less experienced. In short, as Tennant and Pogson (1995) demonstrate, Levinson provides intriguing leads for exploring learning and change in the adult years.

The Social Context

Stage theories, in general, see development emerging from internal maturation plus appropriate external experiences. But the emphasis is usually on internal factors. Other theorists give greater weight to external forces. Neugarten (1979; 1987), for example, emphasizes the importance of "life-events," and the "timing-of-life-events." In this formulation, "normative life events" are those which are expected and supported within a society, such as graduation, marriage, parenthood, and retirement. "Nonnormative life events" are those which are unexpected or unsupported, such as not being able to find employment, early widowhood, or forced early retirement. Research suggests that nonnormative events are much more stressful than normative events. Nonnormative events are arising with greater frequency in today's fast-changing age (Rosenfeld and Stark, 1987).

Individual Differences

In addition to theories which emphasize external circumstances, some theories highlight individual differences. Shein (1978), for example, does not look at career development as a simple progression from early to middle to late stages. Rather, he argues that individuals have "career anchors," self-perceptions of talents, abilities, motives, and values. These anchors, in turn, influence when and how people make career decisions.

He identifies major career anchors such as (a) managerial competence, (b) technical or functional, (c) security/stability, (d) creativity/entrepreneurship, and (e) autonomy/independence. Development is then likely within one of these domains as the individual tries to maximize the opportunities within the perceived value cluster.

In short, individual differences may be especially important in charting pathways of entirement. On one hand, the parameters of human plasticity seem to be well charted (Merlin, 1991; Ornstein, 1993; Seligman, 1993). Humans cannot be molded into just any form, no matter how determined the individual, no matter the amount of external pressure applied. At the same time, the complexity of human development can be richly surprising.

The Evolving Self

Csikszentmihalyi (1993) places the development of the self in a broad evolutionary framework, arguing that the natural flow of development is toward harmonious complexity. In other words, the self becomes increasingly complex and differentiated; but at the same time it becomes more integrated. This natural flow may be blocked or diverted. But individuals who are most likely to be satisfied with their own long-term development are those who achieve a high degree of integrated complexity. An additional corollary is that the end product is likely to be unique, given the enormous diversity found within the human species.

He offers four "axioms" for self-development:

1. *You are a part of everything around you: the air, the earth, and the seas; the past and the future.* Bringing disorder on any of these diminishes the self.

2. *You shall not deny your uniqueness.* Your own configuration of complexity is like no other.
3. *You are responsible for your actions.* If you let yourself be controlled only by "genes and memes," you miss the opportunity to be yourself.
4. *You shall be more than what you are.* The self is a creative construct, which is never completely finished.

This approach builds on his earlier research exploring optimal experience, a body of research important in understanding high levels of achievement (Csikszentmihalyi, 1990). This research drew on data from many cultures around the world. And it taps into an apparently universal source of intrinsic motivation. In brief, enjoyment comes when individuals engage in a challenging task, one that is thoroughly involving, one that provides clear goals and good feedback. This "flow" experience means that the individual learns and the self develops.

Csikszentmihalyi (1993) argues, in fact, that wisdom is one of the attributes of the evolving self, and he tries to specify what is meant by "wisdom." First, wisdom seems to be a cognitive skill, a way of knowing. Second, it is usually seen as a virtue; it is a special way of acting that is acknowledged to be socially desirable. Finally, it is a "personal good" in that the practice of wisdom leads to inner serenity and enjoyment for the wise one. In short, wisdom involves a higher, broader, deeper view.

We noted earlier that Erikson's final stages of life included "generativity," giving back to others and future generations, and, finally, WISDOM. In this view, this is where the integrated self finally finds joy and peace.

Working Wisdom

Aubrey and Cohen (1995) have tried to operationalize "wisdom" further, particularly in the context of the "learning organization" of the future. They begin with the premise that wisdom will be increasingly important for the success both of individuals and of institutions. They distinguish among "information," "knowledge," and "wisdom." For them, information involves collecting data and acquiring experience. Knowledge involves selecting information and giving it form. Wisdom means selecting knowledge, making it learnable, and putting it to work. This they see as the key challenge of the future.

They note that self-managed learning requires aspirations and goals; self-awareness; reflection; and trust, that is, the ability to accept and build on feedback. They then lay out "five skills of wisdom" which operate in the workplace: accompany, sow, catalyze, show, and harvest. They see these as the tools that managers need to facilitate learning in the individual and in the organization as a whole.

In summary, we obviously can now draw on a rich literature concerning human development. Some approaches, in particular, lend themselves to presentation as useful, teachable skills and strategies.

The Road Ahead

Given the challenges ahead, educational institutions, formal and informal, will generate new ways to respond to learner demands. Corporations will probably spend more on in-house training, such as GE's Crotonville. Many companies will link up with local colleges and universities to provide on-site educational opportunities. And managers themselves will increasingly be asked to assume the role of learning leader. Training companies will continue to proliferate, and on-line learning opportunities will expand. Other organizations, which originally pursued a different mission, will turn attention to learner needs. For example, Club Med is now designing learning centers to augment its traditional carefree, getaway resorts (Aubrey and Cohen, 1995:159).

Finally, individuals and grassroot networks will increasingly design their own means to pursue wisdom. One example is the WIT network. WIT stands for "Wisewomen in Training" (Sheehy, 1995:399). Eight to twelve women gather to discuss what they have learned in life, what they can learn from each other, and how they can apply this for themselves and others. While this started with women, there seems to be no reason why it could not be extended to wiseones in general.

In this chapter, we have reviewed a concept called "entirement," which draws attention to personal involvement in lifelong development. We have reviewed some of the research literature which might guide an entirement quest. We also have identified a few possible signposts for those who wish to cultivate their own appetite for wisdom.

Section Two

Lessons from Europe

7

Lessons from Rethinking High-Speed Management: Successful Adaptation of American Theory to an European Company

Giuseppe Raimondi

This chapter can be classified as a case study summarizing and focusing upon the main constituencies of organizational transformation undertaken in a small Italian firm, IPR-Immuno Pharmacology Research S.P.A., which operates in the field of in vitro diagnostics. Such a transformation has as its main prerequisites the high-speed management (HSM) set of theories which have been assumed to be a dynamic guide in order to transform in depth a firm while taking into account three principal variables: (1) the firm itself, (2) the field of diagnostics in which the firm operates, and (3) the social/economic context into which the firm is embedded.

What follows is the examination of the three variables deeply connected with the HSM set of theories, with particular regard to an "organizational mechanism" called "integration-coordination-control" (ICC), by which organizations may achieve a better efficiency.

It was necessary that the mechanism be applied to IPR in a flexible way, considering the three variables already shown as organizational independent variables with which the ICC mechanism had to be interfaced. What follows is the result of this transformation.

The "Integration-Coordination-Control" Mechanism

In the late 1980s, Drs. D. Cushman and S. King theorized that due to the rapidly changing business climate organizations had to adapt to respond to market stimuli speeding up their process of adjustment to their surrounding environment via a new form of communication.

This theory was grounded upon a set of theories called "high-speed management" and was to be used as an organizational tool in which communication is the key factor in successfully coping with such a changing environment. Basically, the variables which can determine the environmental volatility have to be attributed to the level and quality of competition in a certain economic segment. In addition, the organizational difficulty in coping with environment can be dramatically increased by the presence of the so-called recession, by means of an economic crisis whose effects may make the organizational survival harder in itself.

However, what makes the recession the hardest element an organization has to face is, in the end, the lack of original, creative, and effective tools that predict and, in many cases, take advantage of the recession's effects. In this sense, HSM represents a formidable tool against recession due to the ICC mechanism which, in turn, represents the essence of HSM. Cushman and King state:

> Successful firms are differentiated from unsuccessful firms by the integration, coordination, and control they exert over organizational activities, the amount of investment they are willing to make in information and communication systems, and the cumulative force of the types of competitive advantage they could obtain relative to their competitors. (Cushman and King, 1992:33)

It is fundamental at this point to better define the ICC mechanism because of the key role it plays in the case study examined here.

Cushman and King consider ICC a powerful tool which triggers important transformations to render organizations innovative, flexible, and rapid in response. Integration refers to how the organizational integration processes take place:

> Successful organizations are able to focus their energies and resources . . . such a focused response requires the use of information and communication to integrate people, technologies, and resources into a common stream of activities. (Cushman and King, 1992:37).

However,

> reciprocal coordination processes are at the core of effective high-speed management processes. They are essential for a product to be produced rapidly and in the hand of satisfied custom-

ers worldwide at low cost, and with high quality and high value. (Cushman and King, 1992:6)

Finally,

At the heart of a high-speed management organizational control system is the need to audit information and communication flow processes and then to continuously improve a firm's performance by seeking feedback from the stakeholders involved. (Cushman and King, 1995:37)

To support this view, Drs. Cushman and King have been studying a great number of public and private corporations, including GE, Toyota, and IBM. Their analysis suggests that

the basic function of management appears to be the coalignment, not merely of people in coalitions but of institutional action—of technology and task environment into a viable system, and of the organizational design appropriate to it. Management when it works best keeps the organization at the nexus of several streams of necessary action. (Cushman and King, 1992:35)

However, such a wide case study does not take into account small firms, as if they were marginal to the topic. Therefore, in order to verify whether HSM could have been applied to companies smaller than multinationals but still coping with a rapidly changing business climate, the ICC mechanism was utilized as a tool to manage a deep organizational change in a small Italian firm dealing with in vitro diagnostics.

IPR-Immuno Pharmacology Research S.p.A.— The Company

Founded in 1986, IPR is a small company which researches, manufactures, and markets diagnostic kits mainly in the field of immunology, food intolerances, and infectious diseases. Our attention will not be focused upon technical aspects of the products and their correlated technology, since the purpose of this chapter is to depict the process of organizational transformation without regard to the intimate nature of the manufactured goods.

However, in order to better orient the reader, it must be said that the "core production" is constituted by ELISA (Enzyme Linked Immunosorbent Assay) test kits mainly destined to hospitals and private laboratories.

Figure 7.1

From its foundation in 1986 until 1992 when the transformation began, IPR had a simple and entrepreneurial structure as shown in Figure 7.1.

As can be easily inferred, the main focus of the company was placed in the "strategic apex" embodied by the president, who personally took care of virtually everything from marketing strategies to supervising sales representatives' results, to controlling the production line. It is evident that the strategic apex was the main location where all the vital communication and information were concentrated and spread throughout the company.

It is also clear that such a configuration could not have been maintained longer than the initial stage for two main reasons: (1) the impact of the growth of superior products on the market, and (2) the instability of the field of diagnostics in Italy and in the world which called for a profound transformation of the company.

Before taking into account the organizational change which began in 1992, the field of diagnostics should be better framed in order to substantiate what has been examined up to this point.

The in Vitro Diagnostic World Market

For in vitro diagnostic manufacturers 1993 proved to be a difficult year. Many reported low sales in 1993 versus 1992. Most of the companies that reported higher sales had only minimal sales growth. Overall, it is estimated that worldwide sales of in vitro diagnostic products grew 4.5 percent to $13.9 billion U.S. (see Tables 7.1 and 7.2), well below historic growth rates of 7 to 10 percent annually.

Table 7.1 **WORLDWIDE SALES OF IN VITRO DIAGNOSTIC PRODUCTS BY TEST CATEGORY 1988–1998 (IN MILLION U.S. DOLLARS)**

Category	1988	1992	1993	1998	Growth (% Year) 1988–93	1993–98
Clinical Chemistry	4200	5300	5400	6700	5	4
Hematology	1100	1570	1650	2200	8	6
Immunoassay	2550	4500	5875	7500	14	9
Microbiology	700	875	925	1350	6	8
Blood Grouping	195	175	180	195	(2)	2
Urinalysis	260	300	310	360	4	3
Histology	215	275	285	400	6	7
Miscellaneous	220	260	275	320	5	3
Total	9449	13300	13900	19025	8	6

Table 7.2 **SALES OF IN VITRO DIAGNOSTIC PRODUCTS BY GEOGRAPHIC REGION 1988–1998 (IN MILLION U.S. DOLLARS)**

Category	1988	1992	1993	1998	Growth (% Year) 1988–93	1993–98
North America	3900	5450	5750	8200	8	7
Europe	3430	4860	5050	6700	8	6
Japan	1550	2115	2150	2625	7	4
Rest of the World	560	875	950	1500	11	10
Total	9440	13300	13900	19025	8	6

Three factors account for the slower growth sales:

1. a stronger U.S. dollar resulted in lower reported sales when U.S. companies converted their overseas sales to dollars;
2. continued cost-containment pressures, especially in international markets, adversely affected in vitro diagnostic sales; and
3. in the United States there were long delays in FDA approval of new tests.

The North American market remains the largest geographic segment, with total sales of 5.8 billion US $. The Japanese market, estimated at $2.1 billion U.S., has had essentially no growth in the past two years because of the market saturation and cuts in reimbursement for many routine tests. The European in vitro diagnostics market, estimated at $5 billion U.S., has also been hard hit by health reform measures. Three European countries can be taken into account in explaining such an evolution:

Italy

In Italy, which has been one of the most attractive markets for manufacturers, patients will now have to pay for a portion of their diagnostic testing. This requirement has caused physicians and both private and public laboratories to be more selective about ordering diagnostic tests, thereby slowing the demand for in vitro diagnostics products. In addition, in an attempt to reduce high health care debts, the Italian health care service has made substantial cuts in its capital budget for medical equipment.

Germany

In Germany, the government has attempted to curb health care spending by imposing budget restrictions on certain diagnostic tests. If doctors exceed the budget, they bear the loss.

France

In France, the government is considering penalizing physicians if they exceed recommended testing limits for various classes of patients. Limits have been set on the volume of tests private clinical laboratories can perform. Also, the government has cut reimbursement on numerous tests in recent years and has placed ceilings on the volume of tests that private laboratories can perform.

The Economic/Cultural Context

The third factor to consider in organizational change is the economic/cultural context. Among the long list of issues that a problematic field like this can raise, one has been chosen as central for the purpose because it represents the fundamental prerequisite of any theoretical consideration and its subsequent practical action of organizational transformation contextually located in the Italian scenario: the "Italian system."

The Italian system refers to that great number of Italian micro-companies which are effectively the backbone of the Italian economy.

These small firms, which very often have a dense concentration of high technology, can be considered as the historical heritage of the Italian Renaissance's productive system when thousands of entrepreneurial firms were capable of expressing quality and creativity via a number of innovative products at a very competitive price. This was due to their unusual organizational structure within which a great deal of interactive communication occurred among highly skilled laborers.

Thus, the third factor is essentially constituted by individuals with a profound historical background whose position in a rearranged organization had to mirror that one belonging to the reinterpretation of the firm of the Italian Renaissance.

Indeed, now that we listed the three prerequisites, it is time to see and check how the organizational transformation was implemented at IPR.

How to Change

It has been assumed that the process of transformation of a small Italian firm fueled by HSM rested on the analysis of the firm itself, the market where it operates, and the economic/cultural context. Now our attention will be drawn by the process of transformation itself that, as we already know, began in 1992 with a precise goal, to determine and list all operative functions an organization such as IPR had to perform.

Analysis of Organizational Functions at IPR

Passing from one organizational structure to another one presupposes the exhaustive analysis via an appropriate list of the primary organizational functions an organization such as IPR should perform. This is a sort of theoretical exercise that helps to track what was performed effectively in the existing organization and what was not. It also can be viewed as a chart for visualizing the optimal configuration of the firm according to what we have assumed up to this point.

It is useless to say that once we track this sort of map, the sum of the functions coming out from the list does not guarantee an effective performance of the firm; instead, functions have to be interfaced with the "mechanism" of ICC we assumed as central for the HSM set of theories and for the reconfiguration of *any* firm.

Figure 7.2   STRATEGIC APEX

Manufacturing	Marketing (Domestic)	Marketing (Foreign)	Research and Development	Human Resources and Communication
Raw Materials Production (Assembly Line) Packing Delivering	Determination of the Core Production Positioning of the Core Production in Terms of Quality-Price Segmentation of Potential Customers Targeting Old and New Customers with Appropriate Communication Comparison with Competitors in Terms of Products/Services Monitoring Sales, Sales Trends, Customers' Needs	Scanning the World Market Determination of the Best Strategy of Penetration Examining Differences and Affinities Between IPR and Main Competitors over Every Single Regional Market in Terms of Prices/Performances	Monitoring the State of Art of the External Research Units Verifying the Regular Flow of New Products	Creation of a New Corporate Image Elaboration of the Illustrated Material Advertising Public Relations
	SALES REPRESENTATIVES		EXTERNAL RESEARCH UNITS	

To begin with, the entire span of organizational functions was divided into five specific fields, each of them subdivided in a number of micro-functions, as shown in Figure 7.2:

What we have seen easily can be compared to a traditional organigram of a midsize to large corporation with five different departments having tens of people operating inside. Achieving a better degree of ICC within such a company is a matter of

1. focusing the organizational energies and resources in order to produce an innovative, flexible, efficient, and rapid response to environmental changes;
2. co-aligning the organizational activities via the use of information and communication processes; and

3. planning, benchmarking, and monitoring all organizational functions through auditing and correcting the organizational performance.

Instead, in our case, Figure 7.2 refers to a small organization whose job division does not pass through hundreds of people, but has to be conveyed via a limited number of individuals. Achieving a better degree of ICC in such a situation posed a question: How did one apply and verify the ICC "mechanism" derived from the HSM set of theories in a small company that had to perform all of the activities of a big one, utilizing few people?

A New Concept of a Small Firm: The Updated Version of the Italian Renaissance Firm

As already mentioned, taking into account the economic/cultural context was essential to fuel and direct the process of organizational change of the Italian firm, according to the HSM set of theories. Such a context was made by two components:

1. the environment in which the firm operates (i.e., in our case, the diagnostic field); and
2. the historical background belonging to the Italian organizational tradition, whose main and original experience is represented by the small entrepreneurial firms of the Renaissance.

Therefore, the process of transformation implemented began from the examination of the main functions which, at their turn, represented the basic constituencies of the new division of labor within the organization to be performed by a new team of few people.

The main difference between such an organization and those examined by Drs. Cushman and King is the size which requires a process of adaptation of the ICC "mechanism" normally applied to big corporations.

In other words, in small companies, individuals, rather than departments, have to be integrated, coordinated, and controlled. This point of view allows us to look at the small firm as an aggregation of a few people whose set of activities "makes the company."

In our case, the individual had to be rediscovered as the basic functional cell around which building a new concept of company performing not only functions related to productivity, but also having a sort of "social functions" connected to the past represented by the traditional Italian way manufacturing. Such was the Italian Renaissance firm, where the advantage over competitors was the result of the obsessive research for excellence in all activities performed. The main result of this process was the added value to production in terms of quality, creativity, and originality.

IPR was changed according to these parameters and has become a reality where individuals are "poles" of a wider network, performing their jobs in more than one of the five fields depicted in Figure 7.3. This configuration allows the operators a great latitude of independence from the department requirements, practicing a set of distinct and multidisciplinary skills, inaugurating a model of a firm where individuals are entrepreneurs for themselves in charge of performing apparently noncompatible functions.

Thus, Figure 7.3 already examined becomes the following:

Figure 7.3 STRATEGIC APEX

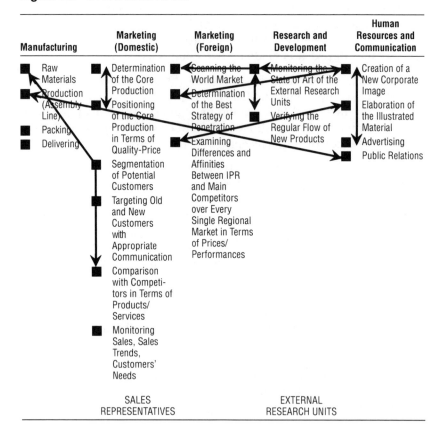

The lines and arrows unify what we previously called "microfunctions" (set of activities within the organization) and resemble those jobs performed by each individual.

The main result of this "nonaggregated" firm is that there is no organizational mechanism that can be over-imposed upon the structure because there is no codified structure upon which to apply something else. In other words, what we took the liberty to call a ICC "mechanism" does not work in the "traditional" manner in a firm such as IPR since both the integration and the coordination are automatically carried out by each individual within the organizational network. As in the Renaissance age, everyone has been trained to achieve the best in regard to his/her set of potentialities which are not relegated to one specific field/department.

Consequently, the integration/coordination processes are managed by individuals and covered in weekly teamwork sessions where topics ranging from market strategies to product development are discussed and automatically integrated and coordinated *by virtue of their attainment to the principal goals set out by the Strategic Apex at the beginning of the year.*

Therefore, such a company has become a sort of laboratory where constant quality control is pursued and applied to each activity, a multipolar network where the process of control is merely given by market results.

The Anti-gliadin Case

In order to substantiate what has been described up to this point, it can be useful to illustrate by means of a practical case how IPR coped successfully with its environment utilizing HSM as a tool.

Such a case refers to a particular diagnostic kit belonging to the "food intolerances" panel called IgA/IgG/IgM Anti-Gliadin. It is capable of detecting anti-gliadin antibodies whose appearance is a precise marker of the development of the coeliac disease, one of the fastest growing pathologies in Western countries. This malfunction is based upon the incapability of the human body to process gluten present in food, possibly leading the patient to death. Therefore, recognizing and detecting the coeliac disease in time, without resorting to time-consuming and painful biopsies, is essential to save the lives of those patients, especially children, who show the coeliac disease symptoms.

A few months after its foundation in 1986 IPR, in connection with one of the most authoritative scientists in the field of food intolerances, developed an innovative diagnostic system based upon the ELISA technique through which the coeliac disease could be detected in half the time normally required by current diagnostics. It had a terrific accuracy and was cost effective. Despite the commercial potentialities of the kit, its penetration among main users (mainly pediatricians, gastroenterologists, and immunopathologists) would have required enormous investments of financial resources and energies normally invested in the introduction of a new product in a specific market segment. In fact, what was needed was the replacement of the traditional diagnostic system with the IPR's new ELISA kit. IPR, at that time, was not structured to handle the changeover.

Above all, the majority of the Anti-Gliadin targets were constituted by public hospitals which typically operated through automated and expensive instruments usually provided by the diagnostic system's manufacturer at no cost to the customer. Given these prerequisites, IPR did not have many chances to be successful in this specific market, even with such an innovative product. As a consequence, the commercialization of the Anti-Gliadin test kit was marginalized to few and selected users operating without automatation.

Needless to say, the IPR test kit was almost immediately closed by two diagnostics multinationals operating within the Italian territory even though the IPR test kit was protected by an international patent. It seems that this is the story of a market failure; instead, the Anti-Gliadin case can be rightly regarded as the success of a team action.

In late 1993, when the "new" IPR came out, one of the first issues raised by the internal team was, of course, the Anti-Gliadin one. The very first Anti-Gliadin meeting was essential to reveal the company's strategic profile: the cloning of the IPR's kit by competitors had to be viewed as a great advantage, since the major effort to persuade the users to switch from the old diagnostic system to the new ELISA was successfully pursued by such competitors. Now, IPR had to follow a simple route: develop an improved ELISA kit to be run on the instruments already provided by its competitors.

In short, the effort of IPR can be summarized in three steps.

First, from the very beginning, it was decided by the strategic apex that 50 percent of the internal resources and time had to be devoted to an exhaustive screening of the Anti-Gliadin users over domestic territories, utilizing specific data banks. All information was gathered and reassembled into the IPR computer network to allow the internal team a step-by-step monitoring action directed toward every single Anti-Gliadin user "belonging" to the IPR's main competitors. This file integrated all pieces of information useful to tracking the Italian Anti-Gliadin customers, together with their needs and purchasing behavior.

Second, the IPR's Anti-Gliadin needed to be updated since it had been developed and released in 1986. The three-step Anti-Gliadin program was communicated in a special meeting to the external research unit in charge of developing new food intolerances products. In eight hours a new version of the Anti-Gliadin test kit was designed to have a set of unique competitive advantages over those of competitors. The production flow was reviewed and rationalized in a new process which allowed a 25 percent savings in costs. Within three months, thanks to the continuous coordination between the internal team and the external research unit, the improved version of the Anti-Gliadin test kit was ready to be launched in the marketplace. It was better and cheaper than the similar top-rated test kit. Valuable information was communicated in 24 hours to all of IPR's sales force together with the list of all potential targets to be visited. In the following six months, the IPR's Anti-Gliadin had conquered 50 percent of the Italian market and had become the new standard for every competitor in the field.

Third, a new control system was implemented at IPR to record the degree of satisfaction with the product and the needs and expectations of all customers. In the Anti-Gliadin segment, such an internal system recently revealed that 90 percent of users are going to adopt another test to complete the detection of the coeliac disease through a new detection called "Anti-Endomysial." Again, IPR is ready to launch another innovative test kit to meet the expectations of all potential customers. At the end of 1995, IPR held the best and cheapest Anti-Endomysial test kit in the world market. The new control system, which is giving extraordinarily good market results, is merely the result of the control that the internal IPR team is continuously exerting on itself, which, at its turn, has been theoretically and practically framed as the main heritage of the Italian Renaissance's productive system: the capability of each individual to integrate-coordinate-control her/himself according to a larger schemata within which individuality is not lost but is aware of being the substantial part of a larger interdependent context.

Conclusions

The so-called new interpretations of a small Italian firm under the lens of history and heritage may be amusing to scholars, academicians, and businessmen in the field of organizational communication. Not amusing are the results IPR has been achieving in the past two years. While many diagnostic firms all over the world are experiencing a tremendous depression in terms of sales and gross margins, IPR experienced a sales growth of 35 percent from 1993 to 1994 and nearly doubled its sales in the first half of 1995.

Apart from any consideration which may classify the organizational "models" proposed as nonelegant or unconventional, it can be said that the combination of the economic Italian tradition with the best American school of thought in the field of organizational communication has yielded those fruits all private and public companies are struggling to achieve: sales growth, geographical expansion, harmony, and respect in the workplace.

8

Lessons in Communicating Change in Transition: Some Dilemmas and Strategic Choices

Artur Czynczyk, Robert MacDougall, and Krzysztof Obloj

This chapter looks at the emergence of organizational communication strategies designed to cope with the newly competitive, swiftly changing economic environment which continues to develop in Poland after the last vestiges of Communist rule were finally dissolved in 1989. First, a short history of transition in Poland is outlined. This section will include a very brief recount of the fall of communism; the rapid transformation into a democratic state and emergent market economy; a recession which might be conceived of as partially "induced"; and the attendant openness which subsequently developed with respect to foreign investors. Next, there will be a discussion focused upon the emergence of multinationals in Poland and the dilemmas—concerning corporate communication strategy—they continue to encounter. This section includes a discussion of the positive and negative aspects of "greenfield" projects, acquisitions, and joint ventures in the aforementioned milieu.

Organizational communication dynamics are then addressed. First, the question of utilizing foreign, or local, communicators as the agents of change is discussed by highlighting the positive and negative features of each. Next, the pros and cons of how a shift to market economy principles effects communication within the organization leads to the final section which looks at the topic of corporate culture. The suggestion is that, unlike a natural (e.g., societal or civic) culture, which encompasses and perhaps even directs the "development" of the individual, the development of an organization's culture has some clearly definable, consensually attainable "ends." Finally, a prescriptive measure designed to develop and implement a customized application of these strategies (depending upon the specifics of organizational structure) in the form of a management development center, established by a large multinational company operating in Poland is outlined and discussed.

Transition in Poland

The Polish recession itself was very specific. It was induced by a swift transition from a centrally planned to a market-oriented economy. In this sense, the lessons we can learn from such a recession are also rather specific. However, these lessons have some universal meanings which are applicable in different environments. It is possible to outline briefly the series of changes leading up to the transition in Poland from a planned to a market-driven economy.

Critics predicted the fall of communism in Eastern Europe early. The suggestion was that the very concept ran counter to underlying human tendencies (e.g., personal autonomy, freedom of choice, and self-expression) which together allowed greater control over one's environment. History demonstrated that collective interest could not be maintained reliably under an imposed system for very long. Inevitably, this would break down in light of subdivision, coalignment, and personal or special interest. Control had to be kept manageable and localized. The state's resources could be utilized toward *focusing* and *promoting* a particular goal (e.g., the maintenance of Communist ideals and a planned economy). However, *effective control* of this process always ended up being negligible. There seem to be have been some more subconscious forces at work as well. Catholicism and Communism are ideologically incongruous. Between 1989 and 1990 about 95 percent of Poland's population was Catholic, as it remains today (in principle anyway). Even if they did not embrace the totality of the faith, many people felt as though they were unable, at a very fundamental level, to accept the precepts espoused by party leaders.

But the beginning of the end of communism in Poland actually occurred around 1956, when industrial workers first demonstrated against low wages and generally poor treatment, thereby breaking the long silence of fear and reticence. In 1968, when student uprisings signaled further discontent—this time surrounding state censorship—it became apparent that the end was merely a question of time. In 1976 workers protested against price changes. This was a significant point in the transition because it was the first time intellectuals and workers joined forces to oppose "the establishment." In the late 1970s, underground publishing houses began disseminating

officially banned literature. In 1980 *Solidarnosc,* with its independent
trade unions, was established. Orwell's *Pig Farm* and *1984* became
legal to read in 1984. During the mid to late eighties the government
tried to recuperate the system. It failed; there was no turning back.
In 1989, the first non-Communist prime minister came to power. The
rest is, as they say, history.

The subsequent transformation into a democratic state and
market economy occurred very quickly. The move to an open marketplace was guided under the auspices of the Balcerowicz plan. As
expected, a planned or centralized economy was the cause of many
difficulties. Under this system, centralized decisions were made with
respect to where, what, and how to invest. However, the vast majority of these decisions were based upon political, not economic interest. The Balcerowicz plan, rooted firmly upon economic theory, was
put into effect January 1, 1990. This set of policies explicitly stated
intentions to actively pursue the establishment of a free market-
driven economy. The first move was to reduce the out-of-control
inflation which had plagued the country for decades. This was accomplished by raising the *nominal* interest rate so as to make the
actual rate a positive figure. To do this, the nominal rate would first
have to approach the then current rate of inflation (about 70 percent per month!).

This is what is implied by a *partially induced recession.* An
attempt to stop inflation by raising interest rates (literally, the price
of money) prompts consumers to stop spending because their money
loses value. When the Balcerowicz plan was enacted in 1990, Poland's
inflation rate was an outrageous 586 percent per annum. In one year,
due to the encompassing reforms, it dropped to 70.3 percent. It has
steadily decreased ever since: 43 percent in 1992; 35.3 percent in
1993; 32.2 percent in 1994 (today, Poland's inflation rate fluctuates
between 22 and 25 percent, a much more manageable figure). The
second move eliminated the need to get state permission to open a
business. After this, the market immediately opened up to competition from all sides. Next, the zloty became internally convertible.
Now, anyone operating a legitimate business and paying taxes could
exchange Polish zloty for foreign currency. Prior to the Balcerowicz
plan, this "privilege" had been reserved for the government alone.

When the Polish marketplace began to feel the energy of the
competitive dynamic this very quickly led to an attendant openness
with respect to foreign investment. Outdated manufacturing facilities, unmotivated workers, and a relative unfamiliarity with Western
business practices made the modern equipment, cutting-edge

expertise, management skills, and shrewd business acumen of outsiders sought-after "commodities" giving way to increased competitive advantage in areas ranging from imported produce to consumer
electronics, to heavy industry (Johnson and Loveman, 1995:50). Today, the influx of foreign investment continues to grow at a steady
pace. Multinationals such as Coca-Cola, IKEA, Nestle, and ABB are
establishing large manufacturing facilities and retail outlets around
the country. Having outlined the factors leading up to this phenomenon, the next section addresses some of the advantages and pit-
falls associated with the several strategies employed by
multinationals in Poland.

Multinationals in Poland: Some Dilemmas

There are several ways to invest in the new economic environment
in Poland. Three popular means will be examined here, the positive
and negative attributes of each: the greenfield project vs. the acquisition vs. the joint venture. A *greenfield project* is an all-encompass-
ing affair, wherein the new facility is often quite literally begun in the
middle of some recently purchased farm pasture at the outskirts of
an industrial/economic/social center. The attraction to "locals" here
typically is that the influx of new jobs will bolster the economy.
Naturally, there are some variables which may alter this positive
effect. There may be a direct competitor across the way who will
now have to compete for employees; there may be a tendency by
the new project owners to hire their own (nonlocal) people; it may
be the case that the project was moved due to recent, "strict" local
ordinances in the previous location which hampered production,
and so on. Generally speaking, however, introduction of a greenfield
project is sought after by local interests. From the management perspective, the greenfield again presents positive and negative issues.

On the positive side, the project leaders have a unique opportunity to create an entirely new system of priorities and values.
Handpicking personnel allows for a greater possibility of mobilizing
a finely tuned organizational culture. Communication problems can
be forestalled if, from the outset, like-minded individuals are employed, not to mention the fact that there will be better control over
managerial, accounting, and manufacturing processes. In addition,
the facility itself can be designed "ergonomically." That is, office
space, servicing facilities, and production areas can be integrated so
as to make for smoother functioning of the entire organization, both

in the physical layout of the facility and in its logistical design (*who is put where*).

With a "ground up" operation such as this, far less paperwork is required and subsequently generated, scrutinized, and deliberated over as well. The reduction of bureaucratic "red tape" gives rise to advantages which are too numerous to outline here. In short, efficiency both at the macro and at the micro levels will be greater. The most salient negative issue associated with greenfield projects is the massive initial investiture. If the appropriate research has been done, however, the probability of recuperating the investment will be high. There are numerous case studies that scrutinize the pros and cons of greenfields, but this chapter is limited to a general picture (as is the case with the next two strategies).

Another common method is the *acquisition,* which also has both positive and negative characteristics. First, there is one potentially negative issue. Where the greenfield allows one to design the infrastructure to suit individual needs, after an acquisition, the newly acquired facility and surrounding property may be more of a burden than a blessing. Reworking, demolition, and/or upgrading all require large sums of money and time. But again, generally speaking, this does not drain the wallet as fast as a greenfield. One positive aspect in all of this, naturally, is that the foundation—both infrastructure and personnel—is already there. However, a more serious problem which arises is one of monitoring and control. The acquired personnel may represent the greatest dilemma encountered when trying to maximize organizational flexibility, efficiency, and speed.

The *joint venture* is a third means of entering a local market. The benefits here are numerous, assuming the transition goes smoothly and the whole affair is injected with a little luck. With the meeting of minds (and money) often comes new possibility, insight, ideas, and perspective—all of which can bring unprecedented good fortune. However, with such a hybrid strategy comes an equally diverse set of problems. As opposed to an acquisition, where management's role is one of delegation (very direct and one-way), in a joint venture, management (that is, both camps) must be willing to engage in discourse and dialogue. There must be a reconceptualization concerning who and what has been created. The hope, ideally speaking, of course, is to recognize that for all practical purposes the two firms are in effect no longer two entities, but rather a single *organism* with the same interests, goals, and aspirations.

Both in joint ventures and in acquisitions, redundant and/or obsolete personnel and equipment pose serious restructuring issues.

In an acquisition, however, this is perhaps not *as great* a concern (as the implicit assumption is that one firm is *taking over,* or *assuming control of,* another). The prioritization of interests and concern will predictably lie with the new owner. In a joint venture, however, this clear stratification of power and interest should be less salient. But the decision to opt for one of these three strategies is only the first task. In fact, the success of these initial decisions is heavily dependent upon the wisdom with which a group chooses to solve subsequent problems that arise.

Thus, in order to deal with the problems surrounding organizational change just outlined, some mechanism of communication must be put in place and successfully employed so that the new organization's internal structure helps to maximize its *fit* within this new external environment. Foreign firms have been investing in Poland for about five years now. It is still very much an exploratory time typified by trial and error at all levels. Having looked at some of the choices to be made with respect to the configuration of an organization, along with its relation to the surrounding geographical, social, political, and economic environments, it will now prove helpful to explicate the dynamics of change management with respect to maximizing the fit of *internal* processes.

The Change Matrix

In order to better understand the theory and practice proffered shortly, those multiple issues confronting the change specialist can be represented graphically in a four-cell matrix similar in appearance to the competing values framework (see Figure 8.1). The matrix describes a range of strategic choices an organization's decision-making body faces with respect to relaying a message designed to implement important changes, whatever they may be. The first issue concerns the problem of agency, or the *who* question. Where agency is at issue, there are really only two discrete choices that can be made. Either import some type of specialist (often a foreigner), or utilize local resources and delegate the task to the best insider. Now, while the answer to the initial question of who to choose is fairly simple, the problems associated with either choice which may arise later are not. Nonetheless, once this dilemma has been satisfactorily alleviated, the *what* question must be answered.

This is not as discrete a choice as *who,* nor is it any easier to satisfy. The options here run more along a spectrum ranging be-

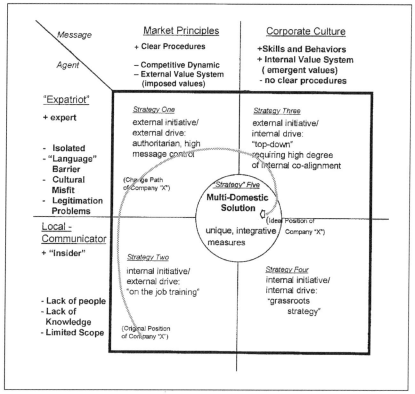

Figure 8.1. The Change Matrix

tween the external drive of the *marketplace,* and the more internal concept of *'corporate culture.'* Therefore, and specifically where Poland is the stage, it is first necessary to describe *market principle.* With respect to the society under analysis, the market principle, indeed, a "market economy" can be considered a *message* to be transmitted (via policy, infrastructure, strategy, example, etc.). Corporate culture is the next way to approach the formidable task of communicating change. Communication should achieve, with some degree of satisfaction, the ends it sought (e.g., the rapid design and implementation of a market economy). However, communication does not begin and end with mere transmission. That is, it must additionally result in some *intended change* of behavior (not just changed behavior). Otherwise, it is not communication, but rather *miscommunication,* or misinformation since the message is somehow obstructed—its ends not achieved.

Therefore, communication must consist of—indeed it requires—more than mere transmission. *Reception* is a necessary part of the formula. The message must be integrated into the consciousness of the agent before some desired behavior can be reliably performed. In light of this, it can be said that while Poland has officially (explicitly) been transformed into a market economy, the question naturally remains: To what degree has this concept become an *implicit* idea, completely absorbed into the mindset of the agents involved? The suggestion here is that 45 years of Communist rule coupled with a planned economy created a *tyrannizing image* (Weaver, 1964) which five years of democracy and market economics have yet to entirely dispel.

Agents of Change: The Messengers

For the above reasons, the intervention of agents who have already integrated market economy principles into their consciousness, and thus can reliably perform (and systematically exemplify) the required tasks, may be required. Perhaps this is the *who* question. One way of achieving this is to import the expertise of "expatriates," individuals steeped and therefore naturally versed in the intricacies of market principles and adept at their attendant economic/business strategies. The solution initially seems straightforward. A firm need merely hire one or more of these individuals to fill the appropriate management/decision-making position. As simple as this means of gaining expert knowledge may be, several problems can, and often do, arise. First, the expatriate manager can become isolated in a figurative "ivory tower," effectively shut out from the rest of the organization. Individuals lower in the hierarchy may alienate this individual, coming to view the expatriate leader as an out-of-touch figurehead without any valuable knowledge.

Second, a language barrier may pose several obvious and significant problems. More often than not, where a foreign language is involved, two-way marginalization and feelings of resentment accompany. Third, an intercultural misfit can cause additional tension during personal interaction. What is more, this "perspective problem" often urges the individual (both expatriate and native) to decrease attempts to participate in interaction and recede back into his or her own *modus operandi* since that way of doing things is familiar, seems functional, and appears to keep things going. The problem of "interperspectival translation" leads to the ultimate dilemma associated with the importation of expatriates. These three factors taken together lead quite systematically to the fourth and most problematic issue—that of *legitimation.*

The assumption, a natural one, is that the foreigner is out of touch. Speeches, presentations, and other "direct" forms of communication may not glean much interest. The response may be "Why *this* program?" and "Why *this* strategy?" Attempts by this outsider to foster support for a given plan, and mobilize action to carry it out, very often are confronted with obstacles which are some combination of contempt, derision, and resistance. This dilemma is, of course, closely associated to the language issue. That actors share conceptions of how behaviors are oriented toward others and the world around them implies that they understand a language. The term *language* here refers to a complete symbolic system, including verbal, gestural, and conceptual representation. For this reason, even if the expatriate manager is fluent in the local tongue, there can be far greater problems lurking "subtextually." So, while importing an expert can satisfy the transmission problem, reception and a necessary integration of the message become the new issues.

The next agent-based strategy is an attempt to rely on local communicators to ensure reception of the message so that isolation, language, cultural, and the subsequent legitimation problems are circumvented. While these reception obstacles can usually be avoided by using local people, new problems arise with respect to the transmission of good messages—ones that contain useful and relevant information. That is, the number of experts from the local area is going to be very, very small. There is a distinct lack of available people in Poland who can be considered experts in market economy strategies. Few have experienced the dynamics of such a situation (e.g., a full-fledged market economy). Studying economics at Yale or Stanford in the United States may well provide the requisite theoretical base and conceptual skills, but such an education tends not to provide practical experience (along with the associated and very necessary mind-set which develops out of this experience).

Three problems, then, become manifest when local communicators are employed. First, there is the problem of locating and eliciting the co-operation of individuals who might initially be considered qualified for the position. Once they are found and "enlisted," only one hurdle has been surmounted. Second, there is little likelihood that, once the leadership process begins, the individual may find that he or she does not possess the necessary skills to convert the concepts learned—back in the United States perhaps?—

into practical, behavior-guiding action. Third, a consequence of the second (knowledge) issue, is the limited scope and subsequent applicability of that expertise which they do in fact possess. The assumption here is that true expertise or *wisdom* is not some enigmatic, mystical quality, but rather that it can only come about after a very careful and very comprehensive fusion of *knowledge* and *experience*. Such are the dilemmas associated with answering the *who* question, and subsequently developing agent-based change strategies.

Now on to the issue of message-based change strategies and an attempt to answer the *what* question. Methods of changing behavior in an organization ultimately consist of a blend of agents (messengers) and agencies (messages). After all, someone must be the *messenger.* But there can be implicit yet obvious priorities set in the way one emphasizes the employment of agents and the direction of messages. Clearly, it is always a synergy. But, with respect to the change agent, one of the ideas in all of this talk of message which follows shortly is to decrease the probability that they will be shot—figuratively speaking of course. Indeed, the old adage, *shoot the messenger,* can actually be a handy means of motivating action when it comes to reminding one of the bad side effects stemming from misdirected, poorly managed change scenarios.

Agencies of Change: The Messages

In what follows, an attempt will be made to flesh out the pros and cons both of internal and of external message strategies. It is a fairly systematic process-in theory anyway. With an external drive mechanism such as the marketplace comes a particular set of issues which are quite different from those which arise when a more internal drive mechanism (e.g., the cultivation of some set of values and other cultural variables) is applied. Several problems manifest themselves when it comes time for opting one change strategy over another. The first approach is to base change on the dynamics of the external environment.

Concerning the structuring of communication within an organization, the principles which underlie conduct in the free market lead to an emphasis on deductive thinking and direct (or at least explicit) communication and the imposition of values closely aligned with those of the marketplace. Among the concerns at issue are an awareness of global economic trends with their fundamental competitive dynamic. In light of this, there is a subsequent need for continuous improvement and fast reaction time so a firm can stay in step with sporadic changes in the global economic milieu. Even a willingness to adopt some *discontinuous* strategies for dealing with this dynamic may be required. That is, people may have to learn entirely new ways of doing (and thinking about) certain things— such as designing and building cars, investing money, or perhaps working with "peers" halfway around the world via satellite). Those are known changes with determinate ends. There is also sometimes a need to initiate unknown changes with multiple consequences, however, spacial constraints preclude their discussion here.

Structuring an organization in accordance to a set of external parameters, such as the global marketplace, which are not directly controllable from within the organization creates the need to impose a high degree of formality and standardization so that communication becomes, in effect, obligatory. This first strategy—opting for an emphasis on market principles—sets certain mechanisms in motion from which a fairly specific organizational structure emerges. This, of course, includes the establishment of large marketing and investment segments which have ready access to timely information concerning stock movements, demographics, consumer trends, and so on. Along with this will be required a myriad of specialists (economists, accountants, marketing experts, and computer specialists) and their support personnel.

One can see the bureaucracy forming already. The more segments and levels the organization has, the more *cultural gaps* or *context/experience interfaces* there are to be bridged. These are really sub-cultures—relatively discrete functional units within which highly context-specific value systems (based on unique experiences) are established. While a corporate culture of some form does inevitably emerge from these particular allocations and values, it is more a by-product of the valuation process. Put simply, the organization is designed with the market, not the organization, in mind. Such a structure, of course, has both advantages and shortcomings.

One positive side to all of this will be a steady link to the external environment. Timely knowledge of a competitor's status provides certain obvious advantages (latest technology advancements, advertising scenarios, investment trends, etc.). All of these can help to direct one's progress. But with the somewhat recent emergence of "virtual corporations" such as Nike, IKEA, Polaris, UST, and Intel, things are changing. Such an organization can base its entire strategy on the market, without having to worry much about cultural interfaces. Since only marketing, accounting, a group of advertising executives, and maybe a handful of designers make up such companies there is no need to justify corporate strategy as communication trickles "down the line."

Why? Because there is no "line," no real hierarchy. This is especially the case where the large wholesale companies are concerned. But what happens if one is not a big outsourcer? Indeed, one of the prerequisites to being allowed into the Eastern European market is that things such as production and manufacturing stay local. In this case, value chains span the gambit (from R and D, purchasing, manufacturing, and distribution, to accounting, marketing, sales and service). Here is where a market-based strategy creates problems and where the *multinational* in Eastern Europe should be concerned. Especially where the need for vertical integration is high, attention to cultural issues must increase proportionately, not inversely, as is most often the case.

Therefore, this text now focuses on one of the most serious shortcomings associated with an external drive mechanism such as the marketplace: the problem of *imposed values.* An imposed value is one which is often misunderstood—not because the person expected to abide by it is stupid, but because he or she has had no experience with it. As far as the individual knows, it is intended to enhance the situation of someone else (most likely someone above him or her). As suggested earlier, a value which is forced onto a group invariably loses *traction* (or the ability to direct behavior) since there is no built-in means of reinforcement.

This lack of reinforcement comes about because, usually, only a small percentage of an organization has ready and continual access to the vital signs of the marketplace. For those market analysts, advertisers, economists, and sales associates, this is a good thing. But what of the rest of the organization? What of the researchers in the lab, the stockperson in the warehouse, the frontline worker at the assembly plant, or the frontline supervisor? They would very likely have trouble translating and understanding this information even if they had ready access to it. This understanding hinges also upon changes in the environment or marketplace. If new corporate goals are being set every month or so to keep astride of these changes, then it becomes that much harder to relay the information "down the line." The increasingly frequent number of discontinuous changes makes things even more difficult. How might this be dealt with? But if values cannot be imposed, if it is difficult to guide behavior externally, then maybe direction from within is the way to go.

The suggestion here is that values are not a "one-shot affair." They cannot be injected into a system and relied upon to do the job. A value requires reinforcement and maintenance; it requires cultivation. It requires active, repeated bolstering through experience with specific, practical behavior. This is a fundamental shortcoming of market-driven strategies. The placement of a value system (onto a large number of individuals working within a range of context/experience dynamics) leads to communication problems which can only be alleviated by more introspective strategies.

Before continuing, it should be emphasized that there are never wholly market driven, nor wholly internal (culturally) driven ways of prompting changes in an organization. It is always a synergy. The approaches are artificially abstracted here for ease of explanation. Every organization utilizes some awareness of the marketplace. Likewise, all organizations exhibit, to varying degrees, some form of culture. The very fact that the group has remained together for any length of time and co-ordinated processes or action in such a way as to produce some product or service attests to the "culture's" existence. The next questions become What problems are associated with the introduction of a good culture? and How can we make a corporate culture really hum?

As was just implied, a communication strategy designed around market principles must be relatively formal with a clear structure which can be referred to when clarification is required. Its sequence of plans, strategies, and prescribable measures obliges the receiver to attend to the message or quit the game. Today's increasingly competitive global economy presumes that companies have worked the concept of continuous improvement into their respective managerial systems. A big downside to an external drive mechanism like the marketplace, however, is that only the upper layer of an organization tends to keep abreast of the often unpredictable changes involved. In light of this, the necessary behavior modification which must be directed down through the entire organization comes in punctuated bursts (such as information seminars, process-improvement workshops, or innovation campaigns) which interrupt the "natural" progression of activity within the system since this information is not usually attended to by those interests. Such change programs are likely to be ill advised, perfunctory, and lacking specific direction.

Typically, these programs are not accompanied by a great enough sense of immediacy and importance. From the average employee's perspective such strategies can be bewildering, tedious, bothersome—even a complete waste of their time. The reason for this, often, is due to the manner in which these meetings, seminars, or "workgroup" sessions are conducted—as one-way, direct, "talk-down shows" where an outside consultant is trucked in, delivers a three-hour spiel, hands out a pack of comment cards, then hops on a plane to the next job. Employees are often not told what the seminar is really all about. A blurb in the company newsletter merely states that it will be held on such and such a date, time, and place. So, in addition to no real importance given to the process, there also seems to be a lack of vision surrounding the whole affair. Subsequently, the line supervisor, floor manager, and project engineer ponder what it is all about.

In short, external drivers are inherently bad at creating urgency, guiding action, and demonstrating vision. With this awareness comes an understanding that some internal mechanism must be present and seriously attended to before the consolidation of practical action can become a realistic goal. One way to increase the stability and cohesiveness of an organization is to turn toward internally directed change.

An alternative message strategy can emerge from within the organization itself. When configured properly, an organization's inherent value system (or corporate culture) can reliably guide constructive, practical action. The development of skills and behaviors which lead to the establishment of a high-performance organization is a subtle task. Touched on briefly in the previous section, a value is (generally speaking) not something which can be pulled out of thin air and *imposed onto* behavior. A value *emerges from* a specific behavior which has proven itself reliable, efficient, and productive. The context/experience/value relationship is a good way to conceive of this process of value formation and reinforcement (Larkin and Larkin, 1994; MacDougall, 1995).

To establish and maintain a value there must first be an inquiry into and description of the behavior or experience which seems to work best in a given context or task situation. If there does not seem to be any good examples of appropriate behavior, then a benchmarking process should be the first order of business. Benchmarking would be employed to locate examples of *valuable,* practical behavior. This sometimes requires a search outside the organization. However, only an accurate description of such behavior can lead to wise prescription. The attempt to build a Communist state—with its planned economy—might be considered a prescription which failed, in part, because of faulty observation and description beforehand. That is, it seemed as though this idea could work, in theory. Applied in practice, however, the idea came up against opposition at multiple levels, including those both of social and of subjective consciousness. Hence, the ability (potential) to prescribe with success may be one feature which differentiates organizational or corporate cultures from "natural," "ethnic," or "societal" cultures.

In reference to societal culture (in this instance, "Polish civil life," which includes the personal expression of the individual citizen), the effects of the changes outlined at the beginning of this chapter seem to be following a relatively stable course from a constricted, or restrictive, to a generally more open and expressive posture. Since there are no rigid, clearly definable *ends* toward which the society or the individual must necessarily aspire, these courses or trends can be said to have no real prescriptive measures applicable to them. Particularly where the individual is concerned, there are not any stringent procedures which can reliably and universally enhance their "quality." The reason for this is that the elements which might comprise a "quality person" are multiply realizable and difficult to measure. In other words, the notion of what a good or productive citizen should be comprised in the new Poland is very much a context-dependant, highly subjective ideal.

In corporate or organizational culture, however, this intractability is reduced dramatically, becoming much more of a quantifiable, measurable target system. Where the corporate culture of a large business organization in the milieu of a still immature yet burgeoning market economy is concerned, there are some very tangible, clearly definable ends toward which an agent can and perhaps should aspire. What it means to become a highly productive, efficient, and, of course, profitable firm is not such an ambiguous, subjectively based ideal. There *are* some prescriptions, that if followed, *can* enhance the overall quality of the organization. In light of this, a construct can be put in place which functions to normalize what might be considered ideal behavior.

The previous discussion suggested that attention to the marketplace, as a means of motivating action, brings with it a need for deductive thinking in the form of analysis (explanation), forecasting (prediction), and implementation (control). This last step is where market-driven approaches run into trouble. Unless one is content to follow trends *after* they have become proven effective and beneficial and thereby function in a passive, or at least re-active role, some risks will have to be taken. Indeed, market analysis and prediction are very probablistic enterprises. So, in the case of market-driven approaches, either the analysis or the prediction (or worse, both) may be missing or faulty. What is more, as suggested in the previous section, even while an analysis of the marketplace may lead to an accurate, perhaps ingenious, set of predictions, this in no way ensures that the subsequent corporate strategies which are formulated are themselves appropriate or will be successfully implemented in the organization. Concerning successful implementation then, because of the perspective and translation problems inherent to a hierarchical structure, a large number of individuals may not be amenable to this form of control.

Reliance on an internal mechanism, conversely, requires a more inductive strategy. The reason for this is that the "installation" of a corporate culture is (or can be) similar to a greenfield project—a totally ground-up affair. Just as a greenfield results in a complete system which is *known,* a corporate culture and its value systems can be generated from those processes which are familiar and understandable. In contrast to deduction, induction is a process of reasoning which begins with the collection of information. From this data, a set of assumptions is generated. This can lead to a very stable set of prescriptions.

This is also the case in management science. However, the whole process must be predicated by a very holistic, open, diagnostic approach to leadership. For instance, when designing a change program, accurate diagnosis is initially required to determine the maturity of one's underlings (Kerr and Jarmier, 1978b). There are two types of maturity in this case: *psychological* and *task* maturity. Psychological maturity of course refers to the emotional and analytical stability of the individual. Task maturity, in turn, refers to the degree of skill or expertise one needs to perform certain work. If workers are low on these qualities they can be given orders (told exactly what to do). This is termed a "telling style" of leadership. When they are high on these qualities one simply "delegates" and stands back, letting them do their jobs. Naturally, this second situation is the more desirable (Kerr and Jarmier, 1978; Cushman and King, 1995).

Now the problems. Perhaps the singly most misunderstood concept in management science today, with all its talk of corporate culture, is the notion of *empowerment.* To begin with, people should have power only over those things they do in and around their job. If frontline workers are expressing an interest in managerial affairs or corporate strategy on a consistent basis, such individuals *should be heard.* If the ideas sound good, they *should be listened to.* What is more, they should be moved because they are in the wrong place in the organization.

However, assume that the individual is comfortable in his or her position in the organization (one based on skill and ability). When this is the situation, the individual should, once again, have power only over those things associated with the context he or she is in and the behaviors and actions (tasks) he or she experiences. So, how is this precarious balance achieved? Empower with respect to *means,* and set the targets or *ends* yourself. If it has not already, the best (most *valued*) way of doing the job will emerge. This is what is implied when the establishment and maintenance of a corporate culture are inductive processes. This, additionally, is what is meant by empowerment.

What follows is a discussion on how to design change strategies, based on the particularities of a problem, which are custom fitted to a respective organization. Certain variables have already been decided upon. That is, an organization probably has its location established in a distinct socioeconomic environment; most of its personnel in place; some type of cultural system; and a general notion with respect to corporate strategy—one which has been in place and (at least) functioning for some period of time. Given these particular facts, a variety of strategies or change paths can be plotted.

The Multidomestic Solution (Theory and Method)

The two kinds of messengers (expatriate and local) and two kinds of messages (outside and internal) were explicated in some detail. In light of this, it seems that there exist four possibilities for initiating a change strategy which can be actively emphasized. These are only *emphases* to varying degrees. They are not pure, wholly discrete strategies. The four cells of the change matrix (see Fig. 8.1) allow for these iterations. The problem can be (1) described by an *outsider* (expatriate) and also prescribed from *without* (the market); (2) described by an *insider* (local) and prescribed from *without;* (3) described by an *outsider* and prescribed from *within* (culturally); and (4) described by an *insider* and prescribed from *within* (sometimes referred to as a "grassroots strategy").

Now, based upon which combinations seem to have been used by the organization in the past, coupled with accurate information about situational factors (e.g. local environment), a new change path can be plotted which will greatly enhance both the internal and the external performances of the organization. The solution can improve conditions within, as well as make the organization ideally suited to the environment, thereby maximizing its degree of *fitness*. Extending the Darwinian metaphor for a moment, the fitness of an organism is most directly assessed during times of change. Where today's Poland is the stage, change is continuous. Organizational performance is being rigorously put to the test. It therefore becomes necessary to design unique strategies which emphasize the following issues: (1) the development of local expertise; (2) the communicative competence of expatriate leader; (3) an attendance to the local environment; (4) the careful translation of market principles; (5) an awareness and support of corporate culture; and (6) a generally holistic and integrative strategy with respect to balancing the first five issues so as to create a highly responsive, productive organization.

Where lacking, the development of local expertise must be actively pursued. This, of course, can be initiated by first importing a foreign expert and attempting a "learn-as-you-earn strategy." The problems associated with on-the-job training (strategy two) of this type have been drawn out in some detail in the previous sections. A grassroots approach (strategy four) has its own obstacles. The limited scope of insiders combined with an overly familiar (tried and true) way of doing things can lead nowhere fast. Stagnation is a common course where there is a refusal to step out of the forest to view the trees.

A multidomestic approach presupposes both of these to be temporary situations. In other words, it is acknowledged that the gaining of market awareness and some of those attendant business skills are desirable at all levels of the organization. A multidomestic approach attempts to integrate local awareness into the larger global dynamic. What is more, it attempts to instill these values into the day-to-day activity of the organization. Ideally, these myriad perspectives become a single, internalized, even habitual way of thinking.

Such a movement brings with it a more macrolevel internalization. Whereas the notions of 'market principle' and 'corporate culture' have hitherto been discussed as discrete, perhaps even mutually exclusive, concepts, the multidomestic strategy (in uniquely integrating disparate principles based upon current status) attempts to reconcile and redirect the various forces.

This chapter concludes with a detailed look at one organization's attempt to systematically realize such multidomestic solutions. This can be considered a practical application of the theoretical responses to the problems outlined in the previous section. A continuously unique set of integrative, holistic prescriptions, in the form of one global company's management development center, will draw out this hybrid strategy.

The Management Development Center

Major transitions are only achieved when education and skills provide a path to success. It should be the purpose of a management development center to create such paths by providing education and skills. A thoughtful reflection on how this can be accomplished after the fact leads to the model presented in this section. This model has significant implications for all pathfinders, whatever their environment.

The Management Development Center (MDC) is a "living example" where the strategies previously enumerated are effectively being operationalized into behavior. Theory is turning into practice. The development center is a small organization, consisting of only sixteen full-time staff members. This makes for a very flexible, responsive organization. Cross-functional teams are the rule, not the exception at the MDC. The roles actually performed are not well reflected with a quick look at work description, job title, or business card. People at the MDC are diversified in their ability and functions to an extremely high level by any standard, East or West.

For instance, the "marketing" person performs the predictable tasks, but also does course syllabus design and qualitative research on privatization in Poland and takes part in the design of an internal MBA program, stocks the facility's library, and helps to decide upon the purchasing of office supplies and equipment. It is interesting to note that, concerning business cards, this individual and several others did not even have a title listed, simply a name. Simply put during an interview, "Actually, it was difficult to find titles for some of us which seemed satisfactory; we do so many things."

One individual's business card reads "Management Development and Training." Performing duties involving the development of "soft skills" (e.g., negotiation, facilitation, conflict resolution, decision making, etc.), she performs what might be traditional tasks for the job. But she also is involved in the design of simulation games intended to hone accounting, marketing, and finance competencies. In addition there is *presently* a research and consulting component which centers around the role of supervisors. This includes the design, preparation, and implementation of diagnostic techniques which troubleshoot problems in order to develop what she termed "tailor-made" programs.

A third person, the director of special events, oversees management of and conducts extracurricular programs, is the booking agent for entertainment at the MDC facility, performs a public relations function, and is involved with the design of materials utilized in the training programs (among other things). His primary concern? "I'm not sure exactly where I belong in the organizational chart." In other words, his biggest problem seems to be that there are a number of options each day. An innocuous sort of identity crisis may haunt some of these people, but are these not good problems? The typical state of affairs in the business world today is that individuals feel as though they have one-dimensional lives, performing the same monotonous task, day in and day out.

In short, the place has a decidedly flat structure. Subsequently, strategic information is almost instantaneously disseminated. Weekly meetings—more like brainstorming sessions typified by free association and punctuated with feisty exchanges—include everyone from the director of the facility to service and maintenance personnel. At one particular meeting the latter had the "floor" the majority of the hour, offering valuable insights on such matters as finance allocation, bookkeeping methods, and cost control—in every respect, an organic, open system. Concerning corporate culture and value systems, there is a clear homogeneity.

Market awareness is maintained continuously. For instance, there is one particularly interesting interoffice "policy" at the MDC. From both the facility's and individual employee subscriptions (a collection of perhaps two dozen national and international social, political, business, and economic publications), any article, chapter, pamphlet, or even cartoon "which seems interesting" is readily photocopied and distributed. Key passages are highlighted, with comments penciled in the margins. This dynamic most accurately could be described as "inquisitive and enthusiastic." Criticisms, concerns, and other feedback tend to fill whatever idle moments arise with lively debate. People at the MDC are very enthusiastic about learning, not just teaching and consulting. Relationships among employees and their clients indicate an open recognition that more heads are better than one. A dynamic of open, two-way information exchange is developed and maintained because it has been proven to work. Multilevel and bidirectional communication have developed out of felt need, not obligation. The value emerged from the behavior, not some proclamation.

The idea was to design a culture that embodies and continuously exemplifies what has been dubbed the "multidomestic" ideal. The entire facility—offices, classrooms, cafeteria, fitness center, a forty-five room "hotel," lounge, sunroom, and even a mock-up Irish pub—are housed within a single building. Because of this, the small number of MDC insiders appears to expand rapidly when programs are in session. But there is also a good deal of "on location" work. That is, MDC people travel to manufacturing facilities and business locations not only for research and diagnostics, but for in-house training sessions as well. In both cases, the initial sixteen become rather elusive, mingling with and becoming part of a larger system, including experts, lecturers, and participants both from within and from outside the parent organization.

The MDC puts concepts such as 'cross-functional teamwork,' 'networking,' 'benchmarking,' and 'outsourcing' into active practice. A variety of experts are invited to teach seminars and run short programs (negotiation, team building, process improvement, customer focus, marketing strategies, conflict resolution, general communication skills, personal efficiency, human-resources management, leadership training, etc.). The management center relies heavily upon partners within the parent firm to disseminate insider know-how and also maintains close external partnerships, working extensively with leading business, management, and communication schools such as Poland's own International School of Management, the Department of Organizational Communication at the State University of New York at Albany, and MIT.

While unique and specifically designed around the apparent needs of the organization, a "typical" development plan proceeds as follows. The parent firm first delegates a business location which will receive consultation. As is the case in the effective treatment of alcoholism, diabetes, near-sightedness, dyslexia, or any ailment, the whole process must begin with a recognition from "within" that a problem indeed exists. This often is more difficult than it sounds. Denial, arrogance, and self-delusion may even be more prevalent in organizational entities than in individual ones.

Nonetheless, once this recognition problem is surmounted, a diagnostics team is sent in. This team conducts an on-site visit or a series of visits. A communication audit is performed by way of surveys, Q+As, monitoring, and participant observation. From the data obtained, a "prognosis" is presented to the appropriate overseeing body. Based upon subsequent feedback, alteration, and fine tuning, a set of prescriptions is developed which will determine what kind of program, or series of programs, is most applicable to the situation.

Change either can be managed or it can be consuming. Management practices can be either accidental or principled. Ultimately, the outcome of change can be either productive or destructive. When change is managed, principled, and constructive, it is learning. This is precisely what education centers should be about. However, when change is consuming, it is likely that it was dealt with in an unprincipled, destructive fashion. The result is most often fear and permanent job loss. This chapter has argued that (1) one must learn not to fear change but to see it as an opportunity; (2) that the principles governing change help one understand market dynamics; (3) that one must initially learn the specific entry points along the change continuum to be a constructive agent of change, and finally; (4) that change can be *designed* to be successful.

9

Lessons from Recession in Central and Eastern Europe: From Survival to Continuous Improvement

Andrzej K. Kozminski

Introduction

The main objective of this chapter is to challenge conventional wisdom and widespread opinion that post-Communist countries of Central and Eastern Europe are the last places in the world where well-managed companies and good managers can be found who can teach us some lessons regarding recession.

Few are ready to accept such facts as Czech Skoda being in the recent past the most profitable subsidiary of Volkswagen or Polish Polkolor being the lowest-cost and highest-quality producer of color television picture tubes for the French consumer electronics giant Thomson. Studies of such companies show that many of them are managed by predominantly local managerial teams and that companies relying heavily on expatriates are much less successful (Kozminski, 1995).

The general public is even less likely to believe that entirely local companies can perform well under entirely local management. Examples: Kwidzyn paper mill in Poland, the lowest-cost high-volume paper mill in Europe *before* acquisition by International Paper (*Business Strategy,* 1993); Sloven Fotona, one of the most advanced producers of laser systems in Europe; and landmark Czech crystal manufacturer Moser.

In order to understand the lessons from the best-run companies in the post-Communist countries, one has to take into consideration specific conditions of transition and specific sets of managerial actions taken at different stages of dramatic enterprise restructuring.

Four such stages have been identified: (1) fight for survival; (2) functional restructuring; (3) process restructuring; and (4) continuous improvement.

The analysis presented below is based on dozens of in-depth studies of Central and Eastern enterprises in transition conducted by this author (Kozminski, 1993; 1995; 1995a), and other researchers (Abell, 1992: Burawoy and Handley, 1992; McDonald, 1993; Lawrence and Vlachoutsicos, 1993; Johnson, Kotchen, and Loveman, 1995), as well as on the author's extensive experience in consulting, management development, and training.

Point of Departure: Fight for Survival

The day after the fall of communism, enterprises in Central and Eastern Europe found themselves in an almost impossible situation. They were suddenly and abruptly exposed to a destructive combination of external threats resulting from the collapse of communism and internal weaknesses inherited from communism.

Among external threats the following should be mentioned:

- "Wild capitalism" resulting from market competition combined with a nonexistent legal framework of market economy (clear property rights, contracts enforcement, law-and-order enforcement, stable tax system etc.);
- Destruction of the communist "common market" (COMECON), combined with failing internal demand (due to unavoidable austerity measures) and protectionist measures introduced by the European Union in order to stop imports of "sensitive goods" from Central and Eastern Europe (U.S. General Accounting Office 1995:35);
- Foreign competition due to sudden abolition of the trade barriers and "internal convertibility" of local currencies;
- Destruction and/or fragmentation of distribution channels existing under communism;
- "Credit trap" resulting from lunatic investment decisions of former communist governments (such as building in Poland the largest tractor factory in the world: Ursus), and combination of inflation, restrictive monetary policies and lack of mature, efficient, and market-oriented financial intermediaries; and
- Chaotic economic policies of often changing post-communist governments in such vital areas as: trade, industrial and regional development, finance or agriculture. (Lavigne, 1995)

Among inherited internal weaknesses of the post-Communist enterprises, the following should be mentioned:

- Inherited debt burden;
- Over-capacity and over-employment contributing to low productivity along with obsolete technology, old machinery, and poor production and inventory management;
- Obsolete products, unattractive packaging, complete lack of marketing skills and market sensitivity, mind-set of management dominated by deeply entrenched production orientation;
- Lack of financial reporting system;
- Byzantine multilayer hierarchical structures, bureaucracy, red tape, ritualistic, closed organizational cultures (Kozminski, 1995a); and
- Poor work ethic, highly politicized workforce, and confrontational unions.

Even the most promising Central and Eastern European enterprises, such as Hungarian Tungsram acquired in 1989 by GE, were not free of most of these weaknesses after communism. When unsalable inventories, uncollectible accounts and unpaid bills were finally calculated by GE accountants, more than two-thirds of Tungsram official 1988 earnings of $20 million faded away (Greenhouse, 1990). In 1989 or 1990 it would be difficult to identify in the whole region a large or midsize enterprise capable of competing with Western companies on equal grounds.

Specifically, deadly combinations of external threats and internal weaknesses of these enterprises had only two logical outcomes: annihilation or survival on "blood transfusions" (constantly growing government subsidies).

Both outcomes can be also considered as an invitation to parasitic practices such as "black privatization" known also under the name of "appropriation of nomenklatura" and to illegal transfer of state property to former Communist managers and government officials. Formation of private "nomenklatura companies" using state enterprises resources is one form of these practices. "Asset stripping"; sell-out of the state owned assets, with sales proceeds going to private off-shore accounts, is another. An estimated $23 billion left Russia in just such ways in 1993 (Intrilligator, 1995).

Under conditions of a combination of threats induced by transition from planned to market economy and internal weaknesses inherited from the old system, turnaround seemed the most unlikely outcome. It was even more unlikely since very few of the state-owned enterprises could be quickly privatized and acquire "personalized private ownership" through acquisition or strategic investment. Only the most valuable were targeted by global leaders such as ABB, GE, Volkswagen, or Siemens.

However, some enterprises and some local managers took their chances and successfully fought for survival. What can be learned from them?

Certainly they can demonstrate the art of survival in the most hostile and turbulent environment with limited and shrinking resources. Even "dinosaurs" (oversized creations of "socialist industrialization" in low value added, heavy industries) can survive and restructure. Two examples from Poland: Szczecin Shipyard capable of securing $1.2 billion worth of orders from the West (Johnson, Kotchen, and Loveman 1995:62) and Lublin coal mines capable of building stable partnership with local power stations. At the same time, other shipyards and other coal mines are deeply in the red and survive only because of government subsidies. Competent management made the difference.

Three types of managerial actions are essential for survival: political, entrepreneurial, and marketing.

Political Actions

These bring about compromise with the workers and the government. Workers, unions, and management representing them have to be persuaded to accept lay-offs, more efficient work organization, higher quality standards, new compensation systems, and eventually privatization. Without workers' consent none of these is possible. That is why managers starting post-Communist restructuring have to possess political skills and act sometimes as "populist politicians" seeking support from the work force. Young engineers or middle managers who were active in anti-Communist opposition and apolitical technocrats are the best positioned to succeed at that game. Mr. Piotrowski, CEO of Szczecin Shipyar in Poland, personifies the first category; Ms. Brvar, CEO of Sloven Fotona, personifies the second.

Larger enterprises, especially those somewhat related to the public domain (infrastructure, transportation, defense, housing, health care, etc.) cannot be successfully restructured without some form of cooperation from the government. Such cooperation can take the form of credit guarantees, government orders, debt restructuring by government-owned banks, and so on. This is especially true in predominantly government-controlled economies at the beginning of transformation. Political connections and lobbying skills are essential to succeed. Former Polish Prime Minister Jan Bielecki, referring to Szczecin Shipyard, stated: "We were willing to help those enterprises, who helped themselves . . . We felt that Polish Development Bank could help them in a constructive way by assisting in negotiations with creditors" (Johnson, Kotchen, and Loveman, 1995:72).

Entrepreneurial Actions

Sell-out or lease of redundant assets, competitive pricing, sales, business partnerships (agency, service, subcontracting etc.) quickly generate income. Mera Pnefal, Polish industrial automation manufacturer (Kozminski, 1993:89–97) and Uralmash, Russian heavy-machinery manufacturer in Siberia (Boycko, Shleifer, and Vishny, 1995:130), provide examples of such entrepreneurial actions.

Marketing Actions

These involve keeping in touch with existing client base, introducing quick, feasible adjustments of product portfolio, delivery, financing, promotion, packaging, quality, and design. Such "quick-fix" marketing improvements helped the survival of not only companies in consumer industries (food, apparel, cosmetics, appliances, etc.) but also in investment goods (machine tools and industrial automation), and even heavy industries (ship building or coal mining).

That kind of "rescue action" can be based on existing (political) managerial skills, common sense and a minimum of entrepreneurial instinct. Engineers in their 30s, promoted from middle to top management after "the big change" are the most likely to possess those qualities (Kozminski, 1993). Abell (1992:33) indicates four facets of desirable individual characteristics of managers at the early stage of turnaround: (1) energy, drive, perseverance; (2) personal charisma; (3) entrepreneurial creativeness; and (4) ability to impose demands on peers and subordinates.

However, in order to secure survival of their companies, managers have to know well their ways in this very peculiar environment of "the day after communism." A "Western MBA" would not last long in that environment," was one of the comments of a Polish former executive.

Functional Restructuring

Functional restructuring is the next step. Its main objective is to bring the company to an "acceptable" minimum level of performance. Functional restructuring covers marketing, product development, production, purchasing, finance, and service.

In marketing, a careful review of customer needs leading to determination of market trends and economic leverage points plays a decisive role. Szczecin Shipyard in Poland provides an excellent example. A market study led to successful specialization in container ships (Johnson, Kotchen, and Loveman, 1995). A Russian optical manufacturer from St. Petersburg Lomo using McKinesy's advice to redesign its product portfolio is another example (Boycko, Schleifer, Vishny, 1995:129–130).

A shortening of new product development cycles, which were excessively long in the Communist enterprises, provided for "speed to market advantage." Polish appliances manufacturer Zelmer was able to redesign completely its entire product line in one year and because of that kept its market share against foreign competition. Hungarian software firm Graphisoft instantly responding to the specific needs of different segments of the engineering profession (mechanical engineers, architects, etc.) exemplifies "speed to market capability" enabling penetration of the most difficult U.S. market as early as 1990 (Kozminski, 1993:57–58).

The bottom line of production restructuring is improvement of quality, elimination of waste, and reduction of production cycle. At Szczecin Shipyard, it took from two to four years to build a ship. Restructuring brought the time to 11 months, which is among the worldwide industry best for container ships. In less than three years Zamech near Gdansk, Poland, has become ABB's worldwide center of excellence for gas turbines.

Due to the supply uncertainty, Communist enterprises were playing a game of self-sufficiency. This leaves a lot of space for cost improvement through state-of-the-art purchasing and out-sourcing. Gerber saves $800,000 a year buying bananas for its Polish baby food operation directly from the producer, instead of going through German intermediaries as local companies usually do (McDonald, 1993). Swedish furniture manufacturer IKEA is known for its nearly 20-year practice of out-sourcing from the whole region of Central and Eastern Europe.

It has to be noted that under communism, accounting systems were designed to suit the needs of government bureaucracy super-

vising activities of the enterprises. Quite often managers were un-
aware of their enterprises' cost structures, and under "soft financing"
regimes costs were not relevant either. Western accounting and
financial reporting provide information for managerial decision making. ABB introduced its financial reporting system to Polish company Zamech within six months. Local companies have to follow if
they are to survive. Accountants trained in Western accounting standards make in Central and Eastern Europe 10 to 15 times more than
medical doctors.

Difficult and costly access to capital is one of the main weaknesses of post-Communist enterprises. Creative financing is needed
to compensate for it. For example, apparel manufacturers in the
whole region use subcontracting for Western companies, and particularly CMT (cut-make-trim) contracts, as the source of working
capital for other operations.

Service product component and services in general were hope-
lessly underdeveloped in the Communist economies. This situation
shaped for decades people's expectations and that is why service
carries in this environment a particularly strong value-adding potential. The French automobile company Renault, building extensive
network of dealerships and service stations and providing financing
for its customers, is a good example of Western entrants taking
advantage of the local "hunger for service."

Functional managerial skills are scarce in the post-Communist
countries. There are two ways to cope with this problem: First, "import" functional managers from abroad. This way has been selected
by several foreign companies restructuring their acquisitions in the
post-Communist countries. Examples are GE in Hungary and Thomson
in Poland.

Second, selection of local talents with some background in management, and training them on the job with strong support from a
global functional staff of a foreign multinational or foreign or local
training and consulting institutions. This way was adopted by some
other multinationals operating in the region, such as ABB or Gerber.
These multinationals adhere to the "multidomestic" philosophy, stress-
ing local character of their foreign subsidiaries (Taylor, 1991). A similar approach is often adopted by more advanced local firms using
such resources as consulting and training services often financed by
foreign aid funds. Polish earth-moving equipment manufacturer Bumar
Warynski illustrates that approach (Kozminski, 1995a:95–96).

A strategy of functional restructuring based on local managers
supported by foreign experts becomes increasingly popular as local

consulting and training organizations emerge. For example, in the Czech Republic such support of local firms is offered by local consulting and organizational development firm Inventa (founded and run by Czech management experts). The firm helps to sort out functional problems and to organize functions according to Western standards of managerial performance. It also provides training and development for managers.

Foreign firms restructuring their acquisitions in the region are using almost exclusively the best-known consulting and auditing firms. They have all established offices in the regions, and all employ local experts, providing them with skills, upgrading opportunities both abroad and in the home countries. Western-style management education institutions offering executive MBA courses and a wide range of management development services are mushrooming all over the region. The quality of these institutions is highly diversified. Several have developed partnerships with leading schools in the United States and in Europe (Kozminski, 1996). Business schools and management-development institutions provide skills enabling functional restructuring.

Laying off of redundant (particularly clerical) personnel and intensive training in functional skills enable successful functional restructuring only if coupled with basic structural redesign providing for elimination of most of the hierarchical layers of the old structure. For example, when Hungarian lighting sources manufacturer Tungsram was taken over by GE, it had 11 hierarchical levels, and the Zamech Polish turbines manufacturer had 15 when the deal with ABB was struck (Kozminski, 1995). No management functions could be performed properly in such structures.

Process Restructuring

Process restructuring is intended to produce "management for results," "results" meaning performance-level average for global players. Incentive to start process restructuring often comes from internal comparisons between Central or Eastern European subsidies of a multinational company with similar Western operations of the same company. For example, it was discovered that the 1991 profit per worker in ABB Poland companies Zamech and Dolmel were only half of the ABB average. This was one reason why process restructuring was started. Local companies do not have such convenient points of reference, which is why they have to use physical productivity measures. For example, in Szczecin Shipyard between 1991 and 1993, productivity improved from 20 corrected gross tons (CGT) to 28.5, while European productivity leaders Spanish shipyards produced 30 CGT per worker, Korean 40, and Japanese 80 (Johnson, Kotchen, and Loveman, 1995).

Mapping of key processes and identification of key value-adding activities provide management with adequate focus and enable the building of a list of activities, organizational units, and assets to be eliminated, spun-off, merged, and so on.

Communist enterprises notoriously lacked business focus. Their product portfolios were unreasonably wide. For example, before restructuring, Szczecin Shipyard produced more than 30 types of ships, while even the largest Western shipyards were much more focused (Johnson, Kotchen, and Loveman, 1995). The Russian automotive company Zil was known for producing refrigerators, appliances, and even microwave ovens.

Communist enterprises carried out and financed a wide range of social welfare activities unrelated to business. These were employee housing, health care, vocational schooling, recreational and cultural activities, and so on. Some of them were highly appreciated by the employees but considerably increased operational costs. Analysis shows that most of these services could be provided more efficiently by independent specialized agents. Process restructuring in the most advanced enterprises was based among others on such analysis.

Key value-adding processes were often unknown to management when restructuring began. It was a surprise to a number of managers that a poor record on accounts receivable was one of the main sources of a company's financial troubles. Inventory management, quality management, and after-sales service were often neglected by the same token. Proper financial reporting (including activity-based costing) introduced by functional restructuring made process mapping a logical next move.

Redesign of processes followed the analysis based on process identification and mapping. The main objective was to build structures around processes by minimizing subdivision of work flows and nonvalue-adding activities. ABB Poland was particularly successful in spinning off auxiliary, lower-value-adding activities and creating a network of small subcontractors, suppliers, and providers of services working with the company but not exclusively dependent on it (Czynczyk, Dahlberg, and Iggland, 1995). In some cases, external experts were brought in to do the restructuring. For example, experts from Warsaw University Postgraduate Management

Center helped to redesign and put in place new procedures of accounts receivable analysis and litigation for newly privatized shirts manufacturer Wolczanka SA. The same company completely changed its inventory management system in record time.

Process restructuring calls for abandoning traditional functional structures deeply entrenched in organizational cultures and in people's minds. In order to facilitate a shift to process-centered structures in some companies (ABB Poland for example), certain functions (such as purchasing) were kept for some time at the company level and gradually released down to cross-functional teams controlling such processes as building air-cooled generators. Some processes, especially new to traditional post-Communist companies (such as market research at Colgate Palmolive Rumania), are controlled from the beginning by autonomous groups. At Colgate Palmolive in Rumania, 25 people formed strong marketing research group which in two years time after creation started to offer its services to other Palmolive subsidiaries in Central Europe (Filipovic and Baleanu, 1994).

A creative approach is needed to eliminate the burden of social services without compromising workers' well-being and motivation. For example, Szczecin Shipyard, in order to cut operating losses on housing, gave all the apartments (company property) to a local housing cooperative at no charge (Johnson, Kotchen, and Loveman, 1995:63).

Process restructuring calls for process-related motivation and incentive systems. Team-performance-based pay greatly contributed to the success of such enterprises as Szczecin Shipyard, Sloven Fotona, and ABB companies all over the region of Central and Eastern Europe.

Process restructuring is certainly not in everyone's reach in Central and Eastern Europe. In order to start it, the following conditions have to be fulfilled:

1. A local team of competent managers, already "fluent" in functional skills, has to be in place.
2. These managers have to use an actively elaborate system of financial reporting and financial indicators.
3. A top-down, bottom-up, and horizontal (especially cross-functional) communication has to be secured.
4. A competent (in local conditions) and affordable consulting support has to be available.

Cream of the Cream: Continuous Improvement

The best of the best, such as Sloven Fotona, Polish ABB Zamech, or smaller entrepreneurial firms in such areas as software engineering or luxury products such as hand-carved crystal or hand-made high-quality furniture, embark on the way of continuous improvement leading to world-class competitiveness.

Continuous improvement is based on vision and creativity, benchmarking world-class practices, teamwork, and employee empowerment. It seems beyond the imagination of the people, who only 6 years ago emerged from communism. But some of the best companies are already almost there.

Vision results from synergy between local and foreign, from the opening of formerly closed economies and societies. A combination of local talent; local human and material resources; local markets with foreign technology, management and markets lead to innovative business strategies. This applies both to locally and to foreign-owned companies.

At the beginning of transition, most of the foreign companies entered Central and Eastern Europe in search of low-cost labor, which would enable them to produce locally, using imported inputs, and export to the West. This strategy did not work in most cases due to the instability of import duties, the exchange rates, the economic crisis in Europe, and many other factors. Companies which were stuck with this strategy for a longer time (such as GE or Benetton) experienced difficulties and often "got burned" in Central and Eastern Europe.

Other companies discovered local resources: market potential, engineering, management striving to close the gap, and physical plants quickly becoming world class after modernization. This is the logic behind Daewoo's close to $1.5 billion investment in the Polish automobile industry. Korean Daewoo is using a large but antiquated and inefficient Polish automotive industry. Nearly 400,000 new units per year on the Polish market, will be a "springboard" to attack the European market after 2005, when tariffs for automobiles between Poland and Europe will be lifted as authorized by the association treaty signed between Poland and Europe.

Successful operations in the region of such companies as International Paper, ABB, Procter and Gamble, Volkswagen, Siemens, Philip, and many others proves that a unique and quick fit between local and global strategy and local and global resources is a key to

Central and Eastern Europe. It can be discovered only with active participation of local managers and local business partners (Kozminski, 1995).

Local companies entered transition intimidated by their Communist past, with a burning inferiority complex and the fear of the unknown. The ones who were quick to overcome these obstacles developed the "positive under-dog syndrome" of fighting back, learning from the West as quickly as possible, discovering weak points of Western business, such as globalized, stiff promotional strategies; inability to assess market potential; ethnocentrism of expatriate managers, and so on. Ambitious strategies of defending local market share and penetration of the global market also result from the positive under-dog syndrome.

Szczecin Shipyard, which quickly took advantage of its location close to the German seaside and the difficulties of East and West German shipbuilding industry, is a good example of such an attitude. Czech manufacturer of power-generating equipment Skoda Praha is another. Companies of that profile also can be found in the Polish apparel and clothing industry, Hungarian food processing, the Czech mechanical industry, and the Sloven pharmaceutical industry. However, in the same countries and in the same industries hopeless cases and chronic laggards are certainly even easier to find. Ailing Gdansk Shipyard in Poland, producing one-third of Szczecin's tonnage per worker is the best example. What really makes the difference is the change in mind set.

Continuous improvement is not possible without teamwork and employee empowerment. It is hard to imagine this empowerment, taking into consideration Communist organizational cultures based on hierarchy, centralization, suspicion, defensiveness, and inward orientation (Kozminski, 1995a). But the change is happening.

In 1993 two Romanian teams from Colgate Palmolive came into the narrowest choice for the global winner in a company-wide improvements contest (Filipovic and Baleanu, 1994). As a result of the initiative of the local management team Otis St. Petersburg in Russia made a swift adjustment to local market conditions and expanded its portfolio into servicing Soviet-made elevators installed in apartment buildings (Lapin, Kuld, and Shekshnya, 1994). Craftsmen producing by hand replicas of the highest quality of French antique furniture for Styl France in Poland are organized in autonomous work groups (Johnson and Loveman, 1995).

Building up Managerial Competence

Continuous improvement is a culmination of the long process of building up managerial competence and adding skills on the way from survival to continuous improvement through functional restructuring and process restructuring. Western European managers started this journey some 50 years ago. Managers in the post-Communist countries have to be much faster, and some of them know it.

Western management techniques are of key importance in the midway phases of functional restructuring and process restructuring. They do not seem that relevant in the first phase (the fight for survival) and in the last (continuous improvement). To survive and to excel, achieving a perfect fit with the environment and the local content of management are the most important.

There are very few (if any) people who can travel personally all the way from survival to continuous improvement, accumulating quickly all the necessary skills. A feasible way of acquiring new skills and building up managerial competence leads through three parallel tracks:

1. changing top management when passing from one restructuring phase to the next;
2. adding new people (with new skills) to managing teams on all levels;
3. encouraging already employed staff to acquire new skills and to develop skills and capabilities they already possess.

Constant head hunting, training, and investment in human capital are the essence of building up managerial competence, provided that someone has a vision of which skills are needed where and when.

In the case of the most sophisticated multinationals operating in the region, management systems and organizational cultures help to generate such vision. Analysis of successful local companies shows that long-range vision can come from the original CEO, who had enough courage to lead the rescue mission at the first stage of the fight for survival. Sloven Fotona is an example of such a company. It provides an argument for stable, consistent, long-range-oriented leadership by the same person, capable of seeking advice and expertise from others, and building a harmonious and flexible top management team.

However, there are also abundant examples of companies that won the war for survival and declared victory too soon, stopping further restructuring drive. Companies such as cable and wire manufacturer Kable in Poland (McDonald, 1993), are stagnating and risk slipping back into underperformance. This is due to short-sighted, short-run-oriented leadership, which needed "replacement or enlightenment."

In Western companies, watchful boards of directors, representing shareholders' interests, replace burned-out managers who have exhausted their vision. Consultants and staff members are supposed to provide those managers with "enlightenment" and "early warning." In the post-Communist countries such mechanisms are not in place yet, and that is why individual personalized leadership and unconventional resourcefulness and talent are so important.

Common Characteristics of the Best-Run Companies

Ambition is the number one key to success. Best-run companies all over the world (including post-Communist countries) are ambitious companies. Japanese companies are the best example. In the early 1950s the Japanese automotive industry was probably less developed than the Russian, Czech, or Polish. It is hard to believe, but the Japanese had a foolish ambition. Under communism, ambition had negative valence; ambition was something to hide. This heritage is still alive. That is why ambitious companies and managers are the most valuable assets in the restructuring process.

Effective use of existing resources can be identified as the second most important characteristic of the best-run companies in the post-Communist countries of Central and Eastern Europe. Communist economies were by no means underdeveloped; they were misdeveloped. They accumulated considerable resources, although they were ill-structured, existed in the wrong places and times and for the wrong purposes. Nevertheless, these resources existed and still do exist. Most of these resources were misused and wasted. Continuation of misuse and waste under emerging conditions of market economies is a sure recipe for underdevelopment.

Successful companies have mastered the game of efficient use of scarce resources. Human resources—well-educated engineers, workers, and scientists—are the most important. Such resources as physical plants, technology, and brand names also can be put into productive use. For example take brand names in cosmetics (such as Norvea and Stella in Rumania) acquired by Western cosmetics manufactures (such as Colgate Palmolive).

Macroeconomic situations and policies of the post-Communist countries induce extreme caution in the use of credit and financial leverage. Successful post-Communist companies, even with parents with deep pockets such as ABB, finance their restructuring and development themselves. Those who rely on parents' soft financing (e.g., GE's acquisition: Tungsram in Hungary) run a considerable risk of operating losses and excessive drain of capital. GE has invested $620 million in Tungsram and lost most of it (Perlez, 1994).

Personalized ownership means more than technical privatization. Voucher privatization or acquisition by huge anonymous corporate bureaucracy does not necessarily change much in people's attitudes, motivations, and actions (Svejnar, 1995). Personalized ownership means responsibilization, creation of "human size" entities where people psychologically "own" operations and processes and feel personally (also financially) interested and responsible. The best companies in Central and Eastern Europe (such as ABB Zamech and Fotona) know how to achieve that.

All well-run companies in the post-Communist countries are involved in some form of cooperation, alliance, or partnership with Western market leaders. These relationships take highly differentiated forms, from loose and flexible—such as outsourcing or joint marketing—to highly structured—such as joint ownership and joint governance. In all cases, a managerial know-how transfer takes place. This transfer takes many different forms, from highly formalized, to "natural" and informal dissemination of the best practices. It is obvious that standard Western management theories and practices need adaptation to local conditions, mentality, and market requirements.

Conclusion

This is not to say that all, or a majority, or even a large group of companies in the post-Communist countries are well managed. This is only to demonstrate that centers of excellence in management are already emerging. It remains to be seen whether and when a widespread proliferation process will be triggered.

Differences between Western and post-Communist styles of restructuring concern more implementation conditions than objectives and general logic. Restructuring efforts in the post-Communist enterprises of Central and Eastern Europe are carried out in a specific environment. Specificity of this environment can be characterized by institutional immaturity and instability, inflation, shortage of capital, shortage of management skills, collapse and transformation of the markets, fragmentation of distribution channels, and a sudden opening to global competition. This specificity will not fade away quickly through the region. When it does happen, however, cultural specificity of the post-Communist countries will remain. It has two components: "systemic culture," the heritage of the imposed Communist system, and the highly diversified national cultures of Central and Eastern Europe.

Author's Note: Following is a summary of the chapter in graphic form.

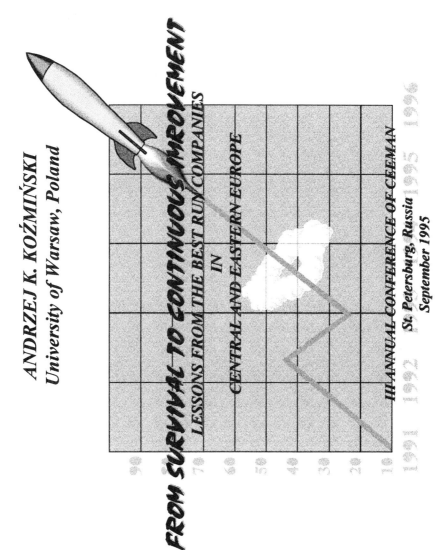

COMMON CHARACTERISTICS OF THE BEST-RUN COMPANIES

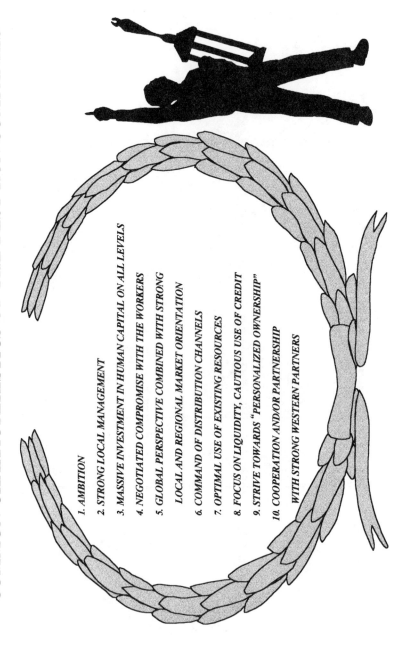

1. AMBITION

2. STRONG LOCAL MANAGEMENT

3. MASSIVE INVESTMENT IN HUMAN CAPITAL ON ALL LEVELS

4. NEGOTIATED COMPROMISE WITH THE WORKERS

5. GLOBAL PERSPECTIVE COMBINED WITH STRONG
   LOCAL AND REGIONAL MARKET ORIENTATION

6. COMMAND OF DISTRIBUTION CHANNELS

7. OPTIMAL USE OF EXISTING RESOURCES

8. FOCUS ON LIQUIDITY, CAUTIOUS USE OF CREDIT

9. STRIVE TOWARDS "PERSONALIZED OWNERSHIP"

10. COOPERATION AND/OR PARTNERSHIP
    WITH STRONG WESTERN PARTNERS

ENTERPRISES: THE DAY AFTER COMMUNISM

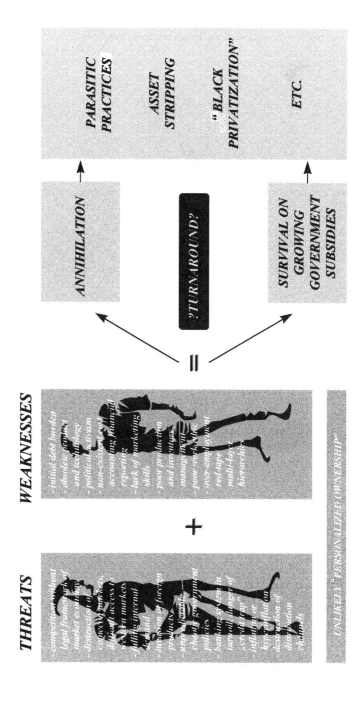

FROM SURVIVAL TO CONTINUOUS IMPROVEMENT

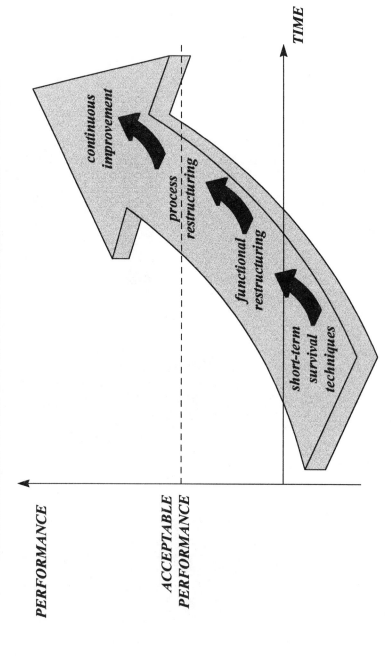

SHORT-TERM SURVIVAL

ACTION

- negotiated compromise with the workers -
- lay-outs
- pressure on the government to ease financial strain, secure temporary protection
- assets sell-out
- competitive pricing (discounts, financing)
- keeping contact with the clients (direct selling, promotional effort, etc.)
- quality, design, packaging improvements
- product portfolio adjustments
- cost reduction, improvement of inventory management

RESULTS

- increased value added
- cost reduction
- protected liquidity
- protected customer loyalty
- decreasing losses
- "survival culture"
- elimination of the "dogs" (non-sellers and slow sellers)

172

FUNCTIONAL RESTRUCTURING

ACTIONS

MARKETING
review of customer needs,
economic leverage points, market trends

DEVELOPMENT
identification of new products,
reduction of product development cycle time

PRODUCTION
factory lay-out, reconstruction of production lines scheduling,
production management

PURCHASING
analysis, selection and development of suppliers

FINANCE
financial indicators, planning, reporting

SERVICE
development of before and after sales services

STRUCTURE RE-DESIGN

flattening of the organizational
structure

HUMAN RESOURCES

elimination of redundant personnel,
training in functional skills

FUNCTIONAL RESTRUCTURING

ACTIONS   **RESULTS**   **FINAL OUTCOMES**

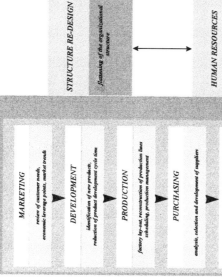

MARKETING
review of customer needs, economic leverage points, market trends

DEVELOPMENT
identification of new products, reduction of product development cycle time

PRODUCTION
factory lay-out, reconstruction of production lines scheduling, production management

PURCHASING
analysis, selection and development of suppliers

FINANCE
financial indicators, planning, reporting

SERVICE
development of before and after sales services

STRUCTURE RE-DESIGN
flattening of the organizational structure

HUMAN RESOURCES
elimination of redundant personnel, training in functional skills

RESULTS
- new products, customer focused product portfolio
- building up company controlled distribution channels
- building up supply network
- building-in service component to increase customer satisfaction
- more adequate workforce size and skills structure
- more decentralized flatter organization
- cost monitoring elimination of money losing operations
- more efficient use of materials, components, energy, labor machinetime and space

FINAL OUTCOMES

MARKET SHARE

RETURN ON ASSETS

VALUE ADDED PER EMPLOYEE

MARKET VALUE OF THE COMPANY

174

PROCESS RESTRUCTURING

ACTIONS

ANALYSIS

mapping of key process and identification of key value adding activities

STRUCTURE RE-DESIGN

around processes by building structure minimizing the sub-division of work flows and non–value adding activities

MOTIVATION

assessment of process ownership and process performance

RESULTS

- spinning off of low value adding and low competence activities
- process-centered horizontal structure
- focused use of resources
- enhanced customer and supplier relations
- development of core competencies
- process-focused motivation

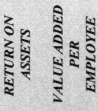

FINAL OUTCOMES

MARKET SHARE

RETURN ON ASSETS

VALUE ADDED PER EMPLOYEE

MARKET VALUE OF THE COMPANY

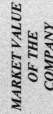

CONTINUOUS IMPROVEMENT

ACTIONS

TRANSFORMATIONAL LEADERSHIP
- COMMITMENT
- VISION
- MOBILIZATION
- INSTITUTIONALIZATION

BENCHMARKING
- SELF-ANALYSIS
- BENCHMARKS IDENTIFICATION
- PERFORMANCE MEASUREMENT
- INCORPORATION OF BEST PRACTICES

TEAM-BUILDING
- MULTI-SKILLED TOP MANAGEMENT
- CROSS-FUNCTIONAL AUTONOMOUS WORK GROUPS

MOTIVATION
- LINKING EVALUATION AND COMPENSATION WITH CUSTOMER SATISFACTION, TEAM WORK AND PROCESS IMPROVEMENTS

NETWORK-BUILDING
- FORMING STRATEGIC ALLIANCES

176

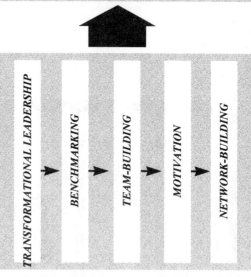

CONTINUOUS IMPROVEMENT

ACTIONS

TRANSFORMATIONAL LEADERSHIP

BENCHMARKING

TEAM-BUILDING

MOTIVATION

NETWORK-BUILDING

RESULTS

- customer focus
- empowerment
- flexibility:
changing roles
responsibilities
measurements,
organizational
structures,
skills
- out-sourcing of
non-core
resources
and competencies
- lean organization

FINAL OUTCOMES

MARKET SHARE

*RETURN OF
ASSETS*

*VALUE ADDED
PER
EMPLOYEE*

*MARKET VALUE
OF THE
COMPANY*

BUILDING UP MANAGERIAL COMPETENCE

SURVIVAL

- political skills
- entrepreneurial skills
- leadership skills
- knowledge of sound business practices
- negotiation skills

+

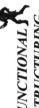

FUNCTIONAL RESTRUCTURING

- functional skills
- market and industry knowledge
- sensitivity to customer needs
- ambition
- quality orientation
- knowledge of principles of management

+

PROCESS RESTRUCTURING

- process mapping skills
- customer and supplier relations skills
- knowledge of market leaders' practices

+

CONTINUOUS IMPROVEMENT

- transformational leadership skills
- teamwork skills
- benchmarking skills
- knowledge of best practices
- alliances formation and network management skills

10

Lessons in How Recession Taught Organizations to Communicate

Bill Quirke

Hard Lessons: How the Recession Taught Organizations to Communicate

The recession of the early 1980s was met with cost cutting and headcount reduction. In the 1990s, with little fat left to cut, organizations have had to confront more fundamental issues. As times have worsened, communication has had to improve. The recession has forced the pace of improving communication and taught lessons that easier times would have avoided.

In the recession of the 1980s, management took the easier way out by focusing on cost cutting and reducing head count. Management did little to change the basic rules by which it played, stuck within the existing model of management, and focused on reducing the cost base. The boom years of the Margaret Thatcher era set the agenda for business communication in Britain. Communication became a key issue and rose high on political and business agendas:

- Margaret Thatcher was remodeled to become a great communicator like Ronald Reagan, and her victory was attributed to careful presentation of her image;
- Saatchi and Saatchi, the advertising agency, was credited with helping the Conservatives win the election through simple clear communication—laying the foundation for their own global success;
- The government's resolve to take on and defeat the power of the unions prompted management to reclaim the right to communicate directly with its workforce, where this had been ceded to the unions;

- The government's privatization campaign meant a huge growth in communication to voters about privatization, to employees as potential shareholders, and to the financial community about newly privatized industries' visions and missions;

- The reforms in health service brought a great investment in communication to win the hearts and minds of voters and employees and to offset the communication initiatives from doctors' and nurses' unions and representatives;

- The increase in acquisitions and divestitures stimulated communication, both internally and in corporate advertising to customers and shareholders.

This was the era of communication, but communication seen as a campaign, a largely one-way communication of presentation and getting the message across.

Setting the Rules for Communication

Communication was viewed as being for the benefit of the communicator. The Marketing and Opinion Research Institute (MORI) research shows that for all the millions spent on internal communication over the past 20 years, employee satisfaction with it has barely improved. The responses of shop-floor workers in a MORI poll demonstrated a continuing deterioration in communication. In 1985, MORI found that one in three working people felt that they could do more work without much effort, but 53 percent believed management was more interested in giving its point of view than in listening to what employees had to say. In 1975 56 percent of them had described themselves as fully or fairly well informed. Ten years later, that figure had fallen to just 37 percent (Walker, 1994).

A 1990 KPMG/CBI study showed that 65 percent of British managers felt their communication was very good, good, or adequate (Fraser, 1991). However, in 1991 a Price Waterhouse/Cranfield School of Management report found managers reluctant to communicate with employees on financial and strategic issues: "Managers seem to concentrate on feeding themselves and each other with information, neglecting the important task of taking their staff and organization with them." (Price Waterhouse, 1991:3)

British managers were clearly more satisfied with communication in their organizations, than were their employees. This satisfaction was rapidly undermined by the pressures of the recession. However, the implicit assumptions beneath traditional internal communication are still with us.

Communication Is Soft and Separate

The dilemma that organizations face is that while internal communication is central to success, managers tend to regard it as peripheral or as an optional "bolt on to" their real job. It is something to be done when there is time and leisure, or something to be delegated to the communications department.

Communication Equals Information

There is a belief that communication is a question of mechanics and a focus on delivering messages. Attention is paid to pumping out news of new developments that may interest the board, but are not relevant or interesting to the people they are addressed to. Information is based on what should interest people, not on what people actually want to know.

Communication Is Seen as an Event, Not as a Process

When there are redundancies, when there is a drive to cut costs, or when a new strategy is launched, senior managers feel there should be a communication program to get the message across. Once that need has passed and the program is completed, it is business as usual, and communication wanes.

Telling the Troops

Senior management often translates communication simply as "telling." There tends to be a built-in assumption that the right to communicate lies with those at the top of the organization. Since seeing the film, leaders want to deliver a stirring General Patton speech and keep asking "What shall we tell the troops?" Most employee communication is like sending people their New Year's resolutions through the mail and expecting them to keep them. Three types of mentality dominate: production line, hierarchical, and megaphone management.

The Production-Line Mentality

Decisions are made at senior levels. They are then passed down the line to the internal communicators to be packaged and distributed as well and as appropriately as possible. There is a manufacturing and production mentality underlying communication. This is an assembly line of communication, in which discrete messages are produced by the specialists, crafted, packaged, and sent out, relegating the communication function, at worst, to the dispatch department.

The Hierarchical Mentality

Though organizational structures may have flattened, the hierarchy mentality is alive and well. At the outset of change, the board goes away for a three-day off-site retreat. The members are the best informed, the most strategically minded, and those who take the long view. When the change is decided, they come back to present the future to their employees. Directors who are best informed get three days away to grapple with and own the strategy. Employees who are least well informed, least involved in background thinking, and critical to the strategy's success get only a two-hour slide presentation, after which they are expected to be enthusiastically committed.

The role of internal communication in this model is that of pushing information down to the troops rather than listening to staff. Passing down information has been largely limited to communicating the company's stance on particular issues, rather than providing context for decisions or responding to issues raised by employees. Communication tends to be, in short, a product crafted to the satisfaction of the supplier, rather than necessarily of value to the internal customer.

Megaphone Management

Companies reviewing their communications spend too much time deciding what it is they want to say, what are their core messages that they want their employees to receive. This usually shows up as a desire to build the chief executive a bigger megaphone, on his or her assumption that if people are not doing what he or she wants them to, it is because they cannot hear him or her. Typically, this involves shopping for new media and imitating the technology employed by another organization, without the spirit that made it work. These approaches to communication held back effective communication when times were good, but they proved a major drawback when times got bad.

Into the Recession

During the boom years, a number of structural changes took place. Britain's manufacturing base had been declining since before the war, and there was a hope that service industries would fill the gap. An end to the North Sea oil revenues meant that there was little money for education and health, which meant that individuals had to start looking at making private provision. The public sector had to change radically, to reduce costs, to demonstrate value, and to cope with the political agenda to reduce the civil service.

Also in the public sector, the government was introducing a financial management initiative, which demanded that armed services and civil servants alike manage their resources more tightly and demonstrate value for money. The white paper which summarized policy becoming law for the health service was published, and the wholesale restructuring of the health service began, seeking a balance between providing a service to apparently unlimited demand and thrashing through the entangled value systems of consultants and nurses.

Black Friday's stock market crash of October 1987 may have triggered a financial meltdown, but this coincided with a number of structural changes that were going on inside organizations:

- The rise in customer focus and consumerism leading to a review of organizational structure.
- The availability of cheaper funds allowing companies to bypass the banks to raise money directly in the market.
- The availability of technology that allowed smaller organizations to reproduce the economies of scale of their larger competitors.
- Deregulation and privatization.
- The balance of power between supplier and customer shifted.
- Organizations reduced in size and restructured.
- The roles of the employee and the manager changed.
- Employee values changed.
- Relationships within the business became more complex.

There has been a fundamental shift in the balance of power that has existed between customer and supplier. With greater choice available, consumers are becoming more fickle and more demanding.

The basis of competition has changed over the past twenty years, and businesses have been driven into untraditional areas in search of a competitive advantage. Many large firms are scrapping layers of middle managers. In British Telecom (BT) over the last 2 years, 5,000 middle managers and 900 senior managers have left as management levels have gone from 12 to 6. During the course of its reduction program to date, IBM has reduced the number of overhead jobs by 20 percent (Survival of the fitest, 1994).

The recession began in Britain at a time when the expectation of prosperity among the middle-class white-collar workers was axiomatic, as the Conservatives drove for privatization and for radical change in Britain's traditions, and house prices steadily climbed, promising prosperity. There was a great deal of political change. The entry into the recession and the pricking of the Thatcherite bubble left precisely those middle-class, middle managers with negative equity in their houses, redundancy, and the shock that their good education no longer promised them a job, never mind a career.

Disillusionment with Conservatism increased, as Britain wrestled with its role in Europe, and with the end of the special relationship with the United States began to see itself as a third-class power. The shift from boom to bust brought with it a shift from aspiration to disillusionment. The value system on which the boom had been built itself seemed questionable, and individuals began to question and realign their values.

The traditional split between white-collar and blue-collar workers changed. The union workers' traditional distrust of management spread to management ranks. Managers realized that loyalty no longer existed and rewrote their psychological contract between employer and employee. Employees realized that the contract between themselves and their employer was being rewritten and that the employer was paying only for work, not for loyalty.

Skepticism within businesses began to increase as employees were faced with two very clear and very different messages—to become the best that they could be in pursuing quality and customer service, with the underlying whisper that there were no more jobs for life and that loyalty was a thing of the past.

The agreement to be a corporate worker, to do what the company asked and climb the corporate ladder was therefore under assault from two sides—the key message to pursue individual survival, and the disillusionment with the Thatcherite values of self-interest. People began to believe that quality of life was more important than quantity of money. The promise of the Thatcher years that there was money for all delivered the realization that there was only money for some. The current stories about sleaze amongst the country's rulers and the revelations that the bosses of privatized industries were receiving large undeserved pay-outs has been the continuing legacy of that disillusionment. Over the last two years, there has been an increasing cynicism about the motives of the country's government, and with it the leadership of their businesses.

There has been no resurgence of the "feel good factor." Rather there is a "feel bad factor," caused by job insecurity and frustration over owning a house worth less than is owed on it and the tearing up of the traditional career contract. It is important that people do not expect to return to another boom, but believe the current situation of hard work and hard-won pay is likely to be the pattern for the foreseeable future.

The traditional distinctions are breaking down as companies become more and more closely involved with their customers and suppliers, with greater collaboration and interdependence. The traditional definition of the employee is also changing. Work life is becoming more complex, driven by the need for more effective cost management by the employer, the need to cater to the varying demands of the customer, and the aspirations and needs of the employee. Key timers, outsourced functions, networkers, flexiworkers, subcontractors, interim managers, franchisees, and telecommuters are all alternatives to the traditional employer/employee relationship.

Having focused for so long on blue-collar productivity, and with the greater proportion of the work force now being white collar, businesses now have to look to increasing white-collar productivity to improve profit. This will mean greater accountability for white-collar workers and more pressure on their time and emotional energy. Employees may not be willing to supply their time and emotional energy. The flattening of corporate structures and the wholesale reduction of management levels means the breaking of the bonds of corporate loyalty.

In the United States and the United Kingdom the numbers of those registered as self-employed, except for farmers, jumped by 75 percent and 50 percent respectively in the late 1980s. In the United States, the number of those in temporary employment almost trebled between 1985 and 1994. The growth in short-term contracts leads to far greater self-interest among individuals who had been working as members of a team or a working group. The concept of a 'career' is fading as people see themselves slipping from a career to a job or simply to work. Working hours have lengthened, and the lunch hour has shrunk to half an hour. Those who set their hours are working longer, with a sharp rise in the number of executives working 10 hours a day or more. The proportion of those who have to work weekends is also rising.

Until the late 1970s white-collar workers' hours had been steadily falling for more than a century. In the late 1970s and early 1980s hours stabilized and then started to rise. Between 1982 and 1993, there was a rise from 41 to 43 hours a week despite a huge rise in part-time work. Two out of 5 managers work 50 hours a week (Heckscher, 1995: Personnel Today, 1994: National Institute of Economic and Social Research, 1995). Cary Cooper, professor of Organizational Psychology, UMIST (January 1, 1995), observes that "people overwork because there is more competition for fewer promotions; and because so many grades have disappeared, there are fewer positions." This has resulted in "presenteeism," the opposite of absenteeism, which consists of people coming in early and staying late to demonstrate their commitment to work.

Employees report that the old feeling of being part of a community is being lost. While the old implicit contract of "jobs for life" is certainly past, the relationship between employer and employee has strayed too far into the hard nosed at the expense of softer values. Employees point to the appeals for their loyalty, commitment, and energy that their managers make, while in the next breath referring them to the small print of their employment contracts.

Employees may recognize that the days of all being part of one happy family are gone, but they also believe that the only other alternative cannot be to become merely a cog in an uncaring machine. Employees will not give that emotional labor to an organization that does not share their values, and whose highest calling is apparently only to increase the return to shareholders. A Gallup poll published in September 1993 shows that people would rather take more time for their personal lives and accept less money. People want more control of their lives and have less tolerance of corporate pressures.

The Impact on Communication

Most organizations found themselves in an increasingly complex game, where revenues dropped, where competition proliferated from nontraditional areas, and where their own employees, having expected increasing wealth and self-determination, struggled to come to terms with the suddenly chillier winds of recession. Employees in organizations were being hit from a number of different directions. They may have been trying to restructure to become more customer focused, to delayer and to become more empowered, and then on top of that they had to cope with a sharply deteriorating economic climate.

Formal and informal communication are shifting from the vertical to the horizontal, from the line-management chain of command to networks of colleagues, suppliers, collaborators, and customers. These are usually between people of similar rank and status, with no line power over each other, and so rely more on collaboration and cooperation. While organizations may be shrinking in terms of numbers, and layers may be being removed, life inside is becoming more complex.

Confronted with change on every front, the typical organization will have strategic-action teams, cross-functional task forces, supplier-quality groups, and new-product-development project teams galore. With an increasing sense of meeting and communication overload, managers rush between meetings, getting their "real" work done in the early morning or late evening when the phones are not ringing.

The drive to internal alliances and cross-departmental cooperation puts a greater onus on how well people are able to get along with each other. They have to bargain, negotiate, and sell instead of making unilateral decisions and issuing commands. The new way gets more done, but it also takes more time. Communication became an imperative, but the old rules were useless in the face of increased demands. The problem was that organizations needed more from communication but were applying outmoded approaches to people who were inclined to give less.

Individuals have responded to the recession and increasing complexity outside by "cocooning" themselves. With fewer people to help or to get support from, in a continually changing environment, people huddle closer together. They identify with their immediate team and their own jobs and job security, to the exclusion of others. The individual's trust in managers two levels above tends to be low, and there is little visibility of managers above that level. Trust tends to be in immediate colleagues and the immediate line boss, unless threat of redundancy has eroded even that. Horizons are lowered, and the focus is more on survival than self-actualization.

At the same time, organizations are trying to widen the horizons of their employees and get them to understand more about the business and the interrelationships within it. The two trends run in opposite directions. MORI tracks organizations undergoing change and compares ratings of communication within these, with communication within more stable organizations.

The norm for credibility of management is 66 percent under normal, stable conditions. For organizations going through change, it drops to 49 percent. Similarly, the norm for understanding of the organization's objectives is 48 percent normally, but in periods of change it drops to 34 percent. Whereas in stable times, the norm for employees feeling are kept informed is 46 percent, in changing companies, that drops to only 33 percent. Finally the norm for stable companies' rating of "I am not able to express my views" is 59 percent, rising to a worrying 75 percent as the company changes. In terms of the visibility of senior management, the stable, normal preference is around 40 percent, but again in times of change, the preference for hearing directly from senior managers rises to over 60 percent. The impact of the recession on communication has worsened employee suspicion and management's credibility (Walker, 1994).

In research among chief executives conducted by People in Business (1991), the most common reason given for the slow pace of change was that people simply did not see the need to change. They did not share the urgency of the need, nor did they feel the pressure on them from the environment. This lack of understanding is the heritage of keeping employees' eyes fixed on their task, and only giving them the information required to do their job.

A common complaint from senior managers is that the majority of their people simply do not appreciate the complexity and the difficulty of the environment in which the organization operates. Worse, they do not seem sufficiently interested in learning about it. They may not share the imperative to make a profit, survive, and thrive, and they may suspect that management is simply "crying wolf."

People will resist going in any direction that they feel violates their concept of 'professionalism.' Employees "decode" all communication they receive, listening for the "real" message. How people listen depends on the organization's culture. In the public sector, for example, there is an acute sensitivity to "business speak" and the suspicion that it shows a betrayal of old values. Values "refract" communication. One may say one thing, but they hear another. Without an understanding of employees' *listening*, companies, however efficient their dissemination of information, are only in control of half of the communication equation.

A number of changes currently under way in the public sector began under conditions of heavy suspicion that basic values were being violated. Reforms in the health service and changes in social services and community care were viewed by the professionals affected as retreat from the values and commitments of the past.

Where there is not a good relationship between those introducing change, and those affected by it, the greater the chance of disbelief and resistance. Where there is a lack of trust, people look for the "real" agenda and the true meaning of the proposed changes. To do that, they use their past experience and put clues and signals into the context they are familiar with.

The climate of trust and relationship inside an organization has a huge impact on communication. Employees opposing any change can see themselves as the resistance, or the loyal opposition, challenging the data and the interpretations, slowing the advance, and defending the values of the organization. They are not resisting; they are protecting. The inclination to communicate only about task-focused issues plays into this mind-set, and aggravates the situation. Managers, more inclined to give tasks than to explain why, undermine the ability of their people to make sense of what is going on around them.

Organizations faced with making change typically set themselves to "sell" the change to their people and become frustrated when their people decline to buy what they are selling. Senior managers tend to focus on what they believe employees need in order to fulfill their tasks, rather than what they need to understand and feel part of the organization. The lesson to be learned is that often the way change is communicated itself creates the apathy and resistance that was feared. The pain managers feel at the hostile reactions they encounter is often self-inflicted, caused by their approach to communicating.

For the kind of responsive, creative, and innovative culture businesses need to foster, new communication channels are needed. The majority of existing communication channels are designed for effective downward communication and are almost exactly *wrong* for the strong upward and horizontal communication.

Communication is often seen as part of the process of implementation when the focus has narrowed, and the emphasis is on details of the task and the implementation plan. The mismatch comes when those at the bottom of the organization only receive narrow communication on the specifics of implementation. Those lower down in the organization have less context as background to the specifics and understand less rationale. Therefore, the less sense the specifics make.

In approaching communication on such a narrow front, managers force their people to look through the wrong end of a telescope, limiting their view to implementation issues. Since, in times of change, people scan the horizon for any sign of impending doom, this forces employees to use informal means of finding out what is going on and hands them over to the grapevine.

The board of directors has been through the thought process and has had the chance to get comfortable with the proposals, evaluating alternatives and understanding why these make sense. The board has the most information and, probably, the greatest level of security about their implications. People lower down in the organization need some change to go through a similar process. For people to accept and cooperate, they have to share the thinking. Announcing the conclusions gives them no chance to do this or to understand the context.

This is increasingly difficult as the company gets closer to implementation. People naturally want answers to their own specific questions. When the threat of redundancy looms, they are unlikely to agree that international expansion is a greater priority than continuing to draw a salary. They do not want the big picture; they want the small picture, and in detail. It is too late then to try to explain the business rationale, as they are now operating on their own personal agenda, and their individual priorities will inevitably be different from those of the business.

Their immediate reactions and questions come from the need for basic security. Then their focus widens progressively to the people around them, and finally to the organization as a whole: Have I got a job? What is this going to mean for me? How is this going to affect my people? How much sense does this make for the business? Without the context, information does not make sense or have the impact it is intended to. Employees will decode and filter communication from their own positions, anticipating that the organization is adopting an adversarial position.

The stage is set for a collision of interests and for communication that seems to be pushing the business agenda at the expense of sensitivity to people's immediate concerns. At a time when managers are announcing the new way ahead, people's heads are filled with much more immediate and apprehensive questions about their own future, which makes it difficult for them to take anything else in. The focus on getting the task done, forcing compliance, taking a position on what actions are right or wrong, and communicating from a value system that is not shared, all add up to creating strong resistance and misunderstanding among the employees.

When times are tough, it is easy to lose sight of what is shared and what connects people and nervously focus on conflicting objectives that divide and create adversarial positions. Focusing communication on the tasks that need to be done can trigger all the defensive adversarial resistance that was most feared.

The grapevine has always been one of the major channels of communication, but the recession has devalued the credibility of formal communication and driven employees into the arms of the grapevine. There are fewer employees, and they keep their noses to the grindstone. They have no understanding of the wider picture and are nervous about job security. This means that ill-informed rumors predicting the worse are all too believable, especially by those who suspect management's hidden agenda and fear their self-interested values. Employees have switched into survival mode, bonding together with their immediate colleagues to unite against the threat—unity in adversity—and are trying to get more out of their lives, despite the increasing amount of hours they have to work.

What Lessons Have Improved Communication?

Top Line, Not Just Bottom Line

The marketing director became the hero of the 1990s, while the 1980s recession was focused on the key role of the finance director. While the recession of the 1980s cut the fat, the recession of the 1990s saw better performance as the only way out. As well as looking at reducing the cost base, the focus switched to growing the top line and revene. Businesses switched to marketing their way out of the recession. The marketing promise made the employees' role in delivering on the promise central to the businesses success.

People Make the Difference

The recession forced companies to compete more fiercely and prompted consumers to ask for more for their money. More demanding customers led to the commoditization of core products, as everything from aircraft engines to motorcars became more and more similar and suppliers sought to provide added value. This added value usually came from employees' knowledge of industry issues, problems facing the customer, and their ability to convert this knowledge into appropriate solutions. Competitive differentiation and added value therefore came from the hearts and minds of employees.

Staff retention became as much an issue as customer attention, as companies realized it was not simply the recruitment costs of replacing employees that hurt business, but rather the loss of the knowledge of customers' needs and the ability to respond to them which resided in the brains of their people. The strategy was clear. Unfortunately, the people were not.

In a survey published by Ingersoll Engineers (August 1993), poor communication was cited as the single substantial barrier to achieving necessary change within organizations: "Managers' apparent resistance to change stems from lack of understanding and the need for more or better communication rather than any underlying wish to oppose change in principle . . . Only when communication and understanding of the benefits of change are achieved will commitment be given and behaviour change."

It seems that now communication does not simply have a role in managing change, but it is also central to making change happen. Reports of failed change initiative after initiative have started to make organizations' leaderships take fresh stock of their situation. Senior management personnel are now trying to get communication right, because they realize that they have got it wrong.

Managers are more and more communicating about task-related issues, trying to get their own jobs done with fewer people. Individual managers are telling their people to keep their heads down and get on with their own jobs, at precisely the time that the rest of the organization is trying to raise its horizons, review, and change how things are done. Perhaps what is more important, managers are forced to neglect their communication with other areas and with colleagues. BP reports that stripping its middle-manager layers has been like taking the shock absorbers off of a car. IBM says it has now taken out so many layers in the organization that managers are too stretched to do cross-functional activities.

Fragmentation

There are a host of forces attacking the bonds of identification that used to bind people together—the drive to get closer to the customer, in smaller, more responsive units, in increasingly complex environments, while employees look to their own security. This tends to fragment the business and works against internal cooperation and understanding at just the time that the business strategy calls for it. While the business strategy may declare "Think global, and act local," local employees think local and act parochial.

Panic and the Quick Fix

Organizations are realizing that communication is vital and that they are failing. In their guilt at earlier rushed and failed communication attempts, they are now in the market looking for better ways of communicating. Unfortunately, since they are under pressure to deliver short-term results, this desire is sometimes for a "fast fix" which attracts them to large-scale, arms-length communication activities such as business television, satellite broadcasting, videos, and e-mail. All of these may be useful for disseminating information, but they are spectacularly ill-suited for creating a trusting relationship and restoring credibility that are needed.

Other managers, perhaps remembering that John Major won re-election as prime minister by forsaking the television studio for the market soapbox, are investing time in talking to people face to face and listening to them in small groups. Operations managers had to learn to communicate. Senior management wanted staff to respond quickly and saw the lag time in that response as a measure of poor communication. They still were not sure how to do it, but they were trying—the flesh might be weak but the spirit was willing.

Delayering Reduces Refraction

Each level of management in an organization tends to bend information coming down and feedback coming back up. Layers in the middle hang on to information, or simply neglect to hand it on, or do not imagine that those below them are interested. In the 1990s recession, the pursuit of quicker responsiveness to the market and a lower cost base meant that communication improved as it was driven by new urgency to perform, had to pass through fewer layers of management, and was being handled by those who wanted to get more from their people.

Process Improvement Extends to Communication

The drive to identify and improve key processes has forced organizations to re-examine their basic assumptions about the communication process. Since process improvement is also based on a continual cycle of planning, doing, checking via feedback, and then revising, this has driven organizations to track feedback from employees and to respond, revise, and improve in response to that feedback.

Internal Customer Focus

Similarly, the shift in businesses from being production focused to being market led and focused on the customer has led them to treat the employee as an internal customer. This has forced employees to begin talking to each other, to re-examine their assumptions and change how they deal with each other.

Benchmarking Brings a Shock

Measurement became an issue, as it was with other processes. Companies shifted from two yearly employee surveys to more regular quarterly updates, with the feedback to the board. Surveys were no longer about whether or not the natives were restless, but whether or not people understood what the organization was trying to achieve and how they could contribute to it.

Seeking Return on Investment

In the continual examination of costs, communication has come under the microscope, and with it the question about what it returns on the financial investment. This has forced communicators to demonstrate how they contribute to business results. It has also highlighted costs not only in financial terms but also in terms of the time for consumption and assimilation among employees.

Line Manager Responsibility

Decentralization as organizations tried to get closer to their market and become more responsive to it finally drove home the realization that communication was a line manager issue not the responsibility of a functional department. Cuts at the corporate center meant that there were simply no communication specialists to whom the responsibility could be abrogated. Regular benchmarking showed progressive deterioration, especially in the areas of perceptions of leadership and trust in the management team.

Flexible Working Brings the Danger of Greater Fragmentation

As companies look more closely at using flexible work forces and mixing and matching full and part timers, the fragmentation threatens to get worse. By 2003, it is estimated that 50 percent of the workforce will be part time, and 70 percent of those will be women. Part timers may see the job as only a part of their lives, which has to fit in with other commitments. They will be working short and irregular hours, and it may not be easy to pull them together in one place as a group. Yet they will increasingly come to represent their company to the customer, and it is vital that they understand what is going on.

Fewer Heads Means Networking Knowledge

Companies want to compete by using the knowledge and expertise of their people. However, they do not want to duplicate experts in lots of locations. Now they want to switch knowledge around the organization wherever it is needed. Communicating knowledge and expertise has become a key strategic issue.

The Stretch Factor

People are now more stretched, as more work is done by fewer people, stretching the working day. There is less time for chat, building relationships, and the social interactions that used to diffuse communication around organizations. Typically, employees receive 70 percent of their information on the grapevine and by corridor communication and informal networking. Head-count reductions have damaged these apparently peripheral activities and have driven social interaction down, eroding the mortar that helps cement different parts of the organization together. One organization found that smokers were more well informed. Those standing outside smoking crossed all grades and had the time and opportunity to swap gossip. Organizations are increasingly engineering greater social contact among their people to rebuild the social cement. Marks and Spencers, Britain's leading retailers, have introduced "parties with a purpose" to mix business and pleasure and build informal contacts among their staff (Quirke, 1995).

Sharing the Thinking, Not the Conclusions

Communication should mirror the thought process that has already gone on within the organization. In a surprising number of cases, the answers to questions raised by staff have already been considered by the team who first mooted the changes. What is needed is to share the thinking. Increasingly, businesses are running regular briefings about their business, progress against strategy, and industry trends. Outside speakers give insights from customers and suppliers, and colleagues provide updates on each other's departments.

Credibility and Trust Are Seen as Assets to Be Protected

Trust is hardest to establish when you need it the most. The recession helped to reduce trust and management's credibility. Credibility is a strategic resource. It takes a long time to build and an extraordinarily short time to lose. Ironically, thanks to the growing awareness of the impact a crisis can have on a business, and the examples of Tylenol, Perrier, and Heinz, senior management are coming cleaner with their people on the real state of the business.

Communication Is Continuous

On average, less than half an organization's employees know where it is going, and half again get any feedback on progress. Now there is a shift to regular, scheduled sessions in more informal surroundings. Companies are starting to keep their people up to date, running monthly team meetings, quarterly business updates, and annual conferences for all, not just management.

Communication Is Given Time

Under time pressure managers tend not to explain the rationale or the intention behind specific changes and neglect to counsel their people who are themselves feeling pressure. Middle managers report that they are caught in the crunch, told by their bosses to communicate, but not allowed the time to do so properly. Increasingly, businesses are planning time for communication in production schedules, budget allocations, and timesheets.

Conclusion

The recession has changed the rules for communication and shifted the context in which communication happens. It has provided the pressure to force organizations to look at how they have communicated and to try to improve communication. The world which we now find ourselves in has very different rules for communication. It imposes higher pressure to increase performance and has changed the structure of organizations in which people meet and communicate. While the lessons from the recession have helped, we find ourselves in the world where the "school of hard knocks" is likely to get harder. At least the recession has left us with a lesson, that there are no final end points to be reached, but a continual process of learning and responding.

Section Three

Lessons from Asia

11

Lessons from Japanese Multinationals and Japan's Government

Donald P. Cushman and Sarah S. King

Although Japan's domestic product is expected to expand as much as 2.5% in 1996, growth will be stunted, perhaps for years, because many factors that usually accompany recoveries simply aren't responding. The recovery isn't creating enough new jobs for Japanese. Property values keep falling. The stock market is stuck at 1990 levels. And consumer confidence remains battered.
(Glain and Sapsford, 1996:A9)

Japan's recovery is in essence suffering from the side effects of some bitter economic lessons. The nation's five-year economic malaise after forty years of economic growth is up against several economic walls. *First,* the high value of the yen relative to the dollar has placed many Japanese products in a competitive disadvantage relative to U.S. products. For example, when the yen was at 80 to the dollar in April 1995, a Toyota Camry was $5,000 more than its chief competitor, the Ford Taurus. In February 1996, the yen was at 106 to the dollar and the Toyota Camry $1,700 more than the Ford Taurus. Such cost differences are characteristic of all Japanese products made principally in Japan (Updike, et al., February 1996:108).

Second, to counter problems caused by the yen, many Japanese manufacturers were expanding production in the United States and in Europe. However, such production shifts are causing a rise in unemployment at home and large additional costs to Japanese firms as they attempt to expand buyouts from early retirements. For example, official unemployment in Japan has risen from 2.0 to 3.5 percent of the labor force. If determination of unemployment in Japan employed U.S. calibration methods, the rise would be from 3.2 to 7.0

201

percent (Glain and Sapsford, 1996:A9). In addition, many Japanese firms have reduced early retirement age to 30 in order to reduce their labor force (Hulme, 1995:6). However, the Japanese government still estimates the need to reduce excess employment in many factories by 500,000 jobs (*The Economist,* March 1995:63).

Third, after $250 billion in government pump priming, the Japanese economy still is faltering. After years of miraculous growth, Japanese output has hardly grown in the last decade. The results have been that more than 1,000 small businesses per month are declaring bankruptcy, property prices are still falling and precipitating a national banking crisis, and flat earnings or large losses in earnings are occurring in Japanese multinational firms (*The Economist,* September 23, 1995:58).

What then are the lessons Japanese multinationals and government have learned from the economic forces retarding recovery and a return to growth? In order to answer this question, let us survey (1) the lessons in general learned by the Japanese firms and the Japanese government and (2) the lessons in particular learned by a Japanese firm, Toyota Motors. Taken collectively, this macro and micro analysis demonstrates Japan's current position in the global economy.

General Lessons Learned by Japan

The nation's five-year economic malaise has forced Japan into a badly needed regimen of restructuring that includes job cuts, a shift of manufacturing overseas, an increase in imports and a move away from traditional business practices such as cross-shareholding.
(Glain and Sapsford, 1996:A9)

The Japanese government has attempted to maintain the yen-to-dollar ratio at about 105 to the dollar. However, such a strategy depends as much on Japan's place in the global economy as on Japanese governmental policy. The private sector realizes that Japan's government cannot always maintain this ratio and has attempted to move production offshore in order to meet U.S. and European demands to do so and to prevent the yen-to-dollar ratio from affecting earnings. For example, by 1997, Toyota expects U.S. production to supply 92 percent of the vehicle sales in the United States (Updike, et al., 1996:100). However, Japan's overall trend has a way to go. In 1995, 26 percent of U.S., 16 percent of Germany, and only 10 percent of Japanese manufacturing was located offshore (Glain and Sapsford, 1996:A9). Leading the way has been SONY, with 50 percent of its production offshore and Toyota with 30 percent (Hulme, 1995:6; Updike, et al., 1996:110). In addition, 25 percent of all Japanese multinational firms' investment in new equipment and expansion for 1997 will be overseas (Pollack, 1996:D7).

The Japanese firms have always been leaders in upgrading their competitiveness by cutting costs through the restructuring of their own firms and suppliers. This process has focused on significantly cutting labor costs in the past five years. Mitsubishi has cut 10 percent of its white-collar employees. Fujitsu closed one plant in Japan. SONY has cut its workforce in Japan primarily through early retirement. Such cutbacks are unheard of in Japan where lifelong employment has been the rule. In addition, most firms have frozen or cut back new hirings. For example, unemployment among new college graduates is up to 8 percent (Glain and Sapsford, 1996:A9).

Finally, Japanese management strategy, long thought to be Japan's chief reason for success, is changing. Lifelong employment is disappearing, bonuses based on performance are replacing the old wage pattern, and the famed Japanese *Keiretsus* are shrinking in importance in the Japanese economy. By 1996, Japan's six largest *Keiretsus* accounted for only 16 percent of Japan's sales, 17 percent of profits, and 4.5 percent of Japan's labor force (Dawkins, 1995:13). By the year 2002, Japanese firms plan to invest 35 percent of their expansion in the United States and 25 percent in Asia, while cutting manufacturing capacity in Japan by 30 percent (Ness and Cucuzza, July-August, 1995:111).

These general trends represent a reordering of the government and private-sector priorities. The results remain to be seen.

Specific Lessons Learned by Japan's Toyota Motors

For the first time since they dipped their toe in the California market in the 1960s, the Japanese now have something to learn from their American competitors. They showed last time that they can learn fast.
(*The Economist*, October 29, 1994:74)

In 1990, the authoritative MIT report *The Machine That Changed the World* called Toyota Motors the "most innovative and efficient automaker in the world." American, European, and Asian manufacturing firms streamed to Toyota City in Japan to observe firsthand how Toyota did it, and then they attempted to imitate the *Kaban* and *Kaisan* system. In 1991, Toyota earned $3.1 billion in profits on $71.6 billion in sales. Toyota produced vehicles at $500 per unit lower than its competitors and ranked third in the world after GM and Ford with 8 percent of the world's car and truck market. The Toyota bank held $22 billion in cash, enough to buy both Ford and Chrysler at 1990 prices, with nearly $5 billion to spare (Taylor, 1990:69).

However, between 1991 and 1995, all this changed, leaving the Toyota Motor Company considering a major overhaul of its vehicle production systems in order to prevent further profit and market share deterioration. Three trends converged to create this crisis. *First,* Japan was hit by its first major recession since World War II, with an 18 percent drop in auto sales in the Japanese market where Toyota held a 32 percent market share in cars and trucks. At the same time, auto sales in the United States and Europe dropped by 20 percent as both regions were mired in recession. Toyota market shares dropped in both markets (Taylor, 1993:79).

Second, between 1991 and 1995, the Japanese yen appreciated 100 percent from 200 to 1 to 100 to 1 against the U.S. dollar, dramatically increasing the cost of all products manufactured in Japan relative to those produced in the United States. This placed Toyota in a difficult position since it platformed over four-fifths of its total production from Japan. In August 1995 with the yen at 100 to 1 against the American dollar, a Toyota Camry sold for $22,000 dollars, while a comparably equipped Taurus sold for $17,000, $5,000 less (Templin and Stern, 1995:A2). Toyota was confronted with three choices in responding to this problem. It could *increase prices* which were already high relative to its American competitors and risk a significant drop in sales while maintaining its margins. It could *substantially cut costs and further reduce its already low margins* in hopes of maintaining market shares. It could *move a significant portion of its production off shore* to the United States to capitalize on the exchange rate and platform from the United States to Japan while closing one or two plants in Japan. However, this was something Toyota had promised the Japanese government, the Japanese people, and its own employees that it would not do. Toyota could, of course, employ combinations of each of these solutions to construct a fourth solution.

Third, and even more humiliating, the Chrysler Corporation of America reengineered its production, accounting, and linkage with supplier systems and replaced Toyota as the world's low-cost producer of cars and trucks. This brought to an end the fifteen-year

Figure 11.1 CHRYSLER'S OLD SYSTEM

dominance of Toyota's lean production (*Kaban* and *Kaisan*) systems. How was this accomplished?

Between 1991 and 1993, Chrysler reengineered its vehicle production system. The firm dismantled its traditionally sequential, component-based process, "where chimney-like functional departments were pretty much worlds unto themselves" (Lutz, 1994).

The company transformed these functional departments into four cross-functional platform teams headed by a strong leader.

The new platform system blurred the lines among customers, suppliers, and functional units. In addition, it created communication among all of these groups in the form of tech clubs or loose gatherings of anyone interested in a given problem. These tech clubs existed both within and between platform groups and included customers and supplies. In the words of Robert Lutz, president of Chrysler Motors,

> We need to keep erasing the line between the people who innovate and the people who implement. We need to make everybody feel that they have the freedom to innovate and invent, just as we also need to make sure that our scientists, who are at the forefront of new technology feel a keen sense of responsibility to the marketplace and to real, live customers. (Lutz, 1994)

Figure 11.2 CHRYSLER'S NEW PLATFORM SYSTEM

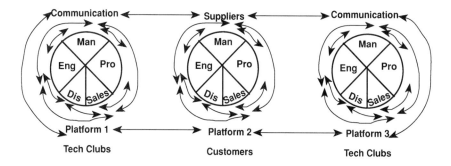

Beginning in 1991, Chrysler implemented an activity-based cost (ABC) accounting system in order to represent more accurately its real cost structure (Ness and Cucuzza, 1995:130). Ness and Cucuzza (1995:131) report that by 1995

> Chrysler estimates that, since it began implementing ABC in 1991, the system has generated hundreds of millions of dollars in benefits by helping simplify product designs and eliminate unproductive, inefficient, or redundant activities. The benefits have been 10 to 20 times greater than the company's investment in the program. At some sites, the savings have been 50 to 100 times the implementation cost.

Such an accounting system should increase the average day-to-day efficiency of decision making and yield more and more savings as each year goes by.

Finally, Chrysler developed a "virtual company" by allowing suppliers to form joint development teams with each other and platform teams in order to innovate in supplying parts. Since 70 percent of all the parts for Chrysler vehicles were outsourced, CATIA, a new computer program, was developed to create a common language and to aid in maintaining effective communication at these numerous interfaces (*Automotive News,* November 21, 1994:6). This virtual company helped develop a number of new innovations. These included a new stamping process which cut stamping costs in half and decreased delivery time to market by months (Brooke, 1994:37) and a new prototyping software process similar to the one employed in developing the Boeing 777, which cut $1 billion out of the $3 billion development cost of vehicles and cut time-to-market by two to three months (Maynard, 1995:B1).

By 1993, this restructuring by Chrysler had yielded the results shown in Table 11.1 and Table 11.2 in terms of increases in per vehicle earnings and declines in time-to-market and development.

Nissan and Volkswagen CEOs paid tribute to Chrysler's accomplishments by turning from Toyota to Chrysler to benchmark production (*The Economist,* October 29, 1994:63). In 1992 and 1993, Toyota's sales rose from $71 billion to $80 and $85 billion. However, since 1990, profits dropped from $3.1 to $1.9 and $1.4 billion, while cash on hand dropped from $22 to $15 billion and Toyota's debt increased by 50 percent (Taylor, 1993:78).

In August 1992, at the age of 63, Totsuro Toyoda assumed the presidency of the Toyota Motor Corporation. Japan was in the midst of a recession, the yen was on the rise against the dollar, and Chrysler

Table 11.1   1993 EARNINGS PER VEHICLE SOLD IN THE UNITED STATES

Firm	Profit/Loss Per Vehicle
Chrysler	$ 828
Toyota	$ 358
Ford	$ 323
Honda	$ 145
GM	– $ 189

Source: Healey, 1994: 6B.

Table 11.2   PRODUCT DEVELOPMENT TIME AND COST OF
AUTOMOBILE COMPANIES, 1993

	Development Time (Month)	$ Billion
Chrysler	31	1.3
Toyota	60	2.0
Ford	84	5.0
GM	NA	NA

Source: Healey, 1994: 63.

had just replaced Toyota as the world's leading low-cost provider of
cars and trucks. By early 1993, Totsuro had designed a strategy to
respond to this crisis. We shall (1) examine the outline of that strategy, (2) explore Toyota's progress in implementation by September
1995, and (3) examine where Toyota still needs to improve.

Toyota's Strategy for a Turnaround

Toyota's turnaround strategy involved a multistage approach. *First,
Toyota would ask its suppliers* to employ the *Kaisan* process to reduce its costs by $1.5 billion between 1993 and 1995. *Second, Toyota
would employ the Kaisan process on its management system* to cut
operating costs by $1.5 billion between 1993 and 1995. *Third, Toyota
would employ its legendary Kaisan system* in a five-year project to
benchmark the Chrysler engineering and development program for
the Neon car and then to integrate those findings into the
reengineering of Toyota's famous lean production system. The aim
was to produce cars and trucks which could compete with American producers even if the yen hit 80 to 1 against the dollar. *Fourth,*

Toyota would expand its design and production facilities in the United States and in Great Britain by doubling their size, increasing offshore production to 1 to 2 million of Toyota's projected 6 million units by the year 2000. *Fifth,* Toyota would expand its platforming of parts and cars from the United States and Great Britain to Asia to help offset the rise in the yen's value. *Sixth,* Toyota would expand its parts and production capability in Southeast Asia in order to take advantage of the most rapidly increasing market in the world. *Finally,* Toyota would explore the point at which it might have to close production facilities in Japan and lay off workers (Taylor, 1993:78–81).

Toyota's Implementation of Its Turnaround Strategy

What has Toyota accomplished in the past two years under Toyoda's leadership? *First,* Toyota supplier teams have cut $1.5 billion in costs. In most cases this involved reducing the quality of materials used and/or cutting expensive but unnecessary frills (*Wall Street Journal* staff, 1995:A5).

Second, Toyota's management teams have cut $1.5 billion in operating costs. This was accomplished by shifting some production offshore, cutting the number of parts and models used in production, and reducing its workforce through attrition. Toyota has doubled the size of its Georgetown, Kentucky, plant, which facility produces its new Avalon car, at a cost of $800 million. This expansion will guarantee that Toyota produces more cars in the United States than it imports, giving Toyota protection against a rise in the yen and/or a trade war (Spindle, Armstrong, and Treece, 1994:54). In addition, Toyota has announced plans to expand by $319 million the production capability of its Derbyshire, England, facility, doubling its production capability to 200,000 cars by 1998. The plant will export Toyota's new redesigned Corolla cars to Europe (*Wall Street Journal* staff, 1995:A5). Toyota announced also that it would reduce its production models from 16 to 8, cutting the diversity of parts required for production. Toyota also cut 2,000 part-time workers at its plants in Toyota City and 1,000 full-time employees through job attrition, reducing the number of its employees from 73,000 to 70,000 (Sapsford, 1994:A10).

Third, Toyota employed its famous *Kaisan* system to reengineer the Toyota production system. Toyota began by benchmarking Chrysler's Neon car production and design center. In September

1994, Toyota held a press conference in which it made public ten limitations of the Neon when compared to the Toyota Tercel:

1. two coats of paint vs. Toyota's standard three;
2. paint thickness varies across car;
3. transmission lacks torque in high gear;
4. engine noise exceeds Toyota standards;
5. stopping power below Toyota standards;
6. rust-prevention omitted;
7. overly complicated instrument panel;
8. interior mirror glued to windshield;
9. unpainted door trim; and
10. no gas tank lock.

(Johnson, 1994:2).

At the same time, Toyota's benchmarking team admired Chrysler's (1) use of platform teams, (2) widespread use of plastic and low-cost steel, (3) development of complete systems from single-source suppliers, (4) low number of parts relative to the other cars in its class, and (5) simplicity of assembly. These features would be integrated into Toyota's reengineering of the Toyota production system (Johnson, 1995b:5).

In February 1995, Toyota announced the implementation of a new Toyota production system in its Miyata and Motomachi plants in Toyota City and plans to expand the implementation to its Georgetown, Kentucky, and Derbyshire, England, plants by 1996. This reengineering effort had six unique features:

1. the new system allowed some work-in-progress to achieve greater flexibility;
2. production lines were organized around tasks;
3. production lines were shorter, so parts moved faster;
4. grouping tasks made the learning curve shorter, so workers could handle several tasks;
5. each line could travel at its own pace, reducing quality problems;
6. automation was cut in half, reducing costs and quality problems; and
7. compared to the past, the lines moved faster, carrying more parts and cutting production time.

Toyota does not publish precise productivity figures. But these new facilities produce 9,000 cars a month, which is more than five times their break-even point. The new plants used value engineering copied from the Chrysler plants where 70 percent of all parts in new models come from parts used in older cars. Platform teams and the benchmarked features which Toyota admired in Chrysler production and design systems were also employed. This reengineering has saved Toyota $1.5 billion in production and design costs. However, Toyota operating profits still remain at 2.1 percent of sales, down from 8 percent in the 1980s (*The Economist,* March 4, 1995:63–64).

Fourth, Toyota has expanded its exports from the United States and Great Britain to Asia. Both cars and parts will be shipped from the United States to Japan (Bremner, et al., 1995:119).

Fifth, Toyota is expanding its production in Thailand, Indonesia, Malaysia, and Vietnam by manufacturing parts and assembling cars in Southeast Asia (Spindle, Armstrong, and Treece, 1994:54; Sapsford, 1994:A1).

Sixth, on May 12, 1995, Toyota indicated that it might be necessary for it to close at least one plant in Japan and lay off its employees. However, Toyota said it would do this only as a last resort (Simson and Reitman, 1995:A5).

Finally, on February 25, 1995, the president of Toyota Motors Corporation, Tatsuro Toyoda, was admitted to the hospital, suffering from hypertension and exhaustion. It was the first instance of a Toyota president being sidelined for illness. In addition to putting in long hours at Toyota, Toyoda was also chairman of the Japanese Automobile Manufacturers Association. This elective post consumed several hours each day. Toyoda had been working at a grueling pace and had pushed himself to the limit. He had also attended the World Auto Forum meeting in Switzerland in January and visited China in February, representing Toyota.

What was the bottom-line effect of this turnaround effort?

Ford, GM, and Chrysler employed continuous improvement programs to decrease operational costs at the same time as Toyota. Ford's program allowed suppliers to cut parts costs by $750 per car and cut $2 billion from a $3 billion product development cost. Ford intended to pass the savings on to its customers by reducing auto costs by 5 percent per year between 1996 and 2000. Chrysler Motors appears to have improved even more, extending its lead over Ford, GM, and Toyota (*USA Today,* August 10, 1995, B1).

Chrysler has increased its lead as the low-cost vehicle provider from $500 to $1,500 per car, while Toyota maintains a lead in consumer satisfaction and loyalty to its products. It is clear from these figures that low-cost production is no longer tied to the cost of

Table 11.3 1994 OPERATING PROFIT PER VEHICLE

Company	Profit Per Vehicle ($)
Chrysler	2,100
Ford	877
GM	621
Toyota	590

Table 11.4 CONSUMER SATISFACTION

Rank	Automakers	Percent (%)
1	Toyota	95.8
16	Ford	87.7
19	Chrysler	86.0

Source: J. D. Power and Associates.

Table 11.5 CONSUMER LOYALTY

Rank	Automakers	Percent (%)
2	Toyota	72.4
8	Ford	64.5
10	Chrysler	61.6

Source: J. D. Power and Associates.

manufacturing, but instead has shifted to design. Therefore, it is unclear whether Toyota's reengineering of its production system and its implementation in Japan and later in the United States and in England will affect significantly its cost competition problems (Okino, 1995:44).

By September 1995, Toyota had attempted to become a more competitive firm. Its CEO was ill from exhaustion, its famous production system had been reengineered, it had shifted production offshore, it was considering closing a plant in Japan. Toyota also had laid off part-time employees, and it was considering the possibility of laying off full-time employees in Japan, and it had lost further ground as the low-cost producer of vehicles. This was a new Toyota corporation indeed.

Toyota Motors' Major Areas
that Still Need Improvement

When Toyota comes out of this current crunch, they are
going to be leaner, meaner, richer, and tougher.
(Abegglen, 1994, in Spindle, Armstrong, and Treece, 1994:55)

For more than a decade, Toyota has been building vehicle factories offshore. Last year, Toyota produced 3.5 million cars, trucks,
and buses in Japan and another million offshore. In the last year,
Toyota has completed expansions allowing for another 600,000 offshore with a capacity of 400,000 more due in the next two years.
Toyota's goal is to capture and to hold 10 percent of the world's
market. However, several problems remain.

First, U.S. automakers had also reengineered both their production and their design facilities at the same time as Toyota. This
reengineering process increased Chrysler's lead over Toyota from
$500 to $1,500 per vehicle (Simson and Reitman, 1995:A5).

Second, many auto analysts do not believe that Toyota is back.
They cite large overcapacity in Japan and an unwillingness to close
at least two and probably three plants in Japan and lay off those
workers. In addition, Toyota has to cut its white-collar workforce by
at least 10,000 workers to remain competitive (Spindle, Armstrong,
Treece, 1994:55).

Third, Toyota seriously needs to rethink the way it engineers
and designs cars and trucks. It has lost contact with the customer. It
has over-engineered its cars; quality, while important to the customer, takes a back seat to low cost, styling, and comfort. In these
areas, Chrysler and Ford are formidable competitors (Spindle,
Armstrong, Treece, 1995:1). However, the need for change is a two-
way street.

On August 11, 1995, sixty-two-year-old Hiroshi Okuda, former
VP for Finance, was named to replace Totsuro Toyoda as the new
CEO of Toyota. He immediately vowed to take back lost market
shares, speed the development of new products, and shift more
production overseas. This was to be accomplished by moving
younger, vital, more dynamic people into positions of power within
the firm (Reitman, 1995, A1). If Detroit thinks it has won, that Toyota
is done, it will have a rude awakening. Toyota will do what it has
always done: get better, and better, and better.

General Conclusions

These then are Japan's general and specific lessons from recession:

1. Attempt to prevent the yen from rising too high relative to the dollar and the mark.
2. Cut production in Japan, and move production offshore.
3. Create new jobs in the construction and small-business sectors to reduce unemployment.
4. Expand investments abroad, particularly in Asia.
5. Restructure private-sector firms to make them more competitive.
6. Change the Japanese management systems.

Specific Conclusions

1. The incremental continuous improvement systems of *Kaban* and *Kaisan* need to be supplemented by a discontinuous change system.
2. Locate manufacturing in all three core markets and use the lowest-cost producers to ship to other markets.
3. Constantly track and benchmark world-class competitors.
4. Exploit a full range of product choices in all markets.
5. Rethink the engineering and design capabilities of Toyota.
6. Develop a global management team.

12

Lessons in Marketing Strategies during Recession from High-Speed Management to Sun Tzu's *Art of War*

Ernest F. Martin, Jr.

The launch of commercial television in North America and Britain in the late 1940s began a period we now can call the "era of classic marketing communication." A nationwide mass audience was readily available, so a few prime time television commercials would reach over half of all the homes at least once. Advertising expenditure skyrocketed, and advertising agencies flourished. High advertising expenditures often were seen as good in their own right, showing the product was progressive, modern, and dynamic. Television advertising was particularly prestigious in business rivalries (Peterson and Toop, 1994).

Marketing was king of business. It was the recipe for corporate and personal success. In 1960, a survey of 170 business presidents ranked marketing competence as most important in the success of America's most well managed companies (Levitt, 1962). Instead of "selling products," business "marketed brands." "Sales directors" changed titles to "marketing directors"; "product managers" were renamed "brand managers." Marketing was "adding value"—that which distinguishes a "brand" from being simply a product. Sometimes the value added was a genuine improvement in physical performance, but most often it was a new and different form of marketing communication—getting the public to see the product in a new light. A product's characteristics often were thought less important than its "brand image." Adding value always involved advertising spending, often justified with the argument of creating a larger market for the product with associated economies of scale in production and lower unit cost.

Throughout the classic marketing era, the "age of the common man" ruled with uniform homogenized tastes, because everyone tuned in to watch the same prime-time network television programs. Mass media served the mass market. As the era progressed, into the 1970s and early 1980s, segmentation of the marketplace—because of "fragmentation" of the mass media with cable, independent television, and VCRs—created mini-homogenized segments.

Throughout the classic marketing era, the manufacturer, as client, ruled. If it could be made, it could be marketed. If it could be marketed, it could be sold. For many product categories, wholesalers and retailers, as distributors, would stock anything "as advertised on TV." Manufacturing companies were big business, and retail was small business.

Throughout the classic marketing era, marketing and advertising became increasingly defined as textbooks, classes in universities, and integration with economics, psychology, sociology and communication made them more intellectual and academic.

Throughout the classic marketing era, advertising magic worked. It was advertising that brought a TV set and other appliances into homes. Advertising brought new cars and a plethora of new products for the home and person—shampoo, toothpaste, pet food, cereal, pain relievers, cosmetics, and much more. The public appetite for new products seemed insatiable. Probing consumer desires grew more and more sophisticated. New discoveries about consumer behavior were made all the time—how advertising worked; emotional and psychological factors in the buying process; color, design and shelf position influencing purchase. It appeared that growth, driven by advertising, would never end.

However, the prolonged recession of the early 1990s amply demonstrated the crisis of classic marketing and advertising. Fundamental changes have altered the face of marketing communication, indeed of all business. An information and communication revolution; the emergence of global corporations and core regional markets as major economic, social, and political forces; and a governmental revolution at local, national and international levels (Cushman and King, 1993), as well as the recession of the early 1990s suggest that the circumstances surrounding marketing and marketing communication have now changed fundamentally, so fundamentally that many of the theories and practices of traditional marketing communication orthodoxy are questionable.

Emerging High-Speed Environment
for Marketing Communication

King and Cushman (1994) point to three trends converging in the late 1980s and continuing in the 1990s. First, information and communication technology dramatically altered how research and development, manufacturing, marketing, and management worked. Second, dramatic increases in world trade, the emergence of a global economy, and the development of three large core markets has been facilitated by the information and communication revolution. Third, the technological breakthroughs and increase in world trade have made success in business difficult because of the volatile business climate characterized by rapidly changing technology, quick market saturation, shrinking product life cycles, and unexpected competition. In addition, there is an emerging trend of revolutionary marketing, which has an impact on all aspects of the marketing communication process.

Impact of Information Technology on Marketing Communication

The information and communication revolution allows firms to track and respond in real time to customers and competitors. Cushman and King (1993) contend that a series of technological breakthroughs allows organizations to track and respond in real time to all aspects of their business environment. New technologies employ computer-aided and telecommunication-linked engineering, manufacturing, resource planning, distribution, marketing, and service processes to allow for the rapid development, production, sales, and service of customized new products at low cost, high quality, and easy service throughout the world (Clancy and Shulman, 1991; Ju and Cushman, 1993; Kotler, 1993). With computers and artificial intelligence systems to provide environmental scanning and test marketing to determine customer desires; to model the product formulation and production with cost, price, profit, and sales potential; to pretest the name, distribution, and marketing communication, the management decision process is cut from years to days (Russell, Adams, and Boundy 1986).

Impact of Three Core Markets and Global Economy

The rise of the global economy is based on a fast-growing "Triad" consisting of the European community (EC), North America (NAFTA), and Asia (Ohmae 1985; Ohmae 1987; Ju and Cushman 1993). The EC and NAFTA are roughly the same status as a core market with both the combined GDP and population being of similar sizes. Asia, still in the formation process as a core of the Triad, is a puzzle box with the largest box being Japan, inside being the four newly industrialized economies (Hong Kong, South Korea, Taiwan, and Singapore), and still further inside the Association of Southeast Asian Nations (ASEAN) (Thailand, Malaysia, the Philippines, and Indonesia). Ju and Cushman (1993) indicate that the initial conceptualization of the Asian core market neglected the booming market economy of China with one of the largest single country GDPs and the largest population in the world. Additionally, India and smaller developing market economies (specifically Vietnam) and the developed economy of Australia can be considered in the Asia core of the Triad. Together, the potential Asia core market is a giant.

Although the three core markets are physically located in separate continents, the internal linkages of business relations and information and communication technologies have led to an interlinked economy (ILE) argued by Ohmae (1990). This means that no national economy or multinational corporation is capable of retaining its competitive advantage if it does not actively participate in the activities within the Triad.

Impact of Volatile Business Environment and Revolutionary Marketing

The business environment is in a continuous state of rapid change, with changing technology, quick market saturation, fragmented mass markets, and unexpected global competition.

The volatility arises from shrinking product life cycles (Cushman and King, 1995) and mass market fragmentation in the entire Triad. The product life cycle (PLC) consists of the stages of development—from development to introduction, through growth, to maturity and decline. Underlying the PLC concept are that the present forms of products have a limited life before a new product (technology) replaces them and they will pass through distinct stages, although the length of each stage varies.

Years ago, the product life cycles for refrigerators took over 30 years to mature, providing considerable time for each phase of the product life cycle to develop. This has changed. The market for microwave ovens took ten years to mature; Citizen's Band radio (CB) four years; computer games, three years (Cushman and King, 1995).

Clancy and Shulman (1991) argue that a marketing revolution is transforming businesses as top managers comprehend marketing's true significance to their companies' future. The demand is for marketing executives to do new things in new ways. Myth and ignorance should be abandoned to using information technology to assist in evaluating hundreds of alternatives to every marketing decision. Marketing is difficult, illustrated by the following example. Perhaps ABC has only seven alternatives for each of a dozen decisions. Usually it has more than seven choices, but sometimes slightly less. For purposes of illustration, the decisions are

1. Market target (7 choices),
2. Positioning (7 choices),
3. Product/packaging configuration (7 choices),
4. Pricing (7 choices),
5. Distribution type/level (7 choices),
6. Promotion spending (7 choices),
7. Promotion schedule (7 choices),
8. Promotion schedule (7 choices),
9. Advertising media spending (7 choices),
10. Advertising media mix (7 choices),
11. Advertising media schedule (7 choices), and
12. Advertising execution (7 choices).

If there are only seven options for each of these twelve marketing decisions, a marketer could develop 13,841,287,201 different marketing programs. Given the laws of probability, 2 percent will be very good programs that companies will want to use; 14 percent will be above average; 68 percent will be average 14 percent will be below average; and 2 percent will be disasters. The odds that a marketing manager will pick one of the terrific successes from the 13.8 billion choices is problematic, which is why most new product introductions and repositioning efforts fail (Clancy and Shulman, 1991). High-speed marketing management can improve the likelihood of success through business's ability to generate information and to use information-processing support to make decisions based on that information. The marketing revolution is management's recognition that for every decision in the marketing mix, the company must evaluate all alternatives in terms of forecasted profitability.

Classic marketing was devoted to "dominating" markets, imposing uniformity of taste on consumers who would be too disparate and segmented for a single brand. It was consumers as a mass, not necessarily as individuals. In fact, marketing was serving to progressively limit choice to fit large-scale production economies and sell enough to justify large advertising budgets.

In the high-speed environment, revolutionary marketing is "individualistic" rather than "mass" oriented. It reflects the ever narrower groups and subgroups within society, becoming aware of their separate identities and separate needs and interests. The "gray" market, "yuppies," "generation X," employed housewives, African Americans, homosexual men, single-parent families, vegetarians, nonsmokers, overweight people, dieters—the list gets longer and longer. Identifies are more numerous and more fluid in the high-speed environment than ever before. These individualistic subgroups have little relation to old class-based economic divisions within society, although there is some correlation with income. Variations of disposable income are important, especially in recessionary times.

The mass markets have largely disappeared, replaced by more narrowly segmented product categories. Consumers who were once happy with general-purpose products are now provided with specialized products designed for a more specific function. During the 1980s, the number of toothpaste brands in the United States rose from 10 to 31 and cereal brands grew from 84 to 150 (Rapp and Collins, 1990). As brands that once dominated their product categories with a single product have added new variants and new competitors spring up, mass-market fragmentation is intensified.

In the high-speed environment, with fragmentation of the mass market, there is no longer one channel of mass communication that can be relied on to communicate with consumers. Television served the role during the classic marketing days. The greater availability of commercial TV vehicles in the high-speed environment, along with cable and satellite vehicles, has been an important factor in TV as a medium in total advertising expenditures, but fragmentation of the mass audience for any one TV vehicle. At the same time, the cost of TV air time has risen faster than other advertising media. Magazines have also been proliferating, with the number of narrowly targeted specialty magazines flooding the news stands. Newspapers have been subdividing into targeted special-interest sections and supplements, effective in reaching narrow audiences, but fragmenting the mass audiences.

In the high-speed environment, power has moved from the manufacturer to the retailer. In the classic mass-market situation, driven by dominant brands, production economies of scale, and controlled market distribution, manufacturers who supplied the retail trade were in power. Retailers were "small business," and manufacturers were "big business." In the 1990s, multiple retailers became bigger businesses than most of their suppliers, generating larger turnovers and larger profits from larger capital bases. The retailer is much more important to a manufacturing supplier than the supplier is to the retailers. No longer do retailers accept gratefully the products created by manufacturers on their terms. The balance of power in many negotiations between supplier and the multiple retailer has shifted.

Retail store groups (such as Marks and Spencer, Toys R Us, Target, and Wal Mart) have their own strong identity and reputation. Brands offered for sale by these stores give their customers the trust and confidence to buy the product—the same qualities that manufacturers have always tried to build into their branded products.

The high-speed marketing environment is an ear of proactive retailing. Retailers are concerned with *presentation* as well as distribution, easy access, and convenience. Store presentation, including merchandising, has always been the main marketing medium for clothing and furniture. Store presentation and merchandising dominate the marketing of others' product categories today. Retailers' reputations are based on a very wide range of products and services rather than on one product or category. Retailers compete with manufacturers' brands with own-label alternatives. The retailer persuades the manufacturer to supply the own-label product, insisting on inclusion of new development work. The retailers can guarantee immediate distribution of the own-label product in all their stores, electronically scan for immediate feedback on reaction from shoppers, and quickly withdraw without damage if it does not sell. In general, retailers have interrupted the manufacturers' communication with customers, interposing themselves between brand manufacturers and shoppers, setting up their own, separate conversation with the public, and often establishing a more intimate and influential, face-to-face relationship with consumers than most manufacturers ever achieved (Peterson and Toop, 1994).

High-speed theory argues that the key to an organization's success is making timely and appropriate adaptations to a complex and ever-changing environment, which spins off new opportunities and new threats. Alert companies monitor the environment for changes to be ready to grasp opportunities and make adaptations. Wong and Whiteley (1991) identify four levels of an Asian marketing environment:

1. The task environment includes the external, yet controllable, institutions which help a company carry out its marketing—suppliers, target markets, marketing intermediaries.
2. The competitive environment includes competitors—those institutions which compete for customers and scarce resources.
3. The public environment includes institutions which monitor or regulate the company—media, government, citizen groups, employees, financial.
4. The macro-environment consists of the major societal forces of the society—culture, economics, law, politics, technology, natural resources, demographics.

Strategic and Tactical Marketing Mix

Strategic marketing in a high-speed environment carefully examines the wants and needs of consumers, develops a product or service that satisfies those needs, prices the offer, makes it available at a particular place or channel of distribution, and develops the integrated marketing communication to create awareness and interest and ultimately lead to the sale. The classic tactical marketing mix consists of four elements (called the four "P's"): (1) product decisions (i.e., product design, shape, color, package, brand symbol); (2) price (i.e., consumer cost level and discount structure); (3) place (distribution channel and length); and (4) promotion (i.e., advertising, public relations, publicity, sales promotion, direct marketing, point-of-purchase, personal selling) (Wong and Whiteley, 1991). Classic marketing communication deals explicitly with the fourth P— promotion—but high-speed marketing communication is more encompassing than only promotion, including communication via any and all of the marketing-mix elements. The basic marketing task is to combine these four Ps into a marketing program to facilitate the exchange with customers in the marketplace.

While traditionally the marketing mix has been viewed as the four Ps of product, price, place, and promotion, Kotler (1993) stresses that the traditional marketing mix consists only of the tactical marketing decisions. The tactical marketing decisions are preceded by strategic marketing's four Ps—probing, partitioning, prioritizing, positioning. The first step is to analyze the marketplace through market research, "probing." The second step is segmentation or "partitioning" the market. As clusters of customers want different things, each cluster should be treated separately. The third step is "prioritizing," ranking the segments to focus on a potentially superior advantage. Target the clusters where there is a preeminent position. The fourth step is "positioning," pinpointing the competitive options in each targeted segment. Kotler argues that by developing the four Ps of strategic marketing, as well as carrying out the four Ps of tactical marketing, the job of marketing will be much easier.

The basic task of strategic marketing is to combine the marketing-mix elements (the four Ps of product, price, place, and promotion), preceded by strategic marketing elements (the four Ps of probing, partitioning, prioritizing, positioning), which provide a situation analysis of the marketing environment into a planned marketing program to increase the odds of exchanges with consumers in the marketplace. Marketers have long recognized the importance of coordinating the marketing-mix elements into a cohesive marketing strategy.

High-Speed Management Response

Rapid environmental change has led to high-speed management for business (Fraker, 1984). High-speed management, as an operative system responding to the volatile business environment, is a set of principles, strategies, and tools for developing a steady flow of new products, making sure they are what the customer wants, designing and manufacturing them with speed and precision, getting them to the market quickly, and servicing them easily in order to make large profits and satisfy customer needs (Cushman and King, 1995). The environment has also led to "high-speed marketing communication."

The term *high-speed management* was first meaningfully used almost a decade ago by Fraker (1984). Cushman and Associates' (Cushman and King, 1993) seminal work structured the theoretical framework. High-speed management is chaotic change management in the current volatile business environment.

The main components of the high-speed management system are

1. a sophisticated information and communication system;
2. environmental scanning;
3. speed to-market;
4. corporate bench marking;
5. value chain;
6. an informal organizational structure;

7. transformational leadership;
8. change-based corporate culture; and
9. teamwork

(Cushman and King, 1995).

All of these components are applicable to high-speed marketing communication.

Information and Communication System

Three major information and communication technologies are used as support tools in high-speed management: computer-mediated communication, virtual reality, and telepresence. Computer-mediated communication may include distinct activities such as the Internet, electronic mail (e-mail), bulletin board systems (BBS), interactive messaging, and file transfer. Systems such as the Internet allow fast and less costly exchange of information and data between customers and organizations. Additionally, systems allow access to information services, data bases, bulletin boards, and thousands of mailing addresses. Virtual reality (VR) is a way for humans to visualize and interact with computers and extremely complex data (Aukstakalnis and Blatner, 1992). While still being developed, virtual reality has been recognized in retaining a firm's competitive advantage (Ju and Cushman, 1993) and will develop as appropriate "individualized" communication in marketing communication. Telepresence originated with remote control machinery. Today it also allows people in geographically distant areas, through the transmission of video and audio signals, to interact in real time (Ju and Cushman, 1993). Telepresence allows real-time electronic kiosks for customer interaction and many other new marketing communication applications. Related to telepresence is the use of FAX on demand in maintaining "individualized" information for customers.

Environmental Scanning

Cushman and King (1995) point out that each industry and market in which a firm operates will contain its own unique underlying dynamics based upon what its competitors are doing to influence sales and the influences to which the firm's customers are responding in buying products. Environment scanning of industry and market forces tracks the organizational strategies, structures, and resources employed by competitors and the tasks, inclinations, products, and potential products that the firm's own customers will want or demand.

Speed-to-Market

A high-speed management system has the general goal of speed-to-market with quality products or services to retain its competitive advantage. In the past General Electric, for example, took three weeks to deliver a custom-made industrial circuit breaker box. Later it took three days. AT and T originally needed two years to design a new telephone. Soon it did the job in one. In the past Motorola turned out electronic pagers three weeks after the factory got the order. Later it took two hours (Ju and Cushman, 1993).

Corporate Benchmarking

Successful companies seeking to be the best must set up specific goals that match the industry's best practices. This requires a firm to perform benchmarking. Benchmarking is a process in which companies target key improvement areas within their firms and study the best practices by others to enhance their own productivity and quality (Kendrick, 1992). Port, Cary, Kelley, and Forest (1992) report that 90 percent of the firms leading their respective market segments in the Fortune International 500 survey attribute major portions of their competitive success to benchmarking.

The benchmarking process is straightforward and simple. A senior manager, for example, starts by deciding what part of an organization to benchmark. The manager then instructs the specialists in that area to map and begin collecting data on that process. Next, management locates a recognized world-class organization which excels in that same business process and offers to exchange information with them. After analyzing the data, a strategic plan is developed to incorporate the most effective approaches employed by the benchmark firm (Ju and Cushman, 1993).

There are various types of benchmarking relating to strategic, process, and customer areas. Strategic benchmarking measures some overall estimate of a firm's effectiveness in creating increased shareholder value given its general corporate strategy and allows a comparison among similar firms that employ differing strategies. Factors could include a total shareholder return on assets, the ratio of a company's market value to book value. Process benchmarking isolates one or more of the firm's primary business processes, such as product development, billing and collection, integrated manufacturing, customer service, and so on. Customer benchmarking involves those using the firm's products. One approach is surveying one's customers regarding what qualities one's own firm and one's competitors' product attributes they consider the most important in influencing their purchase of a product. Then, given this attribute list, a firm benchmarks those attributes and competing firms' product attributes in order to add them to its own product. Generally, customer benchmarking is a four-step process: (1) identify the attributes that influence customer value perceptions; (2) assess corporate performance; (3) analyze competitors' performance and standing; and (4) close gaps between current performance and customer expectations.

Value Chain

The value chain consists of all the discrete activities involved in producing a product or service arranged into functional unit activities and business processes. The functional unit level of a firm's value can typically include design, engineering, purchasing, manufacturing, distribution, sales, and service, with suppliers and customers lying at either end. The business process level of the value chain involves three main processes; product development, product delivery, and customer service and management (Cushman and King, 1993). A firm may obtain competitive advantage and value-added contribution from one or more of these functional unit activities or business processes in the value chain. However, this can be added to (value-added) or canceled out (value diminished) in other functional units or business processes. A primary function of management is to employ information and communication to monitor, evaluate, and improve the value chain in order to gain or retain competitive advantage.

An Informal Organizational Structure

Ju and Cushman (1993) argue that an over-layered hierarchy should be replaced by a simplified structure to enhance speed and responsiveness to market needs. One of the biggest dangers threatening marketing is that classic organizational forms have become institutionalized. Marketing departments have hierarchies of marketing directors, marketing managers, brand managers and, assistant brand managers. Advertising agencies are contacted to do advertising, sales promotion agencies to do sales promotion, direct response agencies to do direct mail, a sponsorship agency to help sponsor suitable sports events, and a public relations consultancy to do media relations. Each of the agencies and consultancies also has its classic institutionalized hierarchy. Peters and Waterman (1982) argues that cutting central staff layers by 50 to 90 percent leads to more responsiveness and better staff work. Less is more, and a lot less is a lot more (Ju and Cushman, 1993). Organizations that follow high-speed management are adaptive organizations, formed by the task, not by a predesigned structure. They have no identifiable top or bottom, beginning or end, and constantly turn in on themselves, in an endless cycle of creation and destruction defined by external environmental variables rather than by internal management logistics (Dumaine, 1991). Traditional structured or formal organizations with a vertical hierarchy and horizontal divisions of functions fit with a predictable stable environment. As the degree of instability of environment gets higher, the organization should move from the formal end to the adaptive end.

Transformational Leadership

The volatile business environment has caused a radical reassessment of the most appropriate type of leadership required to compete successfully. Transformational leaders manage radical change. In the face of environmental uncertainty they develop a vision of what the organization can be, mobilize the organization to accept and work toward achieving the new vision, and institutionalize the changes to last. In stable times, the leadership simply fine tunes existing policies within the integration process. However, a chaotic environment requires the leadership to undertake frame-breaking change (Ju and Cushman, 1993). The recognition comes through scanning the opportunities, threats, construction, and implementation of a new vision before an external crisis forces such change.

Change-Biased Corporate Culture

Ju and Cushman (1993) point out that the term *change-biased corporate culture* is a paradox since culture by nature is conservative and resists change. In marketing communication organizations, rigid planning and budgeting cycles allocate various marketing media and functions with routine procedures that lack "particularity" about the complex special circumstances and particular brand (Peterson and

Toop, 1994) Ju and Cushman (1993) point out that in a volatile environment both cultural stability and flexibility are required within a high-speed management philosophy with two tools available in solving this paradox: high-order values (HOVs) and low-order values (LOVs). HOVs are cultural values that relate to more general organizational goals and management princi[les that remain relatively stable even in a chaotic environment. LOVs are cultural values that relate to specific organizational tasks and management stretegies that are flexible enough to adapt to environmental change. HOVs such as "service to the customer" and "superior performance of all tasks" should not be thrown away. LOVs, including many practices in sales, are subject to change due to environmental change. Ju and Cushman (1993) suggest a change-based corporate culture to respond to environmental contingencies with a solid HOV system and rapid and thorough disengagement from LOVs no matter how rewarding they once were. In short, high-speed management requires a corporate culture that is a mixture of a solid and stable HOV system and a flexible and adaptable LOV system.

Teamwork

In the volatile environment, an organization's ability to effectively achieve coalignment of resources to equal or surpass existing world-class benchmarks is critical. Coalignment is a unique form of organizational interdependence in which each of a firm's subunits or subsystems clearly articulates its needs, concerns, and potential contributions to the organization's functioning in such a manner that management can forge an appropriate value-added configuration and linkage between units (Cushman and King, 1995). Coalignment is operationalized through teamwork with people using information and communication to manage interdependencies at all levels. Teamwork in the context of high-speed management needs commitment on the part of all team members to generate and maintain team spirit. Teamwork in the high-speed management system is characterized by team members' permanent dissatisfaction with products and services, their speedy and effective communication, and a demonstrated consistency in their drive to excel.

High-Speed Marketing Communication Response

Rapid environmental change has not only led to high-speed management responses for business but also has led to high-speed marketing communication responses. The key elements of marketing communication in a high-speed environment are creation and communication of commercial values, exploiting diversity, participatory marketing communication, true branding to avoid diseconomies, flexibility, coherence, consistency, and continuity and strategic integration.

Creation and Communication of Commercial Values

Commercial values are attributes for which consumers or others in the commercial chain (distributors, retailers) will pay. They may be values of existing, identified demand or from generation of a new kind of want or need. The nature of the commercial values has to be communicated. The catch phrase *added value* has meant in recent years merely cosmetic changes by bolting on extraneous attributes to a brand.

Exploiting Diversity

The movement from "mass" to individual markets requires marketing to cater to the rich diversity, creating values relevant to the varied requirements and tastes, celebrating the pluralities. Time is past for lamenting the loss of the old simplicities of a "mass" market—the new diversity is the order of today and tomorrow.

Participatory Marketing Communication

The emergence of dozens of different brand variants, each addressed to a slightly different consumer need, is not enough to exploit the diversity. Individual consumers increasingly want their individuality recognized. High-speed marketing communication provides opportunities for consumers to engage in a dialogue and interaction with the brand rather than just sitting back, passively and patiently absorbing the advertiser's monologue. For example, "cueing" otherwise conventional media advertisements with addresses and telephone numbers to facilitate a direct response is one initial effort. Others include telephone, fax, alternative media such as hypermedia, in-store kiosks, and other approaches.

True Branding to Avoiding Diseconomies

Marketing to diversity is expensive, resulting in significant diseconomies compared with mass generalized requirements.

Developing ways of "remassifying" high-speed marketing activities through integration can maintain scale of economies in otherwise disintegrating situations. Commercial values are not just those for which people will pay, but they are those which it pays a company to offer.

The traditional role of the brand is even more vital for high-speed marketing communication than for classic marketing situations. Branding is the most important technique for packaging commercial values in an identifiable, competitive, reliable, and communicable form. However, the key is true brands rather than a mere commodity with a name stuck on it. Unlike in the past, marketing brands today is more concerned with identifying and exposing values inherent in the product than with simply adding cosmetic value. Psychological and emotional benefits remain as important as ever, but integrated and totally relevent to excellent functional performance, creating a coherent proposition that gives the brand a distinct and distinctive position in its category and market, defining its differences from competitive brands.

Flexibility

High-speed marketing communication requires breaking out of the bonds of hierarchical, segmented, and protective organizational structures and operating procedures. High-speed marketing communication thinking and practice are more flexible, more inductive, and less antiquated than other types.

Coherence, Consistency, and Continuity

Powerful forces of demassification in the volatile business environment pull a brand in different directions. Coherence, consistency, and continuity in everything a brand communicates, in all media and in all vehicles of communication, are essential to avoid creating unnecessary diversity which will confuse the consumer. Coherence, consistency, and continuity apply to the integration of all marketing communication elements.

Strategically Integrated Marketing Communication

In a high-speed environment, companies have recognized the importance of coordination and *integration* of their marketing communication efforts—media advertising, direct marketing, sales promotion, public relations, point-of-purchase, personal selling—to achieve efficiency and effectiveness.

The term *integrated marketing communication* describes the coordination of the various promotional elements with other marketing activities that communicate with a company's customers. Some companies mistakenly view promotional elements—the *promotional mix* of advertising, personal selling, sales promotion, public relations, publicity, point-of-purchase, direct marketing, events and sponsorships—as the sole communication link with customers. This usually leads to suboptimization of the potential total communication effort. In isolation, the various promotional mix and "nonpromotion" elements may work against each other. Successful marketing requires careful integration of all promotional mix elements *and* activities such as corporate identity, product (including product design), price level, and distribution (Fitzgerald, 1988).

The corporate identity, aimed at creating an image of a specific corporate personality in the minds of the general public and favorable images among selected audiences, includes the totality of graphic and design elements in a company.

The product communicates to customers via its size, shape, brand name and symbol, package design and color, and other features. These are product cues to consumers, who only selectively perceive some of the cues. Therefore it is important to have all cues integrated and coordinated to communicate the same message to establish subtle ideas about the total product offering. Price also communicates. The price level can suggest savings or quality and prestige.

Distribution, such as that involving retail stores, also has communication value for consumers. Like people, stores have personalities that are readily perceived. Two stores selling similar products can project different images to prospective customers. Brands of clothing sold exclusively through high-class and status-oriented shopping malls project a higher quality image than those sold in discount shops.

In short, integrated marketing communication is a more global approach to planning marketing and communication programs so that the elements are coordinated in planning and implementation and the consumers' perception is based on a bundle of messages they receive. The synthesis of messages, relying on the synergy of all elements, also avoids duplication of effort or, even worse, conflicting messages to consumers.

Tools of Marketing Communication

Within the promotional mix, marketing communicators have a number of tools, including advertising, direct marketing, sales promotion, public relations, and publicity and personal selling.

Advertising

Advertising is any paid form of nonpersonal communication about a product, organization, service, or idea by an identified source (Alexander, 1965). The term *nonpersonal* indicates involvement of mass media (newspapers, magazines, television, radio, outdoor) whereby a message can be received by large groups of individuals. *Paid* means time or space is bought, as opposed to carried as part of the editorial matter.

Advertising has several advantages in integrated communication programs. First, because it is paid communication, the company controls what it wants to say, how it is said, when it is said, and to some extent, to whom it is sent. For example, Singapore Airlines can purchase time on STAR-TV, including a high proportion of Asian business travelers among its viewers, and air its carefully produced 30-second commercial from 7:00 to 9:00 AM. Second, advertising is a cost-efficient method of communicating with large numbers of people at a relatively per contact cost. Third, advertising can create images and utilize psychological appeals to promote products and services that are difficult to differentiate. Joyce Boutique, one of many Hong Kong upscale fashion stores, utilizes music, close-up and unusual camera angles, and editing to strike responsive chords deep within the potential consumer. Fourth, advertising can create and maintain brand equity (Farquhar, 1990). Brand equity is an intangible value or goodwill resulting from a favorable image, product differentiation, and consumer attachment to a company name, brand name, or trademark. Brand equity allows a product to achieve higher sales volume than it otherwise could. In many cases, a strong company equity position is reinforced through advertising brand image and features. In Asia, large multinationals such as McDonald's, KFC, Coca-Cola, Nike, and Kodak, enjoy strong brand equity that was established and maintained over the years largely through advertising. Fifth, advertising can also reach consumers who have not been moved in other elements of the marketing program, for example, through use of humor.

However, advertising has some disadvantages in the promotional mix. First, the costs of producing and placing advertising can be very high. Second, use of the mass media for advertising is also a disadvantage in the promotional mix because it is difficult for the advertiser to know how well the message has been received. Third, another problem with advertising is its credibility. In Hong Kong, most people consider advertising credible, although there is some indication that credibility problems exist (Martin, et al., 1993). In Western countries, advertising is often treated with skepticism by consumers. It appears that as modernization and higher living standards occur, with the corresponding increase in the amount of advertising the average consumer is exposed to, the credibility of advertising in general suffers. Fourth, advertising can also be ignored by consumers. With many advertisements competing for our attention every day, consumers ignore the majority of them. They selectively process only those ads that are of interest to them. The number of commercials blocked together ("clutter") contributes to this problem, as well as electronic remote controls for channel switching ("zapping") and muting of the sound and VCRs which allow fast forwarding through commercials ("zipping"). Fifth, advertising, or specific advertising message approaches, can also be considered inappropriate in some cultures. In Indonesia, advertising for sanitary napkins, while acceptable in Hong Kong, is considered offensive. Sixth, advertising, as a worldwide institution, is dominated by multinational agencies, predominately from the United States, Britain, and Japan. While trying to "tailor" the advertisements to the local cultural context, many unthinkingly transport their own cultural assumptions as part of the commercial message.

Direct Marketing

In direct marketing, companies communicate directly with consumers to generate a response or an exchange. In some cases the direct marketing is by direct mail, use of the mail-order catalog, telephone, or direct-response television advertisements and programs. Direct marketing requires a high degree of targeting the potential prospects, either through mailing lists or through very selective media placement. It requires that the potential customers have a readily available means of buying the product, usually a credit card. American Express in Hong Kong has successfully used direct marketing to its select list of upscale card holders, all of whom have the means for purchase, both in terms of available credit card and in terms of qualified level of income.

The advantages of direct marketing are many. Direct marketing is a natural augmentation to traditional promotional mix variables in an integrated marketing communication program. It can be used not only to make sales directly, but also to qualify sales leads or to distribute product samples. Direct marketing saves time for the consumer. As the discretionary time of the busy, upwardly mobile Asian shrinks, the convenience of buying through direct marketing becomes a major advantage. Direct marketing allows greater selectivity in targeting marketing communication to specific customers. Direct marketing messages can be customized to fit the needs of particular segments, or even personalized for individual customers. The results of direct marketing are easier to assess since the success or failure is measured through specific actions such as leads generated, requests for information, or the number and size of orders.

There are also disadvantages of direct marketing. When customers are bombarded with unsolicited mail or telephone calls they are less receptive to the efforts. The image of direct marketing can create credibility problems for products and services marketing. The potential prospects list is always somewhat out of date and may have money-wasting duplication. Also, there is often a lack of control over the timing and situation in which the customer receives the message.

Sales Promotion

Sales promotion consists of the marketing activities providing extra value or incentives to the customers, distributors, or sales force to stimulate immediate sales. The two categories of sales promotion are consumer oriented and trade oriented. Consumer-oriented sales promotion uses targets for a consumer and includes tools of couponing, sampling, premiums, rebates, contests, or lucky draws. Trade-oriented sales promotion is targeted at wholesalers, distributors, and retailers—the marketing intermediaries. Tools include promotional and merchandising allowances, sales contests, price discounts, and trade shows. Sales promotion among consumer package-goods companies is often between 60 and 70 percent of the marketing communication budget (Donnelley Marketing, 1992).

The advantages of sales promotion underlie the increasing use of it by marketers. Trade-oriented promotions provide marketing intermediaries with financial incentives to promote certain products. Retailers often demand discounts from manufacturers in exchange for shelf space. Consumer-oriented sales promotion encourages immediate purchase and can stimulate short-term sales. For example, in the retail environment of Hong Kong, where the consumer is "shopping" rather than going out to buy a specific item, sales promotion can be the push to purchase immediately. It can induce trial of a new brand, often by appearing to give the customer a "discount," placing the item "on sale" for price-sensitive consumers. Contests and lucky draws create excitement and may be an additional incentive to get the message noticed.

However, there are disadvantages. If too much emphasis is focused on sales-promotion techniques, the company may become too reliant on short-term market planning and performance. The results may be temporary, and short-term sales may be at the expense of long-term brand equity. The growth of sales promotion can clutter—too many contests, promotional offers, or coupons.

Publicity

Publicity is communication regarding a product, service, or idea that is not directly paid for or run with identified sponsorship. Like advertising, publicity is nonpersonal communication to a mass audience. Unlike advertising, it is not directly paid for, so the company or organization attempts to get the media to provide coverage or run favorable stories. The tools include news releases, press conferences, feature articles, photographs, and videotapes.

The advantages of publicity include credibility and low cost. Publicity is credible because consumers tend to be less skeptical when information comes from a perceived unbiased and objective source such as a newspaper, magazine, or television program. For example, reviewers of movies are usually seen as an unbiased source. The low cost of publicity comes from not directly paying for the time or space in the media. While there are expenses for developing publicity items, the cost is less than that of many other promotional programs.

A major disadvantage is that the company does not control the use or placement of publicity. News releases may be ignored, or information may be aired on television when the target audience is not watching. Also, information about the product might be improperly presented or be too limited in details.

Public Relations

Public relations (PR) is a process of evaluating the public(s) attitudes, planning a program to communicate objectives, and executing actions to earn public understanding and acceptance from the various publics (Moore and Canfield, 1977). Public relations has a broader objective than publicity, with a purpose of establishing and maintaining a positive image of the company among its various publics. Publicity is one of the activities of public relations, but it also can use tools of special publications, community relations, internal communication, fund-raising, and corporate advertising, and various public-affairs activities. Traditionally, public relations has been assigned a supporting rather than primary role in the marketing process. However, many companies and organizations have realized that public relations as an integral part of their integrated marketing communication strategies is a great advantage (Kleiner, 1989).

Personal Selling

Personal selling is person-to-person communication in which a seller attempts to assist or persuade prospective buyers to purchase or act either through face-to-face or some form of telecommunications such as telephone.

Person selling has many advantages. 1) The direct interaction gives the marketing communication flexibility, as the seller can see or hear the potential buyer's reaction to the message and tailor or adapt the message to the specific needs or situation of the customer. 2) Personal selling gives more immediate feedback than most other marketing communication messages. 3) The person selling fits the cultural context of many countries because it can work toward building a relationship, the basis of trust.

Personal selling also has disadvantages. 1) Personal selling has a high cost per contact. Salary draws, commissions, travel and expenses are significant expenditures. 2) It is difficult to reach large audiences through this means because of the time involved. 3) It is difficult to deliver a consistent and uniform message to all customers because different salespeople may deliver different messages. 4) The training of salespeople is a constant process, with a fairly high turnover of people.

Point-of-Purchase (POP)

Point-of-purchase (POP) in a retail store is the time the marketer can influence that purchase choice because the consumer makes product and brand choices with all elements (consumer, money, and product) together (Quelch and Cannon-Bonventre, 1983). A variety of POP communications are used, including various types of signs, mobiles, plaques, banners, shelf tapes, mechanical mannequins, lighted units, plastic reproductions of products, mirror units, checkout units, posters.

The advantages are dominated by the time. With all elements of consumer, money, and product at one point, POP allows a crystallization of other elements, a capstone for integrated marketing communication program. POP occurs at the time and place the consumer is buying. It maximizes impulse buying (unplanned purchases) by attracting the consumer's attention.

There are disadvantages in that materials may go unused by retailers. The POP may not be designed with the retailer's needs in mind, or it may take up too much space for the sales it generates. Also, the materials may be too difficult to set up or have construction defects.

Sponsorship Marketing

Sponsorship marketing is investing in events or causes for the purpose of achieving various company objectives, such as increasing sales volume, enhancing image, or increasing brand awareness (Gardner and Shuman, 1987).

There are several sponsorship advantages and reasons for its rapid growth. First, companies avoid the clutter of traditional advertising. Second, sponsorships help companies respond to consumers' changing media habits. For example, in Hong Kong, television viewing has declined and corporate sponsorships of tennis, football, rugby, and concerts has increased. Third, sponsorships help companies gain the approval of various constituencies, such as stockholders, employees, and society at large. Fourth, events can be tailored for target groups. For example, the Mild 7 Jazz Festival, Salem Open Tennis, Moltavo Concert series, and Nescafe foreign film series appeal to narrowly targeted lifestyle segments. Fifth, sponsorships allow marketing communication when it is prohibited in other media.

There are also disadvantages. The event is shared by several other sponsors—and the image generated is partially a reflection of them. The event may not be a success (or it may be a disappointment), and some of the negatives are attached to the sponsors. The impact is difficult to assess. The amount of exposure is negotiable.

Strategies of War

Classic marketing communication planning was dominated with deploying large-scale resources and large marketing support budgets to achieve a dominant market share of a clearly defined market category in face of competition from brands of somewhat similar size to one's own. The military analogies in the textbooks of the period implicitly modeled attritional trench warfare of the Western Front in World War II when mighty armies fought it out with each other, year in, year out, expending enormous resources for a slight gain of ground in brand share (Peterson and Toop, 1994).

High-speed marketing communication can more effectively draw upon the greater lessons derived from a different framework of strategic warfare. Sun Tzu's military book, *Art of War,* written some 2,500 years ago, exposes principles of great applicability to high-speed marketing. The book is short, some 6,000 Chinese literary characters, but it provides numerous hints about what should and should not be done in warfare (Griffith, 1963; Sadler, 1944). Although it is an influential military treatise, it has found as much application in business in the fields of strategic management, operations, human resources, and marketing (Khoo, 1992).

Sun Tzu constantly stresses planning: "More planning shall give more chances of victory while less planning, less chances of victory. So how about totally without planning? By this measure, I can clearly foresee victory or defeat." (Khoo, 1992:12)

The insistence on planning involves five fundamental factors and seven elements:

> Appraise it (the art of war) in terms of the five fundamental factors and compare the seven elements later named—so you may assess its importance. The first of these factors is the moral law (that which causes the people to be in total accord with their ruler, so that they will follow him in life and unto death without fear for their lives and undaunted by any peril); the second, heaven (the working of natural forces); the third, earth (whether the dis-

tances are great or small, whether the ground is easy or difficult to travel on, whether it is open ground or narrow passes, and the chances of life or death); the fourth, command (the general's stand for virtues of wisdom, sincerity, benevolence, courage, and strictness); and the fifth, doctrine (the way the army is organized in its proper sub-divisions, the graduation of ranks among the offices, the maintenance of supply routes and the control of provisioning for the army). (Khoo, 1992:12–20)

Compare the following elements, appraising them carefully: which ruler possesses the moral law; whose commander has the most ability; which army obtains the advantages of heaven and earth; on which side are regulations and instructions better carried out; which army is the stronger; which has the better trained officers and men; and in which army is there certainty for rewards and punishments being dispensed. (Khoo, 1992:20–21).

Clearly, the applicability to high-speed management and marketing is evident. Components of a high-speed management system directly applicable are environmental scanning, transformational leadership, sophisticated information and communication system, value chain, change-based corporate culture, teamwork, and effective organizational structure. Knowledge of ourselves and our immediate and external operating environments is essential: "If you know yourself and know your enemy, in a hundred battles you will never fear the result. When you know yourself but not your enemy, your chances of winning or losing are equal. If you know neither yourself nor your enemy, you are certain in every battle to be in danger." (Khoo, 1992:22)

Sun Tzu's strategy decisions follow use of acquired knowledge. Overall, one must be capable of anticipating and adapting to changing circumstances: "If one seeks to be victorious he must modify his tactics according to the enemy situation." Many strategies can be utilized from Sun Tzu, generally falling into three categories: overtly offensive strategies, covertly offensive strategies, and defensive strategies. The choice, drawing from Sun Tzu, depends on whether it is worthwhile to fight, one is strong enough to fight, one is weak in defense although strong enough to fight, or it is a situation with no option.

Overtly Offensive Strategy

Direct open attack is to be hard and swift, based on superiority in numbers with forces concentrated. The territory cannot be too wide to avoid spreading resources too thin. In concentrating forces, avoid taking on more than one competitor at a time. Keep something in reserve; do not commit all funds in the concentrated attack.

Covertly Offensive Strategy

Covert offensive strategy means keeping a low profile while making offensive moves. Quietly attack the competitors' strategy to prevent competitive alliances. When there is an opportunity, seize it, because another chance may not be available.

Defensive Strategy

Rather than defense being passive acceptance of one's position in the face of stronger rivals, seek the defensive "offense" with the objective of protecting one's market share. Defensive strategy is proactive rather than reactive. Never assume there will not be an attack; always prepare for attack. In defense, be disciplined in consolidating one's strengths. For example, abandon products that are not doing well and replace those entering decline. Monitor every move of the competitor, being wary of the "wait and see" approach. Always be ready to counterattack.

In implementing strategy, Sun Tzu's advice can be grouped into five key concepts.

1. Deception against Competitors.

All warfare is based on deception. Therefore, when capable, pretend to be incapable; when active, inactive; when near, make the enemy believe that you are far away; when far away, that you are near. Hold out baits to lure the enemy; feign disorder and strike him. When he has the advantageous position, prepare against him; when he is strong, avoid him. If he is prone to choleric temper, irritate him. Pretend weakness so that he may become arrogant. If he is at ease, put him under a strain to wear him down. When his forces are united, divide them. Attack when he is unprepared; appear where you are not expected. (Khoo, 1992:158)

2. Secrecy of Plans.

By discovering my enemy's dispositions and at the same time concealing mine from him, I can concentrate my forces while he must divide his forces. Knowing his dispositions, I can use my total strength against a part of his. If he is ignorant of mine, he will have to spread out his forces to defend every point. This will give me superiority in numbers. And if I were to use my superior strength to attack an inferior one, those I deal with will be in dire straits. The enemy must not know where I intend to attack. For if he knows not, he must prepare for possible attack in many places; and in such preparation, his forces shall be so spread out that those I have to fight at any given point will be few. (Khoo, 1992:160)

3. Flexibility in Approach.

When I win a victory, I do not repeat the tactics but respond to circumstances in limitless ways. Thus, the one who can modify his tactics according to the enemy situation shall be victorious and may be called the divine commander. (Khoo, 1992:161)

4. Speed and Timing of Implementation.

Speed is the essence of war.

If victory is long delayed, weapons are blunted and the ardor of the soldiers will be dampened.

The well-timed swoop of a hawk enables it to strike its prey. Therefore, the momentum of one who is skilled in war will be overwhelming and his decision to strike must be well-timed. (Khoo, 1992:163–164)

5. Direct and Indirect Methods with Consumers.

In battle, there are only the direct and indirect methods of fighting but they give an endless combination of maneuvers. For both forces are interlocked and using one will lead to the other; it is like moving in a circle—you can never come to an end. Who can determine when one ends and the other begins?

Generally, in battle, use direct methods to engage the enemy's forces; indirect methods are however needed to secure victory.

Winners are those who know the art of direct and indirect strategies. (Khoo, 1992:164–166)

Examples of High-Speed Marketing Communication Applications

In the high-speed environment, some approaches are drawn from analyzing Sun Tzu's treatise on maneuvers, nine varieties of ground, and nine variables of employing troops.

Extra-Value Offers

Extra-value offers include price cuts, discounts, cash rebates, and giving an extra product free. "Link save" is a strategy that selects products that go together naturally with a discount for both purchases. Scanners at the checkout automatically calculate the "linkage" and communication in store done via stickers on the product and shelf positioning. Examples include frozen apply pie and ice cream or chicken and rise. "Multisave" is a strategy to encourage buying in bulk for a significant discount. "Extra product free" provides a smaller product with the purchase of a larger product, such as hair spray, one for home and one for handbag. "Cash back" on several purchases can maintain brand loyalty over a set period of time.

Coupons

Over 60 percent of customers in the United States and Britain redeem coupons. New technologies with bar codes on coupons have increased the efficiency of redemption. Coupons can kick start a new, improved, or relaunched product. Another strategy is to use a booklet of five coupons, progressively lower in value to establish loyalty and to balance out the fixed costs of printing and distribution with costs of redeeming coupons.

Premiums, Prizes, and Lucky Draws

Promotional lotteries are popular in countries that permit them, such as Italy, Spain, and Hong Kong. These are most effective when used in combination with the mass media for wide awareness.

Partnership

With shrinking margins, promotion can involve two organizations that normally do not deal with each other. These are also called "affinity marketing," "tie-ins," "joint" or "cooperative promotions." The strategy is to jointly mount sales promotion for the common benefit of both companies. For example, a plastic toy can be jointly packaged with laundry detergent.

Social-Concern Promotions

Also called "cause-related" or "public-purpose" promotion, these offer participants a good feeling of having done something to help a world problem. For example, with ten ball point pens purchased, one is donated by the company to school children in rural China.

Sampling

Free samples are perceived by consumers as gifts. There is generally a high proportion of use of the sample. Peterson and Toop (1994) report one study showing 70 percent use of postal samples compared with 40 percent redemption of postal coupons. Paid-for samples are also viable, with the low price and limited customer risk in sampling a new or previously unused product.

Media Interaction

Use of traditional and new media in the high-speed environment requires invitation of a response with involvement and interaction with individuals. Imaginative ways of integrating package with telephone response, television with prizes, and newspapers with instant prizes or coupons restructures for the high-speed marketing environment.

Conclusion

In synthesizing high-speed management theory, high-speed marketing theory and Sun Tzu's theory, key principles are

1. the four Ps: probing, partitioning, prioritizing, positioning;
2. the four Is: individuality, identity, integration, imagination;
3. the four Cs: compatibility, coherence, consistency, change; and
4. the four Ts: true branding, teamwork, transformational leadership, timing.

The high-speed environment has changed, and marketing communication can continue to play a central role in business in the radically changed circumstances. High-speed marketing communication will cater to ever-greater diversity while minimizing diseconomies with true branding. Communication of values will require subtle and flexible use of a wide range of media and techniques. Understanding high-speed marketing communication is of grave importance, much in the same way Sun Tzu recognized the importance of studying war. Marketing communication, like war, is not a transitory aberration but a recurrent conscious act and therefore subject to rational analysis.

13

Lessons in Managing Government Competitiveness

Ron Cullen

Our governments are in deep trouble today. In government after government and public system after public system, reinvention is the only option left. But the lack of a vision—a new paradigm— holds us back.
Osborne and Gaebler, 1993

The recent recession served to crystalize changes in the role of government in many countries. Globalization of the world economy has reduced the sovereignty of individual nations. Some nations have responded more effectively than others. Where effective responses have occurred, nations appear to have created a source of national competitive advantage; where countries have failed to meet standards of performance set by the global community, nations have been disadvantaged as access to global resources has been cut. The implications for national autonomy and development seem clear.

Most recessions since the 1930s can be seen as part of the ongoing business cycle. The challenge for governments was not to solve the problem or to change the role of government; the challenge was to ameliorate the pain of recession, to await and then take credit for the inevitable recovery. Unlike these previous recessions, the recent recession was associated with important and essentially noncyclical shifts in direction in many countries.

These noncyclical changes demand new approaches to the management of nations and new roles for national and regional governments. In recent years, the reform of government and government administration has tended to lag behind reform in the business sector. There can be little doubt that improving the competitiveness of

246 LESSONS FROM THE RECESSION

nations now requires new approaches to government and government administration. While some of these approaches can be adapted from business experience, others cannot. New approaches to government administration must improve the fit between problems and solutions and must reduce the risks of failure to more acceptable levels.

The challenge of implementing change for most governments is the challenge of delivering tangible results while also maintaining a broad support for change. The implementation of change has been constrained by the reality that many nations seem to have become less governable. In addition, systems of government decision making and administration that worked well enough in the past have increasingly become obstacles to national performance. There is a growing realization that countries, to be world-competitive, require a competitive government as well as a comparative business sector.

This chapter proposes a new model of government administration and uses it to examine the changing role of government and the effectiveness of some of the prescriptions for government reform that are now emerging. The analysis suggests that the current crisis in government has been caused by attempts to respond to new global pressures with old values and systems or, alternatively, with tools borrowed piecemeal from the private sector. It is interesting that the solution to the crisis for many governments is to adopt new approaches to government management. These approaches focus on speed, consensus, and performance, three attributes which have been sadly missing from the score sheet of many, though not all, governments in recent years.

Global Trends Are Reshaping National Competitiveness

An isle is emerging that is bigger than a continent—the Interlinked Economy (ILE) of the Triad (the United States, Europe, and Japan), joined by aggressive economies such as Taiwan, Hong Kong, and Singapore.

It is becoming so powerful that it has swallowed most consumers and corporations, made traditional national borders almost disappear, and pushed bureaucrats, politicians, and the military toward the status of declining industries.
Kenichi Ohmae, 1994

Fundamental trends are altering the way in which business must operate to succeed and the way in which wealth is created and distributed between and within nations. These same trends are altering the role of government and the way in which government and the private sector must operate to compete. While Kenichi Ohmae is probably mistaken in forecasting the decline of government, and while he almost certainly overstates the role of markets in the present and future world, he presents a compelling picture of the changes that are underway and of the need for major changes in the role of government.

Five external trends are driving changes in the way in which governments are managed and in the relationship between the private and public sectors: globalisation; competition for scarce resources; technology development and transfer that are altering fundamentally the value chain of many industries and revolutionising approaches to integration and control both in the private and in the public sectors; the need to respond to increasing diversity within and between nations; and the need to manage these issues under the glare of mass information, which highlights differences and inequities in the process of government.

Globalization

The traditional model for external relationships was to manage them to contribute to the domestic economy of a nation by buffering the domestic economy from undesirable external pressures.

The capacity of nations to buffer their values and development from external influences has all but passed. This has created new external threats and opportunities. Governments can no longer respond effectively to recession or deliver economic growth and employment in isolation. Nations need to access global resources and technologies and markets. The price for this access is the need to meet external needs and expectations.

Competition

Nations must compete externally for a share of global resources and for access to markets and technologies. The traditional model for competition conveniently separated the role of government and business: government was required to regulate markets; business and industry groups were required to operate independently to create added value. This approach has proved unable to cope with external changes; in the new global economy, government and industry need to work together to optimize the share of global resources accessed by a nation or region.

Global resources are increasingly allocated by business networks, such as multinationals; by international trade and investment; and by agencies, such as the World Bank, which seek to facilitate development. Nations that fail to respond effectively are accessing a decreasing share of these global resources.

The role of the public sector can no longer be studied separately from the rest of the economy. The way in which the two sectors interact is no longer fixed; it has become a key variable in new approaches to government. The boundaries between the two sectors are changing as integration between the private and public sectors becomes more critical. Government must work with the private sector to gain a share of global resources and to develop the internal resources required to exploit global markets and technologies.

Technology

To compete, nations must access and apply developing technologies in a cost-effective manner. The development of technology has made technology access and technology transfer, the application of new technology and advanced technological information and processes, key issues for the economic competitiveness of nations.

Old technology tends to be reflected in established production values and practices; new technology requires adaptation of those values and practices to facilitate technology transfer.

The traditional model for technology transfer was to develop a technology base hierarchically, starting with low technologies, leading to higher technologies, and then upgrading and developing the base incrementally. These strategies are no longer effective. Pursued in the current global environment, they are a prescription for disaster and economic exploitation.

To develop as part of the global economy, countries need to recognize that many technology changes are necessarily discontinuous; to access technologies strategically at all levels; to apply and exploit technologies to produce competitive advantage; and, finally, to position themselves to exploit emerging technologies.

These strategies in turn require nations to develop international alliances; to reform labor markets; to review approaches to education and training; to accept and manage technological redundancy as a cost of remaining competitive; and to develop public- and private-sector partnerships to access key technologies. Generic skills are no longer enough; governments must ensure that there is a strategic fit between the demand and supply sides of the education and training system.

Diversity

In addition to globalization and competition for resources and markets, governments must manage major increases in the level of diversity among nations, regions, and interest groups. This requires new approaches by governments, which have favored and often sought to engineer common values and which have come to believe that the majority is the whole.

The traditional model for managing diversity was to focus on common values and consensus and to isolate and reduce anomalies. Integration of economic and political factors at the regional and industry levels can no longer be presumed. High response demands devolution. The need for change and for priorities means that difficult political consensus issues must also be devolved.

Increasingly, the old search for consensus is being seen as counterproductive. Nations are learning to manage their affairs within a comfort zone within which key groups are not motivated to oppose change. This requires political systems able to recognize and negotiate needs with interest groups and an administrative system able to deliver results wile managing negative impacts.

The administrative challenge for governments today can be reduced to the twin challenges of meeting public expectations for real impacts rather than rhetoric while simultaneously managing within the comfort zone to accommodate diversity and maintain the scope for change. The myriad of new administrative tools developed in recent times can be seen as responses to these two challenges. The techniques reduce to two new approaches to government administration: performance management and comfort-zone management.

Information

The traditional approach to communication was to control and shape reporting to reinforce established values and approaches. In the 1970s, when the political and entertainment businesses found much common ground, the objective was still to manipulate mass communications to support established priorities and values and to conceal differences and failures. Simple communicable ideas rather than prescriptions for action were the hallmarks of successful governments.

Governments can no longer convince the public that their interests are synonymous with the national or even with the public interest. It is difficult to convince people that they are moving ahead or even leading the world when the nightly telecasts reflect a more compelling reality.

The speed and saturation of today's mass communications have outflanked these old strategies in many countries. Information about the performance of governments is more readily available, as is information about the performance of other nations.

Performance or the lack of it can no longer be hidden, and public expectations are now more demanding. The grand plans and platitudes that characterized much national planning are no longer persuasive, either to key interest groups within a country or to external groups who increasingly require evidence of performance as a prerequisite for investment and trade.

The New Challenge for Government

Who's to say whether Osborne and Gaebler have it right (I think
they mostly do). The point is that government—in America, Japan,
or France—hasn't been reinvented, and the world of commerce
mostly has (though the task is far from finished).
Tom Peters, 1993

Governments have three core roles: they must work with business to optimize the resources available to a country by accessing a share of world resources and building a world-competitive industrial base; they must optimise both the short- and long-term well-being of their citizens by regulating the framework within which these resources are distributed within the country and by addressing the needs of disadvantaged groups; and they must maintain the scope to govern. While these core roles have not changed, the way in which they must be approached is light years removed from approaches which seemed to work well enough even a decade ago.

In defining the role of government, there is a tendency to confuse means with ends. For example, governments address these core roles by leveraging private- and public-sector resources, by regulating markets, by providing infrastructure and services, by addressing access to international markets and research and technology, and by ensuring that the education and training system delivers world-competitive work skills. Governments also need to balance available resources against the growing list of competing needs, and they must avoid waste and deal equitably with citizens and business. In evaluating government competitiveness, it is important to benchmark performance against the three core roles of government before considering the success or failure of particular solutions.

Comparisons of the effectiveness of government between nations tend to be cluttered by various factors. They include differences between political systems, between per capita levels of wealth, and between stages of economic and social development. Comparisons that have been made seem to suggest that effective government management is an important determinant of national performance. The old idea that government can control, regulate, or even service some static notion of national interest seems dead. Government today must be competitive. Competitive government differs from trends to introduce competition into the delivery of government services. The benchmarks are the performance of government in other countries.

It is interesting that the concepts of "speed" and "strategic response" which have proved so powerful in the business sector also seem to be fundamental to improving the performance of the government sector. Except perhaps in times of major crisis, government management has not been noted for its speed of response or for its capacity to monitor external developments. Even where responses involve little more than removing the maze of regulations that prevent the private sector from responding, the evidence suggests that the public sector has difficulty seeing the woods for the trees.

As governments moved to change old approaches and facilitate the move to high-response management, the fragile consensus that supports governance has been severely challenged in many countries. The management and communications changes required to move to a high-speed response model of government are essential parts of the reinvention of government this time around. In the process, concepts of leadership in government management will need to be rewritten.

Benchmarking National Competitiveness

In responding to the external pressures discussed above, nations need to maximize added value. Three assumptions are suggested to benchmark added value: (1) that added value is best measured in

**Figure 13.1   NATIONAL COMPETITIVENESS AND THE ROLE OF
GOVERNMENT IN SELECTED COUNTRIES**

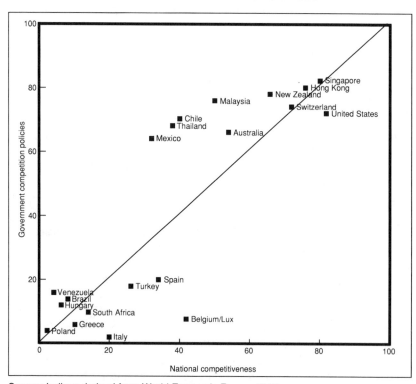

Source: Indices derived from World Economic Forum, 1994.

terms of increased national competitiveness; (2) that the most effective measures are therefore relative measures which compare one country with another; and (3) that comparisons also need to extend to the key factors (access to markets and technology, workforce and management skills, the provision of infrastructure, etc.) which underpin overall national competitiveness.

Nations differ markedly in their effectiveness, and differences are readily benchmarked and communicated. Such information is making it more difficult for nations who seek to buffer and develop differently.

Figure 13.1, National Competitiveness and the Role of Government in Selected Countries, compares evaluations for selected countries on the basis of national competitiveness and the contribution of governments to national competitiveness. The differences between countries are clear from these data, and these differences can be explored in terms of the way in which countries have sought to manage development and change. Three more specific points can be made about these data. First, countries who rank low on the contribution of government policies to competition also rank low on overall national competitiveness. They include Hungary, Poland, Italy and Greece. Second, some countries who rank high on national competitiveness also rank high on the contribution of government policies. They include Singapore, Hong Kong, the United States, New Zealand, and Switzerland. Third, some countries rank in the upper quartile for competition policies but have not yet delivered national competitiveness. They include Malaysia, Chile, Thailand, Australia, and Mexico.

Performance Management: Governments Can Learn from and Adapt Business Solutions

Initial responses to the new global challenges discussed above tended to use old government management solutions; however, they were too insular to address global trends and too process oriented to be strategic. When the need for new approaches to government became apparent, many nations looked to the experience of the business sector.

The search to apply business solutions is not surprising; three out of the four core problems facing public administration today have parallels in the business sector. The three problems which have parallels in the challenges addressed by business in the 1980s are the need to adjust value chains to respond more rapidly; the need to produce real outcomes rather than to consume resources or deliver processes; and the need to rationalize functions and focus on core values. However, attempts to transplant business solutions have created almost as many problems as they have solved.

Current reforms in government administration seek to draw on tools developed to meet the needs of business enterprises. There are three problems with this approach. First, transplanting solutions from one situation to another is always a risky business, especially when the theory surrounding many of the solutions remains underdeveloped. Second, the solutions had frequently failed in particular business situations. Third, the business analogy does not encompass the fourth core problem facing government management today, namely, the need to manage and develop the fragile consensus necessary for governments to govern and to implement change.

While governments can learn from business they cannot be managed as a business. Figure 13.2, Management in Government and Business, contrasts management priorities required to manage the interrelated missions in the public sector with the strategic management model which has assisted the private sector to cope with change. The traditional model of government has been anti-evaluative, and many approaches to government management embrace this rather restrictive value system. While minimizing evaluation may have maintained an uneasy political consensus, the public has become increasingly critical of the failure of governments to deliver on even the simplest reforms. This lowering of expectations has created major opportunities to develop new approaches to public-sector management which shorten cycle time and manage impacts and evaluate performance more directly.

Business solutions require evaluation and a related focus for action which has traditionally been avoided by government administration. This focus can be developed using performance management techniques and can provide a basis for strategic control and evaluation. However, the impacts associated with action planning need to be managed differently. Continuous evaluation needs to be used as a guide to action rather than as evidence of failure. The traditional generalities that surround government programs need to be complemented by a new commitment to action.

There are traps for those who see the business-government analogy in simple terms. For example, attempts to use the traditional plans and budgets developed by governments as a basis for the sort of accountability and evaluation required by new business management solutions seem bound to fail. Plans and budgets developed by government are quite different from the plans and budgets developed by business. Because government plans and budgets must summarize the complex negotiations with interest groups required to maintain the scope to govern, they seldom provide the simple guides to action required to drive conventional business solutions. Attempts to convert government plans and budgets to provide a strategic focus tend to destroy the political consensus required to support change in a complex system.

The idea of empowerment that has driven many successful business reforms must be approached differently in the public sector; devolution of power to act must also be contained by the need to manage comfort zones and diversity. Conventional attempts to centralize the management of comfort zones and decentralize the management of service delivery presume that the fit between these systems can be maintained. Often it cannot.

Figure 13.2 MANAGEMENT IN GOVERNMENT AND BUSINESS

Management Variables	Private Sector	Public Sector
Goals	Externally linked, focused, hierarchical. Renegotiation rare and linked to major external changes.	Political consensus goals tend to be diverse, nonhierarchical, and targeted to comfort-zone maintenance and the solution of common problems. Service delivery and infrastructure goals tend to be general and nonevaluative in order to minimize the impact on comfort zones.
Culture	Uniform and focused to support missions and goals. Developed through communications and by staff selection.	Diverse and focused on simple ideas, a respect for differences, and on the solution of common problems.
Planning	A general mandate both for action and for evaluation.	A vehicle for the negotiation of comfort zones and for demonstrating respect for diverse needs.
Communication	Development of common values. Understanding change. Evaluation of results.	Development of common solutions. Respect for differences. Maintenance of comfort zones.
Budgets	A vehicle for implementation and control.	Ratification of comfort zones. Resources allocated to meet key interests and to provide service delivery and infrastructure objectives.
Core Management Values	Strategic. Performance and results oriented. Devolution of powers to individual managers within agreed plans and a common value system.	Management of the fit between political consensus, service delivery, and resource efficiency and availability. Management of comfort zones. Delivery of services within the constraints generated by the need to manage the impact on comfort zones. Repositioning of the role and functions of the public sector to respond to external change.

Comfort-Zone Management: Governments Can Be Competitive While Managing Diversity and Retaining the Scope to Govern

The changes that are underway are testing the internal consensus for change in many countries and in many political systems. A key element of this model of government is the need to develop and maintain a consensus for change, not in terms of high levels of acceptance for each proposal, but in terms of the maintenance of a comfort zone that recognizes and protects key interests to the point where opposition to key changes is contained. The issue is not simply to develop a political consensus, which is proving difficult enough in many countries, but also to manage a consensus for change among the key interest groups with the capacity to stop each change.

The concept of "comfort-zone management" explains many of the differences between private-sector and public-sector management models. It explains some of the interesting differences between ideas of leadership in the public and private sectors. The difficulty the public sector experiences with performance evaluation and the fascination with processes and inputs are not simply vestiges of old bureaucratic values; they reflect the need to manage the impact of government on a complex system of interest groups.

The techniques for managing comfort zones, including respect for differences and a focus on solutions offering specific value rather than common values, are central to successful public-sector management. While there are some interesting parallels with the values required to manage multinational enterprises, many business solutions do not address these techniques. Many attempts to apply business solutions to government management problems fail to translate the solutions to address even the rudimentary requirements of modern comfort-zone management.

Governments have sought to address the growing problem of managing comfort zones in various ways: some have sought to use participative planning to alter community attitudes and protect key interests; some have used crisis management and temporary coercion; others have used nonpublic processes to support key priorities; and others have sought to remove critical projects from the public sector, by hiding them as part of other programs or by removing them from the public sector by privatizing them.

Toward Competitive Government

Underpinning the ideas discussed above is an emerging paradigm for the management of nations which focuses on speed, consensus, and performance. Most theories of government management are confined to the public sector; most see internal factors as dominant; most are driven by notions of efficiency, equity, or autonomy rather than by the need to respond rapidly to external changes; and most presume an autonomy for nations that today is already an illusion.

There are at least four different approaches to the theory of government. Some theories concentrate on policies, some on political decision making and power, some on public-sector delivery and management, and finally, some on grass roots strategies for altering delivery and removing the blockages which have devastated public-sector performance in recent years. All of these theories underrate the impact of the external trends discussed above.

Each approach has validity, and each in some respects complements the other. Unfortunately, each approach tends to adopt its perspective as dominant and sees the alternatives as raising subordinate issues. No assumption could be more limiting to the development of effective theory. No assumption could be further from the realities faced by governments today.

A New Model of Government

Any new model of government must be able to explore the reasons why some countries are performing more effectively than others; it must shed light on the reasons why business solutions are both effective and ineffective; and it must provide a focus for the development of future ideas and a basis for action.

Three related propositions provide the basis for such a model.

The first is that nations are managing strategic transitions to accommodate new external realities. These solutions are best seen in terms of transitions within a continuum of management responses bounded by three basic modes of management: high production, high autonomy, and high response. Effective responses need to involve trade-offs which shift national management toward the high-response model.

The second is that the successful implementation of change requires new approaches to the management of grassroots impacts both on national competitiveness and on the comfort zones which provide government with the scope to implement change. Government administrative systems must manage both types of impacts at the same time. The tools for ensuring that projects lead to operational outputs and real added value constitute performance management. The tools for ensuring that comfort zones are maintained and resistance to changes minimized constitute comfort-zone management. The keys to these new approaches to management are more flexible approaches to planning, more effective management of impacts, and the management of cycle time to increase the speed of many government responses.

The third is that competitive government must find ways to manage the timing of projects more strategically. The first imperative is to alter lead times to enable government to work with business to exploit windows of opportunity as they arise. The second imperative is to reduce cycle time in order to deliver results before opposition to change erodes support for implementation. Many current reforms in government administration avoid this issue. Some reforms actually increase response time; for example, legislative budgeting and planning processes continue to be developed to increase accountability at almost any cost. Ironically, these developments often commence projects at the wrong time, increase cycle time, and place at risk the very performance they seek to stimulate.

Managing Transitions

Solutions are best seen in terms of transitions within a continuum of management responses bounded by three basic models of management: high production, high autonomy, and high response.

Frameworks developed to analyze organizations can be applied to the management of regions, nations, and groups of nations. Such an analysis provides new insights into the changing role of government; the ways in which the private and public sectors need to interact to respond to changes in markets, technology, and communications; and the role of the political process in developing the consensus required to support change.

Figure 13.3   IMPLEMENTATION-IMPACT MODEL

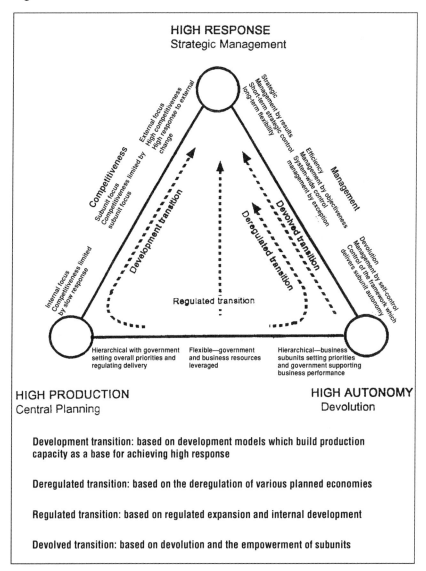

Development transition: based on development models which build production capacity as a base for achieving high response

Deregulated transition: based on the deregulation of various planned economies

Regulated transition: based on regulated expansion and internal development

Devolved transition: based on devolution and the empowerment of subunits

A study of national differences evaluated against various external and internal variables identifies three limiting models of government. Each of the three models of management has different strengths and weaknesses. Each solution requires a different contribution from the public and private sectors. Each faces different transitions to cope with the external changes which all nations must now address. This framework explains differences between nations in terms of transitions rather than static positions. Figure 13.3, a tri-modal model of Government Management, compares a number of different transitions. The transitions are themselves a function of where a nation is placed in the model and where it seeks to move. Within this overall framework, nations can begin the process of managing transitions and of optimizing their performance.

The three limiting modes of management are titled "high response," "high production," and "high autonomy." High-response government monitors and responds to external changes. The objective is to position a nation to exploit external change and optimize national benefits. The challenge is to develop and maintain a consensus for change. High-production government seeks to optimize internal efficiencies through national priorities and planning. The challenge is to buffer the system from external pressures and to develop a culture that supports production priorities. The high-autonomy model optimizes the autonomy of subunits and relies on such units to adapt, respond, and deliver wealth. The high-autonomy model works spectacularly well when there is an effective fit between the priorities of subunits and of the nation. However, attempts to alter the priorities of subunits tend to be seen as eroding autonomy and often are resisted. The challenge is to gain the benefits of high autonomy within a framework of priorities which can co-ordinate effective responses.

The modes do not define three separate types of management but comprise a continuum, within which management changes can be described and within which the mix of management variables must be optimized. Figure 13.4, The Boundaries of Effective Management, explores differences between selected variables. However, in many respects, the three limiting modes are mutually exclusive. The high-production mode necessarily trades off both response and autonomy to achieve its production priority. The high-autonomy mode necessarily trades off production efficiency and response in order to maximize subunit autonomy. The high-response mode necessarily trades off both production efficiency and autonomy in order to respond effectively to external factors. Each of the limiting modes is clearly different. The variables appear to be continuous, and each can be used to rank the three modes.

Figure 13.4   THE BOUNDARIES OF EFFECTIVE MANAGEMENT

	High Production	High Response	High Autonomy
Focus	Focuses on optimizing production. This mode works best when the economy is buffered from external forces. Structures focus on specialization and co-ordination.	The high-response mode increases the power of the environment both over individuals and over enterprises within a nation. The changes required almost always contain an element of discontinuous change.	The high-autonomy mode maximizes the autonomy of individuals and enterprises. Major activities are presumed to occur at other levels. The management role is to provide an environment that supports the activities of subunits.
Management	Management priorities are to eliminate waste and malfunctions by refining processes and structures.	Management aims to implement effective change by focusing on impacts and performance. A major challenge is to use external crises to build and manage political consensus.	Management aims to develop and maintain a consensus about the limits to subunit autonomy and to provide a framework within which subunits can pursue effective change without impacting adversely on other subunits.
Technology	Technology has contributed to coordination and has made work roles less restrictive.	Technology has made the co-ordination required simpler.	Technology has made comparisons between the treatment of subunits easier and has opened up options to increase controls and reduce autonomy.
Objectives	Priorities tend to be imposed through central planning or by major interventions to regulate economic activity.	Dynamic strategic planning which addresses results, key delivery processes, and inputs. Detailed planning must be developed and high-autonomy structures must adjust to new priorities which impact differently on people within a nation.	The focus is away from planning to deliver results and toward the use of planning to develop consensus, explore impacts, and define boundaries and key interests.
Evaluation and control	Exception against plan.	Tight control of short-term impacts, flexible evaluation against long-term threats and opportunities.	Control to protect subunit autonomy and deliver equal treatment.
Government/ business leverage	This solution requires a strong public sector and a subordinate private sector.	This solution requires strategic co-ordination of the public and the private sectors to produce integrated outcomes. The relationships need to be flexible and related to current priorities, and they need to be managed within short performance-oriented cycles.	This mode requires only limited co-ordination between the sectors. The role of government is to buffer the national economy from external forces, negotiate key alliances, provide infrastructure, and ensure that autonomy is protected and people are treated equitably. The private sector operates independently within this overall framework.

The tri-modal model can be used to explore the emerging crisis in government management and to provide some insights into solutions. The model illustrates the dangers of glossing over differences and of assuming that there are either optimal positions for a given nation or optimal solutions for managing all transitions. The transitions required depend upon where, on the model grid, a nation starts, and where it wishes to go. In addition, there are choices about the nature of the transition and the trade-offs required to optimize the management mix.

The general direction that transitions need to address is clear, although not all nations achieve such shifts in practice. The external trends discussed earlier are forcing governments to be more responsive and to dismantle cross-border and internal barriers to performance. This in turn requires a management shift toward the high-response mode.

The nature and extent of these shifts depend on whether a nation needs to develop underlying production strengths and whether it is moving from a position of high production or high autonomy. At least four different transition strategies can be identified.

Each of these transitions can be interpreted as an attempt to respond to external changes by moving toward the high-response mode. Each requires different tools and must address different threats.

Transitions Based on Development Models that Create Competitive Production Capacity as a Base for Achieving High Response

Japan used a development model to achieve many of the characteristics of the high-production mode and then to develop high response through networks of multinational companies. A number of the high-growth Asian economies have chosen this development path. The initial development of high production was based on a development model that buffered external forces and focused internal development, built large efficient companies with clear competitive advantages, and then used those companies to access world markets.

The Singapore transition presents a simpler and interesting variation on this model. As a modern city-state, Singapore has been able to adopt strategies not available to larger, more diverse nations.

The various development models have been remarkably successful. Development goals tend to be accepted initially as a means of catching up with other nations, and acceptance is reinforced when programs deliver added value. The transition is to the left and upward on the model. The key to success is acceptance of overall strategic priorities, the development of production strengths, and the use of early gains to support further change.

The transition requires the development of industry strengths, and the initial development of high response needs to address external opportunities. Empowerment and devolution occurred within this framework.

Three threats need to be neutralized in managing this type of transition. First, nations may not be able to buffer development from global pressures while at the same time accessing critical resources. Second, nations may scan the environment poorly and respond to trends that are not sustained or cannot be exploited. Finally, the strategy depends on maintaining a consensus for focusing resources on national priorities and development. The factors that underpin that consensus are changing. Pressures to open markets and increase autonomy can destroy that consensus.

Transitions Based on the Deregulation of Various Planned Economies

The centrally planned economies of Eastern Europe were buffered from external forces. Central planning was not associated with environmental scanning or benchmarking. The focus tended to be internal.

Recent transitions have opened these economies to internal and external market forces. The results have been sadly predictable. The strategies of benchmarking industry development, which the Asian model used, do not seem to have been employed; instead, privatization programs and open markets were presumed to be the way to increase efficiency. Often, the focus on evaluation and infrastructure support that worked so well in Asia was not present. The key multinationals required to generate wealth in a high-autonomy model did not exist, and strategies to harness existing multinationals to national priorities appear to have met with only limited success.

The transitions appear to have focused on increasing autonomy without increasing production. They have dismantled many of the barriers to change which bedevilled the central-planning model, but they do not appear to have improved the capacity of these nations to respond to external changes. So far, the transition seems to have moved horizontally. Whether the current crises experienced by these transitions will provide the basis to develop production and response strengths in these economies remains an open question. Some countries appear to be improving competitiveness; others look to be regressing to the old central-planning models which will reduce competitiveness over time. The role of government and the approach taken to public-sector management are likely to prove critical for many of these transitions.

Transitions Based on Regulated Expansion and Internal Development

The Western European experience is diverse. However, it is characterized by a tradition of central government and planning and by attempts to maintain a more traditional role for government. While the role of national governments is changing, many of the traditional government roles are simply shifting to the European Community (EC) level. The development strategy has been to buffer national economies from external, particularly non-EC, forces and to develop consensus through central planning while reducing national barriers. Like the development transition discussed earlier, the transition sought is to the left and upward on the model, at least at the overall EC level.

There are parallels and differences with the development-based transitions discussed earlier. The aim of development is similar; however, the focus for subunit development is different. In the European model, the focus is at least in part national rather than industry based. The issues of consensus management and comfort-zone management, which must be addressed to manage such a transition, are clearly more difficult than for the Asian development models.

The model can also be applied to particular nations within the EC. Expansion of markets and competition generated by opening up internal borders offer major opportunities. Consensus at the national level tends to involve government unions and business. The United Kingdom under Thatcher arguably severed many of these constraints and moved to a high-autonomy model. Germany and France retained a centralized model. While the German model appears to focus on a negotiated public-sector–private-sector interface, the French model retains more of the characteristics of the traditional government planning and regulatory model.

There are interesting issues raised by the U.K. transition. The United Kingdom has a more international focus and has sought to become competitive at the cost of employment and various social services. It has reduced the tripartite consensus model and has sought to enable companies access to Europe and the global markets. The breakdown of barriers to the Eastern European countries represents both a major opportunity and a major threat to the transitional consensus process.

Transitions Based on Devolution and the Empowerment of Subunits

The United States is a high-autonomy mode of government with established industrial strengths. The transition sought is upward and to the left on the model. This requires some realignment of industry policies and performance and requires government to address critical infrastructure and support priorities.

The United States fell behind in the competitiveness stakes in the 1970s and 1980s. The response has been to examine and benchmark the competition, and to develop a group of highly effective and large multinational economies. Instead of buffering its economy, the United States opened it and exposed industry to major pressures.

The U.S. government focus has been to manage diversity and achieve political consensus at the national and the regional levels. The process is managed almost independently of the industry policy process discussed above. The focus for response is the multinational corporation. Government has supported the interests of these multinationals and has sought to assist them to access markets. Government has also supported the process by infrastructure and education and training investment and by assisting corporations to gain competitive advantages from various government projects.

The transition to the left produced many challenges. The threats are similar to those faced by all high-autonomy organizations, that gridlock will develop and governments will not be able to deliver needed infrastructure and services, or that the latter will not be coordinated with industry policies and the need to access the global economy.

However, recent improvements in competitiveness suggest that the transition is occurring. The U.S. government has experienced major comfort-zone restraints. It is not surprising that the reform of government has become a major priority to support the current transition.

Managing Implementation

An effective reform strategy needs to be supported with effective implementation strategies and tools. Many governments with a sound agenda for reform have found themselves unable to manage implementation.

Effective national responses to external pressures involve shortening response times and strategically managing ongoing improvements in national competitiveness. Strategic management in open-ended situations must balance the tensions between the need for short-term controls and the need for long-term flexibility. Understanding such processes and benchmarking the performance of nations requires a study of transitions. Managing transitions requires strategies and tools which manage grassroots benefits and other, often unintended, impacts and build an ongoing momentum for future change.

The implementation of change requires new approaches to the management of grassroots impacts, both on national competitiveness and on the comfort zones which provide government with the scope to implement change.

Figure 13.5, Implementation-Impact Model, summarises an implementation model which can be used to explain the high failure rate associated with recent government reform. This model suggests that government administrators must manage both project performance and comfort zones at the same time.

The objective is to manage impacts to maintain each project both in the positive performance zone and in the comfort zone. Governments that trade off popularity for value-added results tend to find that popularity without performance is an increasingly short-lived phenomenon.

Governments that seek change at any cost create conflict and, over time, erode their capacity to govern. Governments pursuing the traditional strategy of compromise to stay out of trouble increasingly find that they achieve neither added value nor popularity. The implementation-impact model provides a useful tool for mapping government implementation performance. However, it is most powerful when used to manage cycle dynamics.

The Management of Cycle Dynamics

The management of cycle dynamics has three components: (1) the management of overall cycle time by engineering government value

Figure 13.5 IMPLEMENTATION-IMPACT MODEL

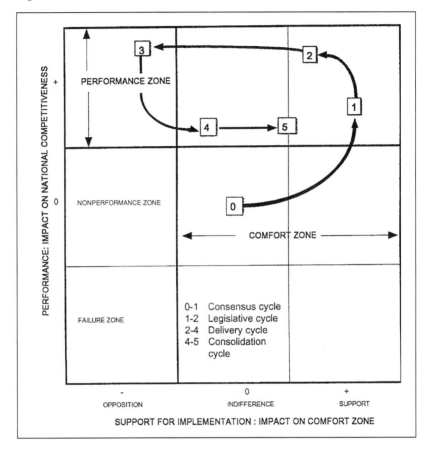

chains to reduce cycle time and enable projects to exploit external events and deliver benefits before initial support erodes; (2) the management of cycle impacts by scheduling impacts on interest groups to maintain perceptions of net added value, even when negative impacts must occur; and (3) the support of the process with pro-active cycle-focused communications strategies that balance expectations against delivery, manage the dynamics of negative impacts, and consolidate project benefits when they are available.

Competitive government must find ways to manage the timing of projects more strategically, to exploit windows of opportunity as they arise, and to reduce cycle time in order to deliver results before opposition to change erodes support for implementation.

As nations pursue transitions to high-performance government, cycle-time management becomes a key variable for managing the fit between the different missions of government. The high-response model requires corporate priorities to be superordinate, restricting, and perhaps threatening to individual priorities. The management challenge is to plan the process to deliver corporate priorities which optimize individual autonomy. This requires shorter cycle times within which specific impacts—positive and negative, real and perceived—can be actively managed. This, in turn, requires new concepts of leadership and communication for the public sector.

Figure 13.5 uses the implementation-impact model to examine movement over time. The numbers divide implementation into four cycles: a consensus cycle (0–1); a legislative cycle (1–2); a delivery cycle (2–4); and a consolidation cycle (4–5).

In managing the consensus cycle (0–1), the challenge is to build support for the changes needed to commit the reforms. Government can usually control information to focus on benefits and to avoid discussion of specific negative impacts. However, history is littered with governments that have oversold solutions only to find that the public rate success a failure. It is important to balance expectations against the prospects of delivery. Timing is often critical to launching projects and building consensus.

In managing the legislative cycle (1–2), the challenge is to access the legislative approvals and resources required to implement change. Where key interest groups seem likely to stop specific projects, trade-offs and negotiations are required. The objective is to gain authorization with minimum trade-offs and constraints. Gaining legislative approval is seldom the end of negotiations with groups opposed to change.

In managing the delivery cycle (2–4), the challenge is to schedule and evaluate both positive and negative impacts to maintain sufficient support to complete reform projects. Managers need to manage the dynamics of project impacts either by bringing forward positive impacts or by shortening cycle time in order to sell end benefits as imminent. Another challenge is to manage negative impacts. Not everyone benefits from every project, and some individuals and interest groups may be disadvantaged. Planning must address these realities and organize timing and communication strategies to neutralize resistance. The added value of a project can diminish considerably during the delivery stage, as constituencies lobby to offset perceived disadvantages. Leadership requires the negotiation of such impacts. The challenge is to position implementation within a comfort zone, which enables implementation to proceed without sacrificing results to the point where reform fails to add value.

In managing the consolidation cycle (4–5), the challenge is to communicate benefits, to manage the gap between public expectations and actual delivery, and to consolidate the benefits by ensuring that opponents cannot erode them too readily. Clearly, this phase can move projects in various directions on the model grid. However, for the purposes of this discussion, a horizontal movement to the right is assumed. This reflects a maintenance of added value and a growing support for reform as benefits are appreciated and understood.

An examination of actual implementation reveals many different cycle patterns. However, three points are relevant to the application of this model to government responses to recession: (1) Governments are rarely able to deliver the added value they first envisage. (2) The extent of the reductions they must accept is determined by the effectiveness of particular reform programs, their capacity to reduce cycle time and achieve short-run control over change, and the threshold levels that define the comfort zone. (3) The chances of a government consolidating to the right on the model depend on whether competitiveness increases, and on the size of the gap between public perceptions of government objectives and the reality of delivery at the grassroots level.

Recessions generally move the comfort-zone threshold to the left on the model, but they also make the process of adding value more difficult, particularly for governments that seek to meet new problems with old solutions.

The Impact of Recession

The recession had two different but related impacts: first, the realization that competitive nations require competitive government stimulated experiments to reform government structures and systems; and second, the failure of many of these experiments to deliver short-term benefits has led many to distrust the traditional processes and rhetoric of governments.

While recession exposed both businesses and governments to new global forces, business responded more flexibly than government. The business response required little more than a development of existing trends. The government response required acceptance that change was discontinuous, requiring new ideas and values to cope with the emerging global economy; these were slow to develop, and many governments in many countries were seen to be impeding change and seeking to protect entrenched positions.

Traditional solutions failed to deliver competitive government. Those who grasped the need for fundamental change sought to transplant business solutions, which solved some problems but often created new ones. This analysis explains some of the problems encountered. There are clear gaps in the tools so far applied. The success of some of the solutions, such as market deregulation and privatization, may be due to rather different causes than those espoused by those who see these tools as solutions in themselves. The dangers of taking solutions developed to support one transition and applying them to nations involved in a different transition seem clear, yet much of the discussion of solutions seems to ignore such differences.

The scope for public-sector change increased as the problems of recession increased and as the public realized that grand promises were no longer credible or feasible. The demands on governments to contribute, rather than impede, national competitiveness and to address the immediate problems of recession grew. Although the comfort zone extended to the left, making key changes possible, many governments were slow to grasp the opportunity for reform.

Instead of decreasing response times and shifting the emphasis to external issues, many governments were driven to reduce response times and focus on internal issues. They were driven by macroeconomic pressures to cut budgets and by attempts to allocate, or avoid the blame for, failure. In many cases, government management increased rather than reduced response times; in some of these cases, the slower response times moved projects out of the comfort zone. A typical government response was to call for sacrifices as the price for future salvation. While the sacrifices were made, the public felt the benefits were not delivered.

Not all of the key changes which have occurred are obvious, and some have been remarkably effective. For example, this analysis suggests that a major factor in deregulation and privatization is the movement of accountability, or at least visible accountability, for many decisions away from governments. This may well make key changes feasible, particularly in high-autonomy nations. However, shortages and queues are seldom solved by adjusting allocation processes. Key decisions must still be made, and, if nations are to become more competitive, the new processes will need to perform.

A number of lessons can be drawn from this analysis of the impact of recession. First, reinvention of government needs to do more than sensitize government services to markets or reduce costs; it must remove the blockages which outmoded approaches to government have created, and it must find new ways for government and business to work together to add value to nations, regions, and cities in an increasingly globalized and pluralistic society.

Second, nations need to address both the strategic and the implementation issues discussed above; audit existing change strategies to ensure that they add value and increase national competitiveness; and audit government management responses to test the fit between the new strategies and the government roles and priorities used to implement them.

Third, at the grass roots, governments now have no option but to review many of the procedures that currently produce inertia and the regulatory fog that, in many countries, subdues all but the most persistent business initiatives. Business also needs to confront the challenges presented by the new global economy. Business development must involve negotiated arrangements with multinationals, to gain their support in delivering national and regional competitiveness. Governments need to develop administrative systems able to address the twin challenges of performance management and comfort-zone management. The various specific tools now becoming available need to be seen as contributing to that process, rather than as prescriptive solutions in their own right. The objective of reform should be the development of a more competitive government.

Fourth, the problems encountered by governments in managing change should not obscure the fact that irreversible change and major reforms of political and administrative processes are now occurring in a number of countries; the reforms are changing the key roles and value chains of government. As governments are compared on the basis of their capacity to add value by assisting their countries to compete in the emerging global economy, the business of government is becoming competitive.

Finally, governments need to guard against the complacency which usually accompanies recovery. The crisis will not disappear, and governments that neglect the need to change will find themselves increasingly disadvantaged compared with those who complete the process. The most effective way to do this is to evaluate government change against the goals of added value and compare and benchmark performance. Any such process must confront the remarkable success of some of the Asian economies and must recognize that those economies today face different challenges from economies that started from a different base and that have pursued essentially different transitions. The objective is not to copy any particular transition; each nation needs to develop strategies suited to its situation and history. However, it seems important to study successful transitions and the government priorities that underpin them. It is also important to develop comparative models that enable practitioners to separate causes from symptoms and that focus on the key issues all nations must now confront.

14

Lessons in Government Communication Strategies of Best Practices in Australia

Robyn Johnston

Introduction

In 1990, at the onset of the recession that then Australian Treasurer Paul Keating said that Australia had to have, Professor of Industrial Relations at Melbourne University Stephen Deery, claimed:

> The real challenge facing Australian industrial relations managers is to create an internal organisational environment in which the key stakeholders—employees, management and unions—are encouraged to focus on the firm's long term competitive position. A flexible approach to work practices, a commitment to skill formation and job security and an ability to facilitate process and product innovation is essential. (1990:15)

This challenge had resulted from Australia's deteriorating position in the increasingly turbulent and competitive global markets. Such conditions meant and continues to mean that Australian organizations can no longer rely on a rich base of natural resources or on traditional trading partners to establish an improved market position. Such conditions have also meant that as Australian organizations emerge from the recession they cannot anticipate a return to stable and predictable work environments which operate with an adversarial model of industrial relations, archaic and restrictive work practices, outmoded organizational structures and management approaches, and a work force unskilled in the use of new technologies and organizational practices. In order to not only compete but also survive long term in such conditions, there is a growing recognition that Australian organizations and employees must adopt new structures and processes which emulate the practices of leading world-class organizations.

This scenario has pressured Australian enterprises to adopt new organizational and management structures and production systems in order to attain the required flexibility and capacity for rapid response. It has required Australian trade unions to develop new approaches to best represent the needs of their members. Such organizational and industrial reforms have meant that both employers and employees are now needing to acquire new sets of skills to equip them to operate in their reformed workplaces. Changes in each of these domains have brought a heightened attention to the practice of organizational communication.

This chapter examines progress in meeting the challenge described by Deery. It discusses some changes that are occurring in the arenas of industrial relations, management practice, and skill formation. It then reports on some of the achievements pertaining to these arenas in selected organizations participating in a Best Practice program, focusing particularly on the role of organizational communication as a key to Australia's emerging successfully from the recession.

Change in the Industrial Relations Arena

Significant change has occurred in the industrial relations arena both at the state and at the federal level in Australia in recent years. This situation has grown out of general recognition that Australia's system of industrial relations, its award and union structures, have limited organizational flexibility and have hindered the ability of Australian enterprises to respond quickly to new economic circumstances. An initial shaping force creating the new industrial relations order has been a series of accords relating to wages policies between the federal government and trade unions which began in 1983 and 1984 and sought to lay the foundations for much-needed microeconomic reform. The accord processes have been pivotal in the development of new levels of co-operation between management and labor which have in turn facilitated industrial relations policy changes and necessitated a change in the nature of the union movement itself.

Changes in the Nature of Unions

The late 1980s through early 1990s marks a period during which the union peak body, the Australian Council of Trade Unions (ACTU),

has enjoyed unprecedented power in influencing economic and social policy making (*Australian Financial Review*, 1989). Paralleling
this growth in influence there has been a substantial decline in trade
union membership in Australia in line with the decline of membership of unions in Britain and Europe.

To counter this situation, the ACTU in 1987 announced a major
program to encourage union amalgamation. Through such amalgamations the union movement hoped to build larger, better resourced
(and better able to recruit), and therefore stronger, unions. Such
rationalizations and the movement toward industry unionism were
seen by the ACTU executive in October 1990 as being better suited
to effective intervention in trade and industry policy. While the pace
of such amalgamation has not been rapid and the goal of 20 super
unions not yet achieved, the 299 unions that had separate identities
in 1987 now number just over 50 in the federal sphere.

Responses have varied about the value of such amalgamations
for increasing the productivity of the Australian work force. Some
writers (e.g., Lansbury and Spillane, 1991; Deery, 1990) argue that
such amalgamation will lead to an improvement in labor relations.
Others, such as Hilmer (1990), claim that the move to the "super
union" is premised on old adversarial philosophies and has little to
offer in terms of creating the organizational flexibility so urgently
needed. In fact, within the Labor movement itself, there are a number of outspoken critics who fear for the loss of identity and effective representation for members of some of the smaller craft-based
unions.

The amalgamation process in itself has not to date resulted in
arresting the decline of union membership, even if it has simplified
negotiation at some workplaces. In a bid to avoid becoming a
marginalized force in the modern Australian workplace in 1995 union
leaders called for the union movement to examine its own management structures and recommended the adoption of more devolu-
tionary management strategies that spread responsibilities and power
throughout union organizations. Additional strategies being recommended to stem the membership decline have included the establishment of new "shop-front" agencies which would take unionism to
nonunionist suburbs and country towns by opening union recruiting
and information and services offices in suburban office malls, employing 500 new recruiting officers and providing discounted air fares
for union members. Such recruitment strategies are attempting to
transform unions into modern service-based organizations (*Australian Financial Review*, 1995).

A New Approach to Industrial Awards

From the mid-1980s the increasingly global nature of competition has seen most major industrialized economies moving to decentralize their wage-bargaining systems. Australia has conformed with this trend.

Initially, in 1987, a bid to promote improved efficiency and productivity in the workplace the Australian Industrial Relations Commission endorsed new approaches to centralized wage fixing with the establishment of a two-tier wage-fixing process. The first tier of this system allowed for a discounted wage increase. A second tier wage increase could be sought by unions under wage-fixing principles that included organizational restructuring and initiatives to increase workplace efficiency. Initiatives in this new category included changes to work and management practices, action to reduce demarcation barriers, advancing multiskilling, training, and retraining, and broad banding and changes to working patterns.

This excursion into decentralized bargaining was continued with the 1988 wage case, which introduced the structural efficiency principle. This principle provided for radical award restructuring and was seen as a way to more extensive workplace reform. Among the dimensions of the structural-efficiency principle were measures which included

- establishing skill-related careers paths which provide an incentive for workers to continue to participate in skill formation;
- creating appropriate relativities between different categories of workers within the award and at an enterprise level;
- ensuring that working patterns and arrangements enhance flexibility and meet the competitive requirements of industry; and
- eliminating impediments to multiskilling and broadening the range of tasks that a worker may be required to perform.

While a full evaluation of the outcomes of the 1988 wage decision is yet to be made, an assessment of 27 workplaces in a number of industries which have sought wage increases through the industrial courts on the basis of the structural efficiency principle has found that broad-ranging changes have been achieved in manufacturing industries and public-sector organizations, including those improving productivity and cutting costs. However, the study showed that measures such as new career structures and enhanced training were still in their early stages (Curtain, Gough, and Kimmer, 1992).

Enterprise Agreements

Some of the organizational flexibility enhancing the possibility of greater productivity is provided though enterprise agreements which also form part of the new industrial-relations mix. The possibility for enterprise bargaining allows unions (and in some cases employees) and employers to conclude agreements that allow for consent awards and certified agreements for specific enterprises. These provisions prohibit arbitration on the terms of the agreement, thus relying entirely on negotiated outcomes. Agreements under this enterprise-bargaining principle must be on the basis of improvements in productivity and efficiency and be for a fixed term.

Initial success in concluding enterprise agreements in the depressed economy of 1991 and early 1992 was limited and continued at a relatively slow pace particularly in the private sector in 1993 (Sloan, 1994). By mid-1994 at a federal level enterprise bargaining had resulted in more than 1,800 workplace agreements and by 1995 covered approximately 56 percent of workers under federal awards with predictions that the volume will increase significantly as procedures become more familiar. Wide-ranging productivity agreements and improvement measures have been incorporated into many of these agreements.

Ferguson (1994) has identified four areas of workplace activity as constituting the improvement measures associated with enterprise agreements. These include

- work organization, which includes functional flexibility, team work, quality assurance, continuous improvement, best-practice strategies, consultative arrangements, and organizational restructuring;
- conditions of employment, including leave arrangements, hours of work, flexible rostering, the contract of employment, part-time employment, and attention to pay and allowances;
- the working environment, including occupational health and safety, absenteeism, disputation, labor turnover, and associated costs; and
- the implementation of training strategies to equip employees with the broad range of skills needed for a comprehensive approach to productivity enhancement.

Such company-based awards have been seen as more likely to provide a greater measure of labor flexibility and lower levels of restrictive labor behaviors (Drago and Wooden, 1989; Curtain, 1988; Dunphy and Stace, 1990). Sloan also highlights the beneficial effectives of such workplace agreements arguing:

> Many of the agreements were "add on" and operate in conjunction with the award particularly in the metals area. At the same time there have been some highly innovative agreements leading to substantial productivity gains and improved benefits for workers. Examples include agreements covering employees in some of the major hotel chains, and others with Alcoa, Optus, and Esso Construction workers at Port Kembla. (1994:26)

These new approaches to restructuring industrial awards and establishing enterprise-based agreements have been achieved by increased work-place consultation which is claimed to have resulted in improved communication between employers and employees (Marchington, 1992 reporting on findings of the Australian Workplace Industrial Relations Survey [AWIRS]).

The accord years have coincided with a period of comparative industrial-relations harmony. The source of such harmony may reside in changes that have emerged in new forms of enterprise awards, new approaches to consultation by management, the potential of new career paths, the decline in interest of employees in union membership, or the depressed economy. As Australia is only now emerging from the recession, with some commentators warning of the possibility of a further plunge into recession, it is still too early to predict the long-term impact of such reforms on industrial and workplace practices. Various parties, including governments and unions, however, are keen to take credit for the so-called gains, which include increases in productivity and savings through reduction of loss of productivity with fewer days of disputation. As the AWIRS indicated in the first benchmark study, it will not be till further longitudinal research is conducted that real outcomes can be determined. However, whatever the reason, the disputation minimization has led to fewer days lost as a result of industrial action at a time of very significant change in workplace behavior and considerable downsizing, and there have been substantial increases in productivity in selected organizations.

Changing Organizational Structures and Management Approaches

The achievement of a more cooperative industrial order in the late 1980s and 1990s with its more collaborative decision-making structures at the enterprise level could be seen as an indication of the adoption of new models of management practice in at least some Australian organizations. The need for such reformed organizational structures and related management practices had been heralded by a range of writers (e.g., Hilmer, 1990; Dunphy and Stace, 1990) commenting on the Australian context in the years leading up to the recession period. The need for organizational reform and new approaches to management continues to be promoted as we move from the recession.

Hilmer (1990), for example, on the basis of evidence gained from 330 workplaces in Australia, covering 200,000 employees, argues:

> We are playing in a new game, one in which globally competitive enterprises, serving customers in unique and constantly changing ways generate the jobs and the profiles that are our national prosperity. But we are still playing by old rules of conduct . . . at many workplaces, particularly in small firms in competitive markets, the rules are ignored. In others regulators, unions and managers are trying to build in the necessary flexibility. (164)

In striving for this necessary flexibility, Hilmer argues that the customer-focused enterprise striving for world-class output should be seen as the new building block for organizational and national prosperity.

Hilmer (1990) advances the position that the actions of governments, unions, and corporate headquarters only guide whether and how individuals will act and that it is not until people at work do something directly or indirectly that an outcome resulting in economic prosperity and jobs is created. He also debunks the myth that most enterprise frontline employees and managers are locked in irreconcilable conflict and advocates that the main reason for regulating work and working conditions should be to improve the relationship between employers and employees, encouraging them to choose methods and patterns of work and pay that fit their own needs and those of their enterprises.

Postrecession evidence of the increasing number of enterprise agreements based on improvement measures and award restructuring initiatives allowing for more flexible work practices determined co-operatively by managers and employees are indicators of a movement in the direction Hilmer was calling for in 1990. Similarly, initiatives concerning worker empowerment and involvement in enterprise decision making discussed later section in this chapter provide some evidence of prosperity of work resulting from "people directly doing something" in Australian enterprises.

Dunphy and Stace (1990) have also argued for a new approach to management and organizational structuring to achieve the necessary "strategic fit" and hence competitiveness in a changing environment. They cite evidence of the emergence of this process in leading organizations in Australia, drawing on a 1989 survey covering 545 public- and private-sector organizations. From this survey, it was shown that 58 percent of organizations had changed their fundamental mission, 65 percent had made significant changes to their business strategy, and 62 percent had made significant change to their corporate goals and objectives in the previous two years.

Among the most common trends related to structural change that are evident in Australian organizations, according to these writers are the move from functional to divisional structures—with high-tech and professional organizations moving to matrix structures; the move to flatter organizations—with the aim of such a move being to lessen the communication distance between top management and the organization's frontline employee; and the move to radical devolution of authority and accountability through the development of profit-accountable strategic business units and project style operations.

Dunphy and Stace provide examples of Australian organizations that have made such structural changes supported by cultural change programs arguing: "The new organisational forms are much more flexible and therefore more able to support innovation and entrepreneurial action even when the organisation is large" (1990:48).

These writers suggest that leadership has a vital role to play in transforming organizations, claiming that the new leadership must be a combination both of transactional and of transformational leadership. They state: "One of the important roles managers play is to identify the expectations of all important stakeholders and to work with their expectations to form a creative synthesis or reformulation of their organisation's mission and strategy" (304).

Recognizing the importance of communication in the transformation process, they argue:

The most central task of management in a time of great change is to "feed the soul" of the organisation by creating new meaning around the identity of the organisation. This involves forming an active relationship with key external stakeholders and those in the organisation creating a dialogue of action and debate from which the new meaning is forged. (206)

Limerick and Cunnington writing as Australia emerged from the recession in 1993 also claim that the arrival of the age of discontinuous change has produced the need for new models of organizational structure and differing management skills. Their message, while not solely for Australian organizations, is based on studies of organizations from Australia and other parts of the world competing successfully in times of turbulence. They argue, in a similar vein, to Hilmer for the replacement of the large hierarchically structured organizations with a smaller network structure providing a flexibility and increased customer focus. Like Dunphy and Stace, these writers suggest that the new sets of skills required by managers in such organizations include a capacity to manage the meaning of their organizations—a position that had been advanced by Weick (1979) when he argued: "Managerial work can be viewed as managing myth, symbols and labels . . . because managers traffic so often in images, the appropriate role for the manager may be evangelist, rather than accountant" (237).

From a study investigating approaches used by Australian CEOs, Limerick and Cunnington found that the following techniques were being used by managers for managing meaning in leading Australian organizations: (1) the careful use of language and slogans; (2) bringing to prominence legends and models; (3) systems and sanctions; and (4) self-modelling (1993:202).

Limerick and Cunnington also argue the need for Australian organizations to become organizations which learn by using, doing, and failure, and, in words reminiscent of Argyris and Schon (1978) and Senge (1993), to engage in double-loop learning, challenging their own basic work-related assumptions. The writers claim that there is a high level of congruency between the creation of action-learning communities within organizations and the model of management necessary for network organizations which will succeed in a period of discontinuity. The writers cite organizations such as ICI (Aust.) and the Department of Education in Queensland (Aust.) as developing an action-learning approach within the units of their organization (223).

The importance of leadership in assisting our recovery from recession has been recognized by the Australian government with its establishment of an Industry Task Force on Leadership and Management Skills in 1991. This task force is expected to make its final report to the government in 1995. In broad terms, the task force was established to advise the Australian government on measures to strengthen the leadership and management skills required in Australian enterprises. Some initial findings from this project reveal that while there is evidence of changing management practice in some organizations, there remains an urgent need to improve the skills of the nation's managers. The Barraclough study which comprised part of the research of the task force has indicated that Australian managers

- lack vision and have a short term perspective
- lack strategic perspective
- are poor at team work
- are inflexible and rigid
- do not have good people skills and are complacent
- do not manage themselves well.
  (Industry Task Force on Leadership and Management Skills, 1994)

From extensive research from a range of task force teams, Ivanoff and Prentice (1994) indicate that management training, education, and development activities are not being given high priority in the majority of Australian businesses surveyed. Ivanoff and Prentice argue that current business support for management development does not approach "best-practice" level and there is little indication that remedial action is being taken to close the gap. They state: "A Catch 22 situation appears to exist in which business will not give management development a high priority, until its impact on the bottom line is proven. However its impact on the bottom line will not be proven until enough business give management development appropriate priority" (Ivanoff and Prentice, 1994)

These researchers report that the reduction in layers of management in many Australian organizations has meant a changing role for frontline managers.

They recommend that given that approximately 60 percent of these managers in Australia do not have formal education and training for management, there is a need for a national initiative to enhance the skills of the new frontline managers. Thus, during the recession period and years surrounding it, there has been significant attention directed to the need for new forms of structure and managerial skills in Australian organizations. There is evidence certainly from some larger organizations of changes both in structure and approach to management, with the emergence of flatter organizations, increased communication with organizational stakeholders and greater participation in decision making by some employees. The level of such participation is not well distributed across all Australian organizations. However, the new approaches to industrial relations are creating increasing opportunity for such participation. There remains a need for continuing attention in this area to promote change with findings from the leadership and management task force indicating an ongoing need for more advanced approaches to management and development within Australia.

A New Focus on Learning

Much as the immediate pre-recession and recession years have stimulated an increased interest in more participative approaches to management and more flexible workplace industrial arrangements, so too these years have seen the emergence of new approaches to skill formation for those in the Australian workforce. A changing culture recognizing the need for ongoing workplace learning has been generated by the introduction of advanced technology, new workplace arrangements, and the need to be more competitive. These new working conditions, which are still at an embryonic stage in many workplaces, require multiskilled workers who can undertake a wider range of tasks and thereby increase their organizations' flexibility and responsiveness.

The union movement, in supporting such workplace reform and the need for upskilled workers, has striven to have workplace training requirements embedded in industrial agreements. The federal government, to nurture a new culture of workplace learning and employee upskilling, has adopted an interventionist approach through its initiation of a raft of discussion papers and policy statements directed to the process of skill formation. These are collectively seen as constituting the Training Reform Agenda. A key element of this agenda has been the establishment of a national competency-based system of training. This system has been supported by an extensive infrastructure which has enabled the development and ratification of industry competency standards. These standards form the bases for the development of national industry training curricula.

In moving from a competency-standards-based approach to skill formation, a broad concept of "competency" has been adopted in that all aspects of work performance (task skills, task-management skills, contingency-management skills and job/role-environment skills) are included. Analysis of the various competency-standards documents clearly shows that industry has identified the importance of communication-related skills as part of workplace competence (Johnston, 1993).

Other elements of this reform agenda include the development of a new qualification system that allows for portability of qualifications throughout Australia, including recognition of competencies gained from workplace-based experience or from nonformal study. The new skill-formation system has been responsible for a reexamination of the roles of education provided in schools, including higher education sectors, and for the closer articulation between the work of education providers. It has also provided industry with a greater voice in the nature and content of training received by employees in formal postcompulsory education institutions.

These radical changes are at early stages of implementation. There still remains much confusion about the changes and their implications. An initial report evaluating the changes has found that

> while there has been increased spending on upskilling of the Australian workforce in Australian business, Australian enterprises at the time the report was compiled did not have a strong commitment to the major components of the reform agenda, particularly competency based training. Many people in industry were turned away by the sheer bureaucracy and rigidity of implementation. (Allan 1994:11)

The report of the evaluation (1994:3) continues:

> the lack of strong commitment of business to the reforms collectively and at an enterprise level (with exceptions) can be traced back to the lack of a full mapping of the means to implement the reforms to the desired ultimate goal. In particular the inadequacy of existing means to engage business can be attributed to the absence of a strong demand side focus in the reform process.

Thus at the macro level, while there has been a committed approach through government intervention to the skill-formation process in keeping with national policies of other major industrialized countries and the new competitors of Asia, this approach has not won the "hearts and minds" of all Australian enterprises. At the same time, the Allan evaluation did signal that there had been a number of impressive success stories, and since the compilation of the report evidence of the implementation of reform-agenda initiatives at enterprise levels is continuing, albeit slowly. Therefore, it would seem that while a changed culture in terms of skill formation is emerging, the real implications of this revolution are yet to be produced.

Best-Practice Initiatives

Thus, in recent years, many Australian organizations have experienced considerable change. Such changes include new approaches to industrial-relations practice, some movement toward more participative-management practice, and a growing awareness of the deficiency of management skills among those who as a result of organizational restructuring have had more management and self-management responsibility thrust upon them, and, the beginnings of a culture that supports ongoing workplace learning underpinned by a national framework for more strategic skill formation. These changes, although significant, have been occurring slowly, and, certainly as Australia entered the recession, particularly slowly. At that time, the Australian Manufacturing Council provided evidence to suggest that Australian industry lagged behind the rest of the world in adopting a new workplace culture (Australian Manufacturing Council, 1990). In a bid to reverse this situation and provide additional impetus to earlier policies and programs of economic reform, the federal government initiated a series of programs and policies. One such program was the Best-Practice Demonstration program. This program was designed to accelerate the introduction of practices that emulated those occurring in leading world enterprises and thereby improve Australian competitive position. Analyses of reports on the processes being adopted and outcomes being achieved by participants in these programs provides evidence of the trends in industrial relations, management, and skill formation discussed earlier in this chapter. Such analyses also reveal the increased emphasis on organizational communication practices that is occurring in Best-Practice organizations as they move toward becoming more competitive. The following section addresses some findings concerning processes associated with best practice in Australian organizations.

The Best Practice Demonstration Program

The Best Practice Program which was announced in March 1991 in an industry paper, "Building a Competitive Australia," aims to accelerate the introduction and dissemination of new ways of working based on international best practice. The program has two central components. It has provided project assistance in terms of financial grants to specific companies, initially to accelerate or introduce change programs. Companies participating in the project commit themselves to demonstrating to wider industry the methods and approaches to best practice they have identified. In this way, the funded companies become role models for other companies, and all Australia benefits.

The initial round of the project in 1991 and 1992 funded Best Practice Programs in 43 large enterprises from the manufacturing, service, or hospitality sectors. Later rounds of funding have been directed to small to medium-size enterprises in high-technology areas and in geographic clustering or networking arrangements. Achievements by participating organizations attained through the program have been reported in a range of sources, including one interim evaluation report on the first round of projects.

The evaluation of the first round of the Best Practice Demonstration program was conducted in 1993. The evaluation found that the program itself had accelerated the adoption of best practice in funded enterprises along with stimulating the adoption of best practice in many enterprises that had applied unsuccessfully for funding. The program has therefore had a catalytic effect on the adoption of best-practice procedures in large Australian enterprises (and there is evidence of similar rates of adoption in small to medium enterprises, with the extension of the program to these sectors in the later rounds of funding). Other findings from this evaluation showed that there have been significant achievements in a range of areas, including the following:

a) Productivity Improvements
   About 30 percent of projects reported improvements in productivity and a further 40 percent reported expectations of improvement within the short term. Indicators for such achievements included improvements in production times, decreases in labour hours per batch, falls in rejections rates, reductions in lead times and wastage rates, increased occupany rates, decreased labour turnover and absenteeism rates.

b) Improved industrial relations
The benefits reported as having already occurred in 65 percent of projects concerned the improvement in management employee relations, with greater worker participation and empowerment reported as having occurred in 50 percent of projects.

c) A more highly skilled workforce
Around 20 percent of funded enterprises reported that the project had contributed to a more highly skilled workforce.

d) Greater organisational flexibility
A third of participants reported greater organisational responsiveness and flexibility.

e) Improvements in Occupational Health
Almost 25 percent of the projects reported an improved Occupational Health and Safety record with improvements including a decrease in time lost as a result of injuries.

f) Accreditation to quality standards
Three projects at the time of the evaluation had achieved accreditation to international and Australian quality standards AS3901/2, ISO9001/2 Ford Q1.

g) Building partnerships with customers and suppliers
More than one third of program participants improved relationships with customers and suppliers.

h) Performance measuring systems
The project survey indicated that a third of the projects had achieved improvement in their performance measurement systems.
(Department of Industrial Relations, 1993:25–29)

Such a study clearly shows that in participating enterprises changing industrial-relations practice, management practice and skill-formation strategies have had an impact and there is evidence of increasing productivity. The interim evaluation only indirectly focused on the communication processes and outcomes. The following section considers analyses of the programs from a communication perspective.

Communication Analyses of the Best-Practice Program

Data for this communication-focused examination came from a set of profiling documents supplied by participating organizations as part of their commitment to the program. These documents were compiled before the interim evaluation study referred to above was completed. While this source of data provides only broad perspectives of initiatives in each of the participating enterprises, it does provide general evidence of major features of best-practice implementation and progress toward outcomes identified in the interim evaluation study. The profile documents were analyzed from three perspectives: the focus of change in participating enterprises; the processes used to effect change; and stated outcomes achieved at the point of compiling the profile. What follows is a report of some of findings from the analysis.

FOCUS OF CHANGE PROGRAMS From an analysis of the content of the profiling statements, it could be seen that the focus of change programs being implemented by participating enterprises varied particularly in relation to specific goals being sought by the enterprises.

Table 14.1 represents the specific goals of the programs most commonly identified through profile documentation. Some organizations highlighted as part of their focus several of the goals shown below.

From Table 14.1 it can be seen that many organizations described their specific program goals in very broad terms. Conversely, several enterprises focused on specific goals of their programs (e.g., improved safety record) with the inference being that the broader outcome of increased competitiveness would be achieved. The high proportion of enterprises nominating increasing competitiveness is to be expected, given that this was the central aim of the project and the basis for gaining acceptance onto the program. It is interesting to note that the issue of quality which is receiving worldwide

Table 14.1   FOCUS OF BEST-PRACTICE PROGRAM

Goal of Change Program	% of Organization
Increase competitiveness	47%
Improvement in quality of product/service	37.5%
Improvement in productivity performance	27.5%
More efficient use of capital equipment	15%
Strengthened customer relationship	22%
Strengthened supplier relationship	10%
Improved safety record	7.5%

attention is a major goal of a large number of participating organizations to enhance their competitiveness. Second, the move to recognize the importance of stakeholders, including customers and suppliers, as part of the production process also fits with a new approach to organizational practice.

PROCESSES USED IN BEST-PRACTICE PROGRAMS Most enterprises identified a raft of initiatives that were at various stages of the implementation as part of the process of achieving best practice. Table 14.2 shows the most commonly identified processes that had been used in implementing the best-practice approach.

Table 14.2 identifies the ten most frequently mentioned approaches used in the process of implementing the Best-Practice project. It should be noted that the above approaches were those that were identified at the time of profile compilation and that other processes, while being used to support the implementation, were not identified in profile data.

Given the trends discussed earlier in this chapter, some of the processes used to implement reform deserve closer consideration. For example, at least 90 percent of organizations in the sample clearly indicated a major undertaking in terms of workplace training in order to achieve best practice. Some of the organizations delivered this training in the workplace. Others provided in-house training but had also established arrangements for articulation of their training

Table 14.2 PROCESSES USED IN IMPLEMENTING BEST PRACTICE

Processes Used	No. of Organizations	% of Organizations
1. Training of staff	36	90%
2. Benchmarking	29	72.5%
3. Enterprise agreements	17	42.5%
4. Establishing work team structure	19	47%
5. Employee participation/empowerment strategies	14	35%
6. Consultative committees	12	30%
7. Continuous improvement strategies	12	30%
8. Communication strategies, e.g., team briefing, seminars	12	30%
9. Training in communication	11	27%
10. TQM quality circles	8	20%

programs with local education providers or had established programs in partnership with them. Twenty-two percent of organizations indicated that they had implemented competency-based training programs, and 20 percent indicated that they had established training in communication as part of the process of workplace reform. This training included programs related to the English language and literacy, as well as programs for improving both interpersonal and team communication to support the greater emphasis on team-based structures. Several enterprises highlighted management-development programs as part of the workplace reform project.

From this analysis it can also be seen that almost half the participating companies identified the establishment of specific enterprise agreements as a significant part of the process, with at least 30 percent of all participating organizations using consultative committees as a further part of the process of achieving workplace reform and best practice. One profile claimed that the development of an enterprise agreement "has enabled a number of product efficiencies to be made and, in part, reflects an improvement in communication, resulting in a win-win outcomes," thereby drawing attention to the importance of communication in the process of establishing enterprise agreements.

Indications that new organizational structures and related management approaches are being adopted in participating organizations can be seen from the significant number of organizations moving from hierarchical functional structures to flatter, team-based cellular structures (47 percent) and by the number of organizations using some form of participative approach to managing, as shown through nomination of the use of formal consultative committees and employee-empowerment strategies, and participative-management and continuous-improvement structures.

A further process that seems to have played a major role in the move to best practice has been the establishing of benchmarks against which to measure improvement. Some organizations cited benchmarking against overseas companies following visits to comparable organizations by management and staff members. In other areas, the benchmarks were established within Australia.

This analysis of processes of implementing best practice nominated by participants certainly reveals a focus being given to workplace communication. This can be seen through the attention being given to various aspects of communication training as discussed earlier. It is also apparent through the establishment of structures for the purposes both of establishing more co-operative industrial relations and of establishing more participative approaches to management. The heightened attention can also be seen through the number of organizations nominating the implementation specific communication strategies as part of the program, such as team briefing, seminars, and regular newsletters.

In citing such findings it should be noted that the processes identified from the profiles in fact represent those processes that are perceived to be most significant to particular organizations. Therefore, the percentages shown may represent only minimum usage as some enterprises may have been using the processes described but failed to identify usage in their profiling statement.

OUTCOMES ACHIEVED THROUGH BEST-PRACTICE IMPLEMENTATION
This research also attempted to identify outcomes of program participation. The profile documents were not a definitive source of data for this kind of information, given that they were compiled partway through program implementation. This in fact could explain why many respondents indicate the achievement of implementation of best-practice processes as program outcomes. Such responses were not included as part of the outcomes analysis.

At the time of compiling the profiles, it would seem that considerable improvements in product/service quality had been achieved. Some of the 42.5 percent of enterprises reporting improvements in quality had received quality accreditation, according to the ASA3900 series standards which agree with ISO 9000 series quality standards.

Table 14.3   OUTCOMES ACHIEVED IN IMPLEMENTING THE BEST-PRACTICE PROGRAM

Outcomes Achieved	% of Organizations
1. Improved quality (including receiving quality accreditation)	42.5%
2. Improved work practices	42.5%
3. Increases in productivity	30%
4. Improved supplier relationships	20%
5. Improved customer satisfaction	25%
6. Improved labor relations	37.5%
7. More efficient use of capital equipment	17.5%
8. Improved safety record	17.5%
9. Increase in contacts (including export contracts)	7%

A large number of the sample reported improved workplace practices as an outcome and improved labor relations, indicating a meeting of some of the challenges posed by Deery (1990). Several organizations reported improvements both in customer and in supplier relationships, and it is interesting to note that some reported this as an outcome although they had not nominated such improvement as a major goal of their participation. A smaller number reported improvements in safety record, and several reported an improved record in winning contracts.

Other outcomes reported by a number of respondents included the establishment of benchmarks, which included not only those that were product related, but also those focusing on human-resource usage and supplier/customer satisfaction, improved work structures, and team work and improved-skills base for future development. These outcomes reflect the more specific findings of the interim evaluation.

Research conducted by Webber (1994) also confirms the increasing attention being paid to organizational communications as part of the best-practice program participation. As part of this research, Webber conducted interviews with selected best-practice enterprises. Several comments of interviewees cited by Webber reflect the significance of communication practice in the implementation of the best-practice program. For example, one respondent claimed that as a result of participation in the best-practice program, "I have been in this business for 10 years but I've heard more in the last 6 months about plant operations than in all the previous time." A second interviewee from another participating organization indicated an increase in organizational understanding as part of a program associated with the best-practice program when he reported: "Through the use of improved team skills, the implementation of the program and having a least one staff member from another area involved in team meetings, cross departmental communication and understanding improved dramatically." A further interviewee from a third enterprise argued: "An important part of the strategy for Best Practice was the improvement of communication and especially listening skills amongst all employees. The emphasis was on 'listening to understand.' It was soon found that some supervisors found it very difficult to listen to shopfloor people have their say." This sample of interview comments mirrors the tenor in many of the profile documents supplied as part of the best-practice program.

OTHER BEST-PRACTICE EVALUATION A further study of Best Manufacturing Practice in Australia and New Zealand completed in 1994 for the Australian Manufacturing Council also sheds further light of the nature of best practice and the impact of such practices in manufacturing sector. This study examined practice in 1,400 manufacturing sites in Australian and New Zealand (including some of the Best-Practice Demonstration program participants) and then focused on the differences in achievement and practice between the top 20 percent (leaders) and the bottom 20 percent (laggers) to identify characteristics of each category. This study found that while no identifiable hierarchy of practices can be recommended to a firm wanting to pursue best practice and that there is no fixed sequence of steps likely to lead to success, a range of elements can be seen as important to change practices in organizations (iv–v).

The following elements were shown from this study to separate leaders from laggers in best practice.

1. Transformation of adversarial approach to a cooperative approach in employee relations. Having fewer numbers of unions on the one site would seem to be one dimension of creating a co-operative working environment. This study showed that leading manufacturing enterprises had fewer unions on-site than laggers. The study also found, through site visits, that while leaders were no more likely than laggers to enter into enterprise-based agreements (EBA), that "successfully negotiated EBA can consolidate or advance the change process." The study also reported that an EBA is less likely to assist in the pursuit of best practice when used to initiate or drive the change process. An enterprise agreement is unlikely to be successful if the essential ingredients for co-operation—open, honest communication and trust—are not there (27).

2. Aspects of people practice. These characterizing more leading manufacturers than laggers included effective top-down and bottom-up communication; self-managing and/or other work teams contributing to factory operations; employee satisfaction regularly measured; organization-wide training and development processes, including career-path planning; employee flexibility, multiskilling, and training are used; excellent occupational health and safety practices; and concepts of the internal customer are well understood. The

salience of communication as the underpinning element of good people practices in best-practice organizations is highlighted in the report by the argument:

> Effective communication underpins excellent people practices. This can be achieved through formal structures such as consultative committees regular meetings, employee newsletters or representational and cross functional teams undertaking activities such as benchmarking and problem solving. It may also be achieved through senior management being highly visible, through an active staff suggestion scheme or through social events and celebrations of achievement at the site. A spirit of trust commitment and cooperation is both assisted by and assists top-down and bottom-up communication. The study shows that leaders are better than laggers in this area. (30)

The study also showed that leading organizations were making a conscious move to a flatter organizational structure and to team-based approaches even though this movement was less pronounced in the Australian and New Zealand group than in an international comparison group. Commitment to training and development processes was also a feature of more leading best-practice organizations as were good occupational health and safety practices.

One of the most significant differentiators between the leaders and the laggers concerned leadership practice. Dimensions of organizational leadership that emerged as part of the mix of best-practice leadership included: senior managers actively encourage change and implement a culture of trust, involvement, and commitment; they show a high degree of unity of purpose; they act as champions of change; they proactively pursue continuous improvement rather than reacting to crisis/firefighting; and they actively use ideas from production operators in assisting management (37).

3. Benchmarking. While this study showed that benchmarking is the single practice that most clearly separated the leaders from the laggers it also revealed that the concept is far from uniformly understood. Some findings about benchmarking practice include the failure of organizations to translate their findings toward establishing improvement,

simplistic approaches to benchmarking using a simple ad hoc approach, or using a system that lacked integration; that Australia and Zealand are most likely to benchmark against sites in the same industry overseas focusing on operating processes and quality procedures, and that only half of the leaders from this study benchmark on human-resource utilisation.

4. Customer focus. The survey indicated a widespread and keen awareness of the importance of customer focus in sustaining competitiveness. Leaders showed a significant edge in disseminating customer requirements to workers and in completing systematic customer-satisfaction measurement and utilizing customer complaints for internal process improvement. Interestingly, the study reported a far less strenuous effort being committed to improving supplier relationships. The report comments: "The relatively low degree of supplier integration revealed by the survey suggests that this may be a largely untapped but vitally important source of competitive advantage for Australia and New Zealand manufacturers" (53).

5. Quality processes are also reported as being well established more frequently in leading best-practice organizations. Significantly, more leaders report standardizing and documenting operating procedures. Further, leaders have had much more success than laggers in instilling in their employees the belief that quality is ultimately an individual responsibility. The survey showed that while quality accreditation was an issue for many respondents, leaders were somewhat more likely to be certified than laggers and that leading sites tended to set themselves quality standards well above the minimum standards prescribed for certification and then continually seek to improve all facets of the operation.

6. The use of newer technology was viewed as more positively contributing to increased competitiveness by leaders. The report concludes that it is clear that advanced technology cannot be viewed as panacea and that its introduction needs to be planned, coordinated, and implemented with other key elements of best manufacturing practices, for example, people practice.

7. Manufacturing strategy. The final element addressed in the report concerns manufacturing strategy. More leaders in

Australia reported clearly articulated mission statements that were supported by employees and comprehensive short- and long-term goals set through structured planning processes. Ninety percent of leaders reported incorporating the concerns and requirements of customers, suppliers, and other stakeholders, including the community, compared with 50 percent of the laggers.

This report suggests that people practices, benchmarking, and leadership are the three elements that most significantly differentiate leaders from laggers. Thus from this study, as in previously discussed studies, there is evidence that among leading best-practice organizations certain sets of behaviors or processes are leading to a greater achievement of desired outcomes.

From each of the sources of data, it becomes obvious that there is evidence of more cooperative workplace climates being established in a bid to achieve marketplace competitiveness through processes such as enterprise agreements, consultative committees, or other communications strategies. There is also evidence of new approaches to management through use of self-managing teams in place of hierarchical, structured divisions; greater consultation by managers of employee opportunities to be part of quality teams; and an increased focus on skill formation, which has included provision for communication training to enable fuller participation in the new organizational structure.

The words of Richard Warburton (1994:10) well summarize the achievements that are occurring as we emerge from the recession following a best-practice pathway:

> As the Australian economy becomes increasingly integrated into the global market, Australian enterprises must become internationally competitive. Enterprises that have acted on this new-found knowledge are succeeding and have changed the way they operate in their quest to be better than best. From the time it was established in 1991 this program has guided Australian companies along the path to achieving international Best Practice. Three years down the track the program is reporting measurable results that are helping many of the 43 participating companies to be internationally competitive. Seventy percent of the Best Practice enterprises report significant productivity gains, 86% say that they have improvements in management-employee relations; 63% point to greater

organisational flexibility and 56% have reached new partnerships with suppliers and customers.

By any standards this is a quantum leap forward.

Conclusion

The position advanced in this chapter is that Australian enterprises (particularly those following best-practice programs) are beginning to play by new rules using new skills. Key stakeholders in organizational life, including government, unions, managers, employers, customers, and suppliers are to varying degrees influencing the development of new workplace practices and a new workplace climate. Australian governments through interventionist approaches to skill formation and industrial relations reform are helping to embed the changing practices. The union movement, through new approaches to their own structure and acceptance of new wage-fixing arrangements and participation in new consultative processes within organizations, are facilitating the movement. Such changes in these various streams of organizational life could be seen as converging as they come into fruition. At the center of this convergence is the new focus and attention falling on the broad area of organizational communication practice. Thus in the new climate, with its greater attention to the process of communication, we are seeing the achievement of positive outcomes for many Australian organizations as they emerge from the recession. The questions now remain whether the momentum of such changes can be maintained and extended to other Australian enterprises and whether that momentum can be sufficiently powerful to allow Australia to regain a more pre-eminent position in a turbulent global marketplace where the best practice goals are continuously being raised.

References

Chapter 2: Lessons in Mass Media Depiction of Economic Conditions during a Recession

Behr, R. L. and Shanto, I. (1985). Television news, real-world cues, and change in the public agenda, *Public Opinion Quarterly,* 49: 38–57.

Bethell, T. (November 30, 1992). Now they tell us, *National Review,* 24–25.

Bodnar, J. (December 1989). How TV sees the economy, *Changing Times,* 89–93.

Business Week. (October 18, 1982). Business thinks TV distorts its image, 26.

Case, T. (June 4, 1994). Corporate liars and unfair business coverage, *Editor & Publisher,* 14–15.

Crossen, C. (1994). *Tainted Truth: The Manipulation of Fact in America.* New York: Simon & Schuster.

Easterbrook, G. (August 21, 1989). The sky is always falling, *The New Republic,* 21–25.

The Economist. (October 24, 1992). Recession or doom? 13–14.

Epstein, E. J. (1973). *News from Nowhere.* New York: Random House.

Evans, F. J. (Winter, 1984). Business and the press: Conflicts over roles, fairness. *Public Relations Review,* 10/4, 33–42.

Fasbinder, J. (October 1987). Do business reporters know their beat? *Public Relations Journal,* 43/10, 14.

Gergen, D. (January 13, 1992). Is the press to blame? *U.S. News & World Report,* 54.

Gersh, D. (January 23, 1993). Economic news still closely read, *Editor & Publisher,* 1, 31.

Harrington, D. E. (Spring, 1989). Economic news on television, *Public Opinion Quarterly,* 53(1): 17–40.

Kaplan, B. D. (June 20, 1993). Americans' view of the economy distorted, *Richmond Times-Dispatch,* A4.

Koretz, G. (October 19, 1992). Voters may have a jaundiced view of the economy, *Business Week,* 22.

Labate, J. (March 23, 1992). Bad news hurts too, *Fortune,* 26.

Ladd, E. C. (November–December, 1992). The U.S. economy: Key data, *The Public Perspective,* 4(1): 22–27.

———. (January–February, 1993). The 1992 election's complex message, *The American Enterprise,* 4(1): 45–51.

Lichter, S. R., and Noyes, R. E. (1995). *Good Intentions Make Bad News.* Lanham: Rowman and Littlefield.

Lichter, S. R., Rothman, S., and Lichter, L. S. (1986). *The Media Elite.* Bethesda: Adler & Adler.

Lichter, S. R., and Smith, T. J. III. (1993). Bad news bears, *Forbes Media Critic,* 1/1, 81–87.

Lipset, S. M. (March 1993). The significance of the 1992 election, *PS: Political Science & Politics,* 7–10.

Mutz, D. (November–December, 1992). Impersonal influence in American politics, *The Public Perspective,* 4(1): 19–21.

Newsweek. (October 29, 1994). *Newsweek* poll: Republicans retain marginal edge over Democrats. News release, mimeo.

Patterson, T. E. (1993). *Out of Order.* New York: Alfred A. Knopf.

Pines, B. Y., with Lamer, T. W. (1994). *Out of Focus.* Washington: Regnery Publishing.

Price, C. (Summer, 1994). The media and the economy, *Cross Sections,* 11(2): 1–4.

Public Relations Journal. (June, 1989). CEOs rate business coverage, 43/6, 14–15.

Reynolds, A. (March–April, 1993). Persistent misreading of U.S. economic performance, *The Public Perspective,* 4(3): 16–18.

Sanders, D., Marsh, D., and Ward, H. (April, 1993). The electoral impact of press coverage of the British economy, 1979–87, *British Journal of Political Science,* 23: 175–210.

Sethi, S. P. (Summer, 1977). The schism between business and American news media, *Journalism Quarterly,* 54(2): 240–47.

Smith, T. J. III. (April, 1988a). Journalism and the Socrates syndrome, *The Quill,* 78(4): 14–20.

———. (1988b). *Moscow Meets Main Street.* Washington: The Media Institute.

———. (1988c). *The Vanishing Economy: Television Coverage of Economic Affairs 1982–1987.* Washington: The Media Institute.

———. (January, 1990). The watchdog's bite. *The American Enterprise,* 1(1): 62–70.

———. (December, 1992). Are we betraying the public trust? *RTNDA Communicator,* 30.

Tuchman, G. (1978). *Making News: A Study in Construction of Reality.* New York, Free Press.

Weaver, P. H. (July, 1984). The networks vs. the recovery. *Commentary,* 35–40.

———. (1994). *News and the Culture of Lying.* New York: Free Press.

Winship, T. (February 1, 1992). Lean even heavier on business news, *Editor & Publisher,* 5.

Wood, W. C. (Winter, 1985). The educational potential of news coverage of economics, *Journal of Economic Education,* 27–35.

Chapter 3: Lessons from Benchmarking Downsizing in IBM

Altany, D. (November 5, 1990). Copycats, *Industry Week,* 11–18.

Baumohl, B. (March 15, 1993). When downsizing becomes dumbsizing, *Time,* 55.

Buck Consultants (July 26, 1988). *Wall Street Journal,* A1.

Business Week (April 24, 1995). Gerstner goes into warp drive, 6.

Byrne, J. A. (May 9, 1994). The pain of downsizing, *Business Week,* 60–69.

Cameron, K. S. (Summer 1994). Strategies for successful organizational downsizing, *Human Resource Management,* 33:189–211.

Cameron, K. S., Freeman, S. J., and Mishra, A. K. (1991). Best practices in white-collar downsizing: Managing contradictions, *Academy of Management Executive,* 5:57–73.

Cascio, W. (1993). Downsizing: What do we know? What have we learned? *Academy of Management Executive,* 7:95–104.

———. (February 1994). The cost of downsizing, *HRMonthly,* 8–13.

Cortese, A. (June 6, 1994). IBM rides into microsoft country, *Business Week,* 111–112.

Cushman, D. P. and King, S. S. (March 13, 1995). High performance organizations? *Internal Communication Focus,* 62–64.

The Economist (April 18, 1995). Still twitching, 56–57.

Eng, P., and Lewyn, M. (February 7, 1994). IBM leans on its sales force, *Business Week,* 110–111.

Fisher, A. B. (May 23, 1988). The downside of downsizing, *Fortune,* 42–53.

Fortune (April 19, 1993). The Fortune 500, 175–278.

———. (April 17, 1995). How's business? Leadership lost—and regained, 217–218.

Hardy, E. S. (April 24, 1995). The Forbes 500s annual directory, *Forbes,* 208–380.

Hays, L. (April 26, 1995). IBM is "gathering momentum," Gerstner says at annual meeting, *Wall Street Journal,* B6.

Hays, L., and Ziegler, B. (April 28, 1995). Warning Signs: Dependence on Big Iron raises query on IBM: Will hot streak last? *Wall Street Journal,* A1, A7.

Henkoff, R. (April 9, 1990). Cost cutting: How to do it right, *Fortune,* 40–49.

Hitt, M. A., Keats, B. W., Harback, H. F., and Nixon, R. D. (1994). Rightsizing: Building and maintaining strategic leadership and long-term competitiveness, *Organizational Dynamics,* 18–32.

Jacob, R. (May 18, 1992). The search for the organization of tomorrow, *Fortune 2*, 91–98.

Jennings, K., and Westfall, F. (1992). Benchmarking for strategic action, *Journal of Business Strategy*, 22–25.

Kirkpatrick, D. (September 19, 1994). What's driving the new PC shakeout, *Fortune*, 109–122.

Larkin, T. J., and Larkin, S. (1994). *Communicating Change: How to Win Employee Support for New Business Directions*. N.Y.: McGraw-Hill, Inc.

McMenamin, B. (March 14, 1994). What kind of duck are you? *Forbes*, 126–128.

Merlo, V. (1995). Observational study of internship experience: International Business Machines Corporation, Tucson, Arizona. Unpublished M.A. project, State University of New York—Albany, New York.

Murray, M. (May 4, 1995). Thanks, goodbye: Amid record profits, companies continue to lay off employees, *Wall Street Journal*, A1, A6.

Port, O., Cary, J., Kelley, K. and Forest. A. (November 30, 1992). Quality, *Business Week*, 66–72.

Robotham, J. (January 18, 1994). Big Blue leaves others in its wake, *The Australian*, 25.

Sagar, I. (May 30, 1994). The few, the true, the blue, *Business Week*, 124–126.

———. (January 30, 1995). IBM's parallel power rangers, *Business Week*, 81–82.

———. (May 1, 1995). "We won't stop . . . until we find our way back," *Business Week*, 116–120.

Sagar, I., and Cortese, A. (April 4, 1994). Lou Gerstner unveils his battle plan, *Business Week*, 96–98.

———. (January 23, 1995). IBM: Why the good news isn't good enough, *Business Week*, 42–43.

Sagar, I., McWilliams, G., and Hof, R. D. (February 7, 1994). IBM leans on its sales force, *Business Week*, 110–111.

Schweiger, D., and Denisi, A. (1991). Communication with employees following a merger: A longitudinal field experiment, *Academy of Management Journal,* 34:110–135.

Sherman, S. (October 3, 1994). Is he too cautious to save IBM? *Fortune,* 78–90.

Shetty, Y. K. (1993). Aiming high: Competitive benchmarking for superior performance, *Long Range Planning,* 25:39–44.

Tadjbachsh, S. (1991). Conflict during downsizing at IBM advanced workstations division, Kingston, New York. Unpublished M.A. project, State University of New York—Albany, New York.

Tungate, M. (1990). Corporate cultures at IBM: The changing tide. Unpublished M.A. project, State University of New York—Albany, New York.

Wall Street Journal (May 3, 1995). IBM software to aid big firms managing remote PC networks, B4.

Weatherly, J. D. (September 1992), Dare to compare for better productivity, *HRMagazine,* 42–46.

Ziegler, B. (February 7, 1995). IBM's O'Malley resigns post at PC division, *Wall Street Journal,* B8.

———. (February 22, 1995). IBM tries, and fails, to fix PC business, *Wall Street Journal,* B1, B6.

———. (April 21, 1995). IBM's earnings climbed sharply in first quarter, *Wall Street Journal,* A3.

Chapter 4: Lessons from Leading Organizational Turnaround at IBM

Altany, D. (November 5, 1990). Copycats, *Industry Week,* 11–18.

Baumohl, B. (March 15, 1993). When downsizing becomes dumbsizing, *Time,* 55.

Bloomberg, F. (May 8, 1995). Company to buy computer service from GE, *Wall Street Journal,* B6.

Buck Consultants (July 26, 1988). *Wall Street Journal,* A1.

Business Week (April 24, 1995). Gerstner goes into warp drive, 6.

Byrne, J. A. (May 9, 1994). The pain of downsizing, *Business Week,* 60–69.

Cameron, K. S. (Summer 1994). Strategies for successful organizational downsizing, *Human Resource Management,* 33:189–211.

Cameron, K. S., Freeman, S. J., and Mishra, A. K. (1991). Best practices in white-collar downsizing: Managing contradictions, *Academy of Management Executive,* 5:57–73.

Carlton, J. (March 22, 1995). Shipments of workstation computers increased 25% world-wide in 1994, *Wall Street Journal,* B6.

Cascio, W. (1993). Downsizing: what do we know? What have we learned? *Academy of Management Executive,* 7:95–104.

———. (February 1994). The cost of downsizing, *HRMonthly,* 8–13.

Cortese, A. (June 6, 1994). IBM rides into microsoft country, *Business Week,* 111–112.

Cushman, D. P., and King, S. S. (March 13, 1995). High performance organizations? *Internal Communication Focus,* 62–64.

The Economist (April 18, 1995). Still twitching, 56–57.

Eng, P. and Lewyn, M. (February 7, 1994). IBM leans on its sales force, *Business Week,* 110–111.

Fisher, A. B. (May 23, 1988). The downside of downsizing, *Fortune,* 42–53.

Fortune (April 19, 1993). The Fortune 500, 175–278.

———. (April 17, 1995). How's business? Leadership lost—and regained, 217–218.

Hardy, E. S. (April 24, 1995). The Forbes 500s annual directory, *Forbes,* 208–380.

Hays, L. (April 26, 1995). IBM is "gathering momentum," Gerstner says at annual meeting, *Wall Street Journal,* B6.

Hays, L., and Ziegler, B. (April 28, 1995). Warning Signs: Dependence on Big Iron raises query on IBM: Will hot streak last? *Wall Street Journal,* A1, A7.

Henkoff, R. (April 9, 1990). Cost cutting: How to do it right, *Fortune,* 40–49.

Hill, G. C. (May 1, 1995). Packard Bell led the U.S. PC market in first quarter: IBM bouncing back, *Wall Street Journal,* B4.

Hitt, M. A., Keats, B. W., Harback, H. F., and Nixon, R. D. (1994). Rightsizing: Building and maintaining strategic leadership and long-term competitiveness, *Organizational Dynamics,* 18–32.

Huey, J. (February 21, 1994). The new post-heroic leadership, *Fortune,* 42–50.

International Business Machines (May 8, 1995). Company to buy computer services business from GE, B4.

Jennings, K., and Westfall, F. (1992). Benchmarking for strategic action, *Journal of Business Strategy,* 22–25.

Kirkpatrick, D. (September 19, 1994). What's driving the new PC shakeout, *Fortune,* 109–122.

Larkin, T. J., and Larkin, S. (1994). *Communicating Change: Reaching and Changing Frontline Employees.* Adapted from *Communicating Change: Winning Employee Support for New Business Goals.* N.Y.: McGraw-Hill, Inc.

McCartney, S. (May 8, 1995). Compaq seeks to join U.S. computer industry's elite, *Wall Street Journal,* B4.

McMenamin, B. (March 14, 1994). What kind of duck are you? *Forbes,* 126–128.

Merlo, V. (1995). Observational study of internship experience: International Business Machines Corporation, Tucson, Arizona. Unpublished M.A. project, State University of New York—Albany, New York.

Moore, A. H. (April 17, 1995). Leadership lost—and regained, *Fortune,* 217–218.

Mossberg, W. S. (February 21, 1995). IBM's Butterfly emerges as a gem of a tiny computer, *Wall Street Journal,* B1.

Murray, M. (May 4, 1995). Thanks, goodbye: Amid record profits, companies continue to lay off employees, *Wall Street Journal,* A1, A6.

New York Times (May 6, 1995). Purchase of a GE Capital computer unit set, 37.

Panettieri, J. C. (March 27, 1995). Like a gale force, *Information Week,* 46–56.

Pope, K. (May 12, 1995). Europe's PC business increased 28.2% in 1st period, outpacing U.S. growth, *Wall Street Journal,* B2.

Robotham, J. (January 18, 1994). Big Blue leaves others in its wake, *The Australian*, 25.

Sagar, I. (May 30, 1994). The few, the true, the blue, *Business Week*, 124–126.

———. (January 30, 1995). IBM's parallel power rangers, *Business Week*, 81–82.

———. (May 1, 1995). "We won't stop . . . until we find our way back," *Business Week*, 116–120.

Sagar, I., and Cortese, A. (April 4, 1994). Lou Gerstner unveils his battle plan, *Business Week*, 96–98.

———. (January 23, 1995). IBM: Why the good news isn't good enough, *Business Week*, 42–43.

Sagar, I., McWilliams, G., and Hof, R. D. (February 7, 1994). IBM leans on its sales force, *Business Week*, 110–111.

Schweiger, D., and Denisi, A. (1991). Communication with employees following a merger: A longitudinal field experiment, *Academy of Management Journal*, 34:110–135.

Sherman, S. (October 3, 1994). Is he too cautious to save IBM? *Fortune*, 78–90.

Shetty, Y. K. (1993). Aiming high: Competitive benchmarking for superior performance, *Long Range Planning*, 25:39–44.

Stedman, C. (December 12, 1994). IBM romances Unix developers, *Computer World*, 1, 121.

Stewart, T. A. (December 13, 1993). Welcome to the revolution, *Fortune*, 66–76.

Tadjbachsh, S. (1991). Conflict during downsizing at IBM advanced workstations division, Kingston, New York. Unpublished M.A. project, State University of New York—Albany, New York.

Tungate, M. (1990). Corporate cultures at IBM: The changing tide. Unpublished M.A. project, State University of New York—Albany, New York.

Wall Street Journal (May 3, 1995). IBM software to aid big firms managing remote PC networks, B4.

Weatherly, J. D. (September 1992), Dare to compare for better productivity, *HRMagazine*, 42–46.

Ziegler, B. (February 7, 1995). IBM's O'Malley resigns post at PC division, *Wall Street Journal*, B8.

———. (February 22, 1995). IBM tries, and fails, to fix PC business, *Wall Street Journal*, B1, B6.

———. (March 6, 1995). Can Butterfly help IBM fly higher? *Wall Street Journal*, B1.

———. (April 21, 1995). IBM's earnings climbed sharply in first quarter, *Wall Street Journal*, A3.

Zuckerman, L. (March 23, 1995). I.B.M. to introduce new computers (Hold the OS/2, please), *New York Times*, D3.

Chapter 5: Lessons in Governmental Budgeting during Recession in the United States

Bay State Skills Corporation. (1986). *The Bay State Skills Corporation: 1981–1986, Evolution and Innovation*. Boston, Massachusetts.

Blaustein, S. J. (1982). UI fund insolvency and debt in Michigan, *The Michigan Economy*, 1:1–8.

Brazer, H. E. (1982). Anatomy of a fiscal crisis: The Michigan case. *Public Budgeting and Finance*, 2:130–142.

Brazer, H. E. and Laren. D. S., eds. (1982). *Michigan's Fiscal and Economic Structure*. Ann Arbor: University of Michigan Press.

Bryan, T. and Howard, D. (1979). Michigan's budget and economic stabilization fund, *Innovations*. Lexington, Ky.: The Council of State Governments, 1–11.

Citizens Research Council of Michigan. (1983). The state fiscal plan, *Council Comments*, 941.

Comparative State Politics Newsletter. (March 1981) 2/2.

Davis, O., Dempster, M. A. H., and Wildavsky, A. (1966). A theory of the budgetary process, *American Political Science Review*, 60(3): 529–547.

Davis, O. A., Dempster, M. A. H., and Wildavsky, A. (1974). Toward a predictive theory of government expenditures: U.S. domestic appropriations. *British Journal of Political Science*, 4/4:419–452.

Gold, S. D., and Ritchie, S. (1993). State policies affecting cities and counties in 1992, *Public Budgeting and Finance,* 13(1):3–18.

Gorwitz, K. (February 4, 1983a). Michigan Population Trends. East Lansing, Michigan: Public Sector Consultants.

———. (March 22, 1983b). East Lansing, Mich.: Public Sector Consultants.

———. (September 1982). Michigan's Current and Projected Population Trends. East Lansing, MI: Public Sector Consultants.

Heckman, J. C. (July 29, 1981b). Budget cutting techniques. Paper presented to the National Conference of State Legislatures, Atlanta, Georgia.

———. (May 11, 1983). Management in a declining economy. Speech prepared for presentation to employees of the State of Michigan.

———. (December 8, 1981a) Michigan's budget reduction experiences. Paper presented to the House Appropriations Committee, State of Maryland.

Hollister, D. (1983a). Michigan's current economic crisis. *Report No. 5.* Lansing: State House of Representatives. February 1983.

———. (1983b). Michigan's current economic crisis. *Report No. 6.* Lansing: State House of Representatives. December 1983.

Hoole, F. W., Handley, D. H., and Ostrom, C. W. (1979). Policy-making models, budgets and international organizations, *Journal of Politics,* 41:923–932.

House, A. (1981). Managing more with less—The public administrator's role in an era of cutbacks. Panel discussion for the Michigan Capital Area Chapter of the American Society for Public Administration, November 18, 1981.

Knott, J. H., and Langley, R. E. (1993). Economic change, tax revenues and budget discretion in state government. Paper presented to the annual national meeting of the American Society for Public Administration.

Lane, H. U. (ed.) (1984). *The World Almanac and Book of Facts, 1985.* New York: Newspaper Enterprise Association, Inc.

Lijphart, A. (1971). Comparative politics and the comparative method, *American Political Science Review,* 65(2):682–693.

Morris, S. R. (1979). *The Legislative Process in Michigan.* Hillsdale, Mich.: Hillsdale Publishers.

Morris, S. R. and Brierly, A. (1991). Testing fair shares in retrenchment. Paper presented at the American Society for Public Administration national conference, Washington, D.C., March 26, 1991.

———. (1990). Budget outcomes in cutback management. Paper presented at the American Society for Public Administration national conference. Los Angeles, April 10, 1990 (with Allen Brierly).

———. (1991). Testing fair shares in retrenchment. Paper presented at the American Society for Public Administration national conference, Washington, D.C., March 26, 1991 (with Allen Brierly).

Mowbray, C. T., Tableman, B., and Gould, R. (1984). Reduction in force: A summary and analysis of one state agency's experience, *New England Journal of Human Services,* 24–33.

Nagel, S. (1980). Series editor's introduction. In *Fiscal Stress and Public Policy,* ed. Charles Levine and Irene Rubin, 8–10. Beverly Hills: Sage.

Natchez, P. B. and Bupp, I. C. (1973). Policy and priority in the budgetary process, *American Political Science Review,* 67(3):951–963.

Osborne, D. (1990). *Laboratories of Democracy.* Cambridge, Mass.: Harvard University Press.

Press, C., and VerBurg, K. (1983). *State and Community Governments in the Federal System* (2nd ed.). New York: Wiley.

Public Sector Conultants, Inc. (1991). Managing state employee displacement. Report prepared for the Michigan Department of Civil Service. Lansing, Mich.: Public Sector Consultants.

Rosen, L. S. and Wang, C.-L. (1983). Michigan. *American Demographics* 15:46–48.

Savage, D. (1992). California's structural deficit crisis, *Public Budgeting and Finance,* 12(2):82–97.

Schick, A. (1980). "Budgetary Adaptations to Resource Scarcity." In *Fiscal Stress and Public Policy,* ed. Charles H. Levine and Irene Rubin. 113–134. Beverly Hills: Sage.

————. (1988). Micro-budgeting adaptations to fiscal stress in industrialized democracies, *Public Administration Review* 48(1):523–533.

The State Journal. Lansing, Michigan. Issues of October 30, 1976, September 30, 1981.

State of Michigan. Hollister, David. (1981–1983). Michigan's current economic crisis. Reports No. 1–6. Lansing: State House of Representatives, February 1981, September 1981, April 1982, October 1982, February 1983, and December 1983.

————. House Taxation Committee. (1983). *The Michigan State Budget: Background and Current Issues.* Lansing: State House of Representatives, February 2, 1983.

State of New York. (1986). *New York State Assembly Program Development Group, Economic Growth and Revitalization,* April 1986.

Wildavsky, A. (1975). *Budgeting: A Comparative Theory of Budgetary Processes.* Boston: Little, Brown.

Wooldridge, B. (1984). Exemplary practices in local financial management: An international perspective, *Public Administration Review,* 44(2):153–161.

Yondorf, B., and Summers, B. J. (1983). *Legislative Budget Procedures in the 50 States.* Legislative Finance Paper No. 21. Denver: National Conference of State Legislatures.

Chapter 6: Lessons for Entirement: Strategies and Skills for Self-Management, Lifelong Development

Aubrey, R., and Cohen, P. M. (1995). *Working Wisdom: Timeless Strategies and Vanguard Strategies for Learning Organizations.* San Francisco: Jossey-Bass.

Berger, K. (1991). *The Developing Person through the Life Span* (3rd ed.). New York: Worth.

Brazelton, T. B. (1992). *Touchpoints.* New York: Addison-Wesley.

Carroll, A. (1994). *Golden Opportunities: A Volunteer Guide for Americans over 50.* Princeton, N.J.: Peterson's.

312   REFERENCES TO CHAPTER 6

Cooley, C. (1902). *Human Nature and the Social Order.* New York: Scribner's.

Csikszentmihalyi, M. (1990). *Flow: The Psychology of Optimal Experience.* New York: Harper & Row.

————. (1993). *The Evolving Self: A Psychology for the Third Millennium.* New York: HarperCollins.

Cushman, D. P., and King, S. S. (1995). *Communication and High-Speed Management.* Albany: State University of New York Press.

Drucker, P. (November 1994). The age of social transformation. *Atlantic Monthly,* 274(5): 53–80.

Erikson, E. H. (1950). *Childhood and society.* New York: Norton.

————. (1987). *A way of looking at things: Selected papers from 1930 to 1980,* S. Schein, ed. New York: Norton.

Flavell, J. H. (1985). *Cognitive development* (2nd ed.). Englewood Cliffs, N.J.: Prentice-Hall.

Freud, S. (1905/1976). Three essays on the theory of sexuality. In J. Strachey (ed. and trans.), *The Standard Edition of the Complete Works of Sigmund Freud* (Vol. 7). London: Hogarth Press. (Original work published 1905.)

Goleman, D. (March 7, 1995). 75 years later, still tracking geniuses, *New York Times.*

Handy, C. (1995). *The empty raincoat: Making sense of the future.* London: Arrow.

Harrison, R. P. (1996). *Entirement: Personal involvement in lifelong development.* Manuscript in preparation. (Available from POB 22541, San Francisco, CA. 94122–0541.)

Kohlberg, L. (1984). *Essays on moral development: Vol. 2. The psychology of moral development.* San Francisco: Harper & Row.

Kubler-Ross, E. (1969). *On death and dying.* New York: Macmillan.

Levinson, D. (1978). *The seasons of a man's life.* New York: Knopf.

————. (1986). A concept of adult development. *American Psychologist,* 41:3–13.

Mead, G. H. (1934). *Mind, self, and society.* Chicago: University of Chicago Press.

Merlin, D. (1991). *Origins of the modern mind: Three stages in the evolution of culture and cognition.* Cambridge, MA: Harvard University Press.

Neugarten, B. (1979). Time, age, and the life cycle. *American Journal of Psychiatry,* 136:887–894.

————. (1987). The changing meaning of age. *Psychology Today,* 21(5):29–33.

Ornstein, R. (1993). *The roots of the self: Unraveling the mystery of who we are.* San Francisco: Harper.

Ornstein, R., and Ehrlich, P. (1989). *New world, new mind: Moving toward conscious evolution.* New York: Doubleday.

Piaget, J. (1977). *The development of thought: Equilibrium of cognitive structures.* New York: Viking Press.

Resnick, B. (1987). *Education and Learning to Think.* Washington, D.C.: National Academy Press.

Rifkin, J. (1995). *The end of work: The decline of the global labor force and the dawn of the post-market era.* Los Angeles: Jeremy P. Tarcher/Putnam.

Rosenfeld, A., and Stark, E. (1987). The prime of our lives. *Psychology Today,* 21(5):62–72.

Sakaiya, T. (1991). *The knowledge-value revolution.* Tokyo: Kodansha.

Schaie, K. W., and Willis, S. L. (1990). *Adult development and aging* (3rd ed.). New York: HarperCollins

Schein, E. H. (1978). *Career dynamics: Matching individual and organizational needs.* Reading, Mass.: Addison-Wesley.

Seligman, M. E. P. (1993). *What you can change and what you can't.* New York: Knopf.

Sheehy, G. (1995). *New passages: Mapping your life across time.* New York: Random House.

Sternberg, R. J. (1989). *The triachic mind: A new theory of human intelligence.* New York: Penguin.

Tennant, M., and Pogson, P. (1995). *Learning and Change in Adult Years: A Developmental Perspective.* San Francisco: Jossey-Bass.

Tichy, N. M., and Sherman, S. (1993). *Control your destiny or someone else will.* New York: Doubleday.

Toffler, A. (1970). *Future shock.* New York: Random House.

———. (1980). *The third wave.* New York: Wm Morrow.

Chapter 7: Lessons from Rethinking High-Speed Management: Successful Adaptation of American Theory to an European Company

Costa, G. (1994). La Svolta Formativa. Un'offerta da Aggiornare per il "Management Snello," *L'Impresa,* 73:44–63.

Cushman, D., and King, S. (1992). *High-Speed Management: Organizational Communication in the 1990's.* An early version of the 1995 publication by SUNY Press.

———. (1993). *High-Speed Management and Organizational Communication in the 1990s: A Reader.* Albany, N.Y.: State University of New York Press.

———. (1995). *Communication and High Speed Management.* Albany, N.Y.: State University of New York Press.

Dioguardi, G. (1993). Nell'Impresa Multicellulare Cresce il Ruolo dell' Innovatore, *L'Impresa,* 93:12–19.

Mariotti, S. (1994). Produzione Snella e Soluzioni Flessibili per il Manufacturing, *L'Impresa,* 11:111–122.

Simoncini, G. (1974). *Città' e Societa' nel Rinascimento.* Torino, Italy: Einaudi.

Chapter 8: Lessons in Communicating Change in Transition: Some Dilemmas and Strategic Choices

Chelminski, D., Czynczyk, A., and Sterniczuk, H. (1994). New forms of state ownership in Poland. In *A Fourth Way? Privatization, Property, and the Emergence of New Market Economies,* ed. Gregory S. Alexander and Grazyna Skłpska. New York, London: Routledge.

Cushman, D. P., and King, S. S. (1995). *Communication and High Speed*

Management. Albany, N.Y.: State University of New York Press.

Czynczyk, A. (April, 1991). Privatization in Poland: Politics, society and the law, *Law and Policy,* 13(2).

Fortune, Global 500 (1994).

Johnson, S., and Loveman, G. (March–April, 1995). Starting over: Poland after communism, *Harvard Business Review,* 44–56.

Kerr, S., and Jarmier, J. M. (1978). Substitutes for leadership: Their meaning and measurement, *Organizational Behavior and Human Performance,* 22:375–403.

Larkin, T. J., and Larkin, S. (1994). *Communicating Change: How to Win Employee Support for New Business Goals.* New York, London: McGraw Hill.

MacDougall, R. C. (1992). The data precedes hypothesis approach to scientific investigation. Unpublished paper.

————. (1995). Competitive benchmarking and the incongruent corporate culture: Accurate prescriptions and unlikely cures (a case study). In *Benchmarking Organizational Communication Processes,* ed. Branislav Kovacic, Albany, N.Y.: State University of New York Press.

Weaver, R. (1964). *Visions of Order: The Cultural Crisis of Our Time.* Baton Rouge: Louisiana State University Press.

Chapter 9: Lessons from Recession in Central and Eastern Europe: From Survival to Continuous Improvement

Abell, D. (1992). *Turnaround in Eastern Europe: In Depth Studies.* New York: United Nations Development Programme.

Boycko, M., Shleifer, A., and Vishny, R. (1995). *Privatizing Russia* Cambridge, Mass., London: The MIT Press.

Burawoy, M., and Hendley, K. (1992). Between "Perestroika" and privatisation: divided strategies and political crisis in a soviet enterprise, *Soviet Studies,* 44(3):371–402.

Business Strategy (1993). Purchasing a plant in Poland, An interview with C. Cato Ealy, 14(2):38–45.

Czynczyk, A., Dahlberg, O., and Iggland, B. (1995). Enterprise restructuring: Rationalization by means of non-core activity reduction. Paper presented at Annual Conference of CECIOS, Warsaw, Poland.

Filipovic, N., and Baleanu, C. (1994). Colgate-Palmolive Rumania SRL—Case study. Brdo pri Kranju, Slovenia: International Executive Development Center.

Greenhouse, S. (December 16, 1990). General Electric running on fast forward in Budapest, *New York Times,* 7–8.

Intrilligator, M. D. (1995). Privatization in Russia has led to criminalization, *Australian Economic Review,* 1.

Johnson, S., Kotchen, D. T., and Loveman, G. (November–December 1995). How one Polish shipyard became a market competitor, *Harvard Business Review,* 53–72.

Johnson, S., and Loveman, G. (March–April 1995). Starting over: Poland after communism, *Harvard Business Review,* 44–56.

Kozminski, A. K. (1993). *Catching Up? Organizational and Management Change in the Ex-Socialist Block.* Albany, N.Y.: State University of New York Press.

———. (1995). Lessons from the restructuring of post-Communist enterprises. In *Communicating Organizational Change: A Management Perspective,* ed. D. Cushman and S. King. Albany, N.Y.: State University of New York Press, 311–328.

———. (1995a). From the Communist "nomenklatura" to transformational leadership: The role of management in the post-Communist enterprises. In *Social Change and Modernization: Lessons from Eastern Europe,* ed. B. Grancelli. Berlin, New York: Walter de Gruyter, 84–105.

———. (1996). Management education in Central and Eastern Europe. In *International Encyclopedia of Business and Management.* London: Routledge.

Lapin, A., Kuld, S., and Shekshnya, S. (1994). Otis—St. Petersburg—case study. St. Petersburg: International Management Institute.

Lavigne, M. (1995). *The Economics of Transition: From Socialist Economy to Market Economy.* New York: St. Martin's Press.

Lawrence, P. R., and Vlachoutsicos, C. A. (January–February 1993). Joint ventures Russia: put locals in charge, *Harvard Business Review*.

McDonald, K. R. (May–June 1993). Why privatization is not enough, *Harvard Business Review*, 49–59.

Perlez, J. (1994). GE finds tough going in Hungary, *The New York Times*.

Svejnar, J. (ed.) (1995). *The Czech Republic and Economic Transition in Eastern Europe*. San Diego: Academic Press.

Taylor, W. (March–April 1991). The logic of global business: An interview with ABB's Percy Barnevik, *Harvard Business Review*, 91–105.

U.S. General Accounting Office. (1995). *Poland: Economic Restructuring and Donor Assistance: Report to Congressional Committees*. Washington, D.C.: GAO/NSIAD-95-150.

Chapter 10: Lessons in How Recession Taught Organizations to Communicate

Cooper, C. (January 1, 1995). Death of the job, *Independent*.

Fraser, R. (1991). Total quality marketing: KPMG/CBI research. London: Kogan Page.

Gallup (September, 1993). Working lives. London: Gallup.

Heckscher, C. (1995). *Management Loyalties in an Age of Corporate Restructuring*. New York: Harper Collins.

Ingersoll Engineers (1993). Creating confidence: Communicating, planning and successful change. London: Ingersoll Engineers Ltd.

National Institute of Economic and Social Research (1995). Household survey. London.

People in Business (1991). Managing change in the 1990s. London: People in Business.

Personnel Today (December, 1994). Survey reported in *Personnel Today*.

The Price Waterhouse Cranfield Survey (1991). *Project Annual Report*. Cranfield: Cranfield Press.

Quirke, B. (1995). *Communicating Corporate Change*. London: McGraw Hill.

Survival of the fittest (1994). London: Institute of Management.

Walker, S. (1994). MORI (Marketing and Opinion Research Institute) database on employee communication. Presentation by Susan Walker. London: MORI.

Chapter 11: Lessons from Japanese Multinationals and Japan's Government

Automotive News (November 21, 1995), 6.

Bremner, B., and Brull, S. (January 22, 1996). At last—Sayanora to the blahs, *Business Week*, 54–55.

Bremner, B., Updike, E., Armstrong, L., and Treece, J. (April 10, 1995). What the strong yen is breeding: Japanese multinationals, *Business Week*, 118–199.

Brooke, L. (August 1994). Stamping the Neon, *Automotive Industry*, 37–38.

Dawkins, W. (November 30, 1995). Loosing of the corporate web, *Financial Times*, 13.

The Economist (October 29, 1994). The car makers' recovery stakes, 73–74.

———. (March 4, 1995). The kindergarten that will change the world, 63–64.

———. (September 23, 1995). Japan's economy, 58–59.

Glain, S., and Sapsford, J. (February 23, 1996). Japan's economic recovery is an empty shell, *The Wall Street Journal*, A9.

Healey, J. (June 24, 1994). Chrysler per car profits leave rivals in dust, *USA Today*, 6, 13.

Hulme, D. (July 1995). SONY responds for multimedia future, *Asian Business*, 6–7.

Johnson, R. (September 1995a). Turned off by Neon, *Automotive News*, 1.

————. (March 1995b). Toyota chief hospitalized for exhaustion, *Automotive News,* 5–8.

Lutz, R. (March–April 1994). Implementing technology change with cross functional teams, *Research Technology and Manufacturing,* 15–18.

McElroy, J. (February 1994). Man of the year: Chrysler's Robert Lutz, *Automotive Industry,* 62–66.

Maynard, M. (August 2, 1995). Chrysler draws on popular designs, *USA Today,* B1.

Ness, J., and Cucuzza, T. (July–August 1995). Tapping the full potential of ABC, *Harvard Business Review,* 130–138.

Okino, K. (February 1995). Toyota changes its famous production system, *Automotive Industry,* 44.

Pollack, D. (January 30, 1996). Beyond the Japanese orbit, *New York Times,* D1.

Reitman, V. (August 11, 1995). Toyota names a new chief likely to shake up global auto business, *The Wall Street Journal,* A1.

Sapsford, J. (February 13, 1994). Surge in pre-tax profits at Toyota shows streamlining has set stage for growth, *Wall Street Journal,* A1.

Simson, R., and Reitman, V. (May 12, 1995). Toyota says it may have to shut down plant in Japan: Layoffs are possible, *Wall Street Journal,* A5.

Spindle, W., Armstrong, L., and Treece, J. (April 4, 1994). Toyota retooled, *Business Week,* 54–57.

Taylor, A. (November 19, 1990). Why Toyota keeps getting better and better and better, *Fortune,* 66–79.

————. (January 20, 1993). How Toyota copes with hard times, *Fortune,* 78–81.

Templin, N., and Stern, G. (August 17, 1995). Weaker yen spells trouble for Detroit, *Wall Street Journal,* A2.

USA Today (August 10, 1995). Ford savings, A1.

Updike, E., Armstrong, L., Kerwin, K., Naughton, K., and Woodruff, D. (February 26, 1996). Japan turns a corner, *Business Week,* 108–112.

Updike, E., Bremner, B., Borrus, A., Woodruff, D., and Armstrong, L. (May 21, 1995). Japan's auto shock, *Business Week,* 44–47.

Wall Street Journal staff (January 17, 1995). Toyota Motors plans to more than double British plant's output, A5.

Womack, J. P., Jones, D. T., and Roos, D. (1990). *The Machine That Changed the World.* New York: Macmillan.

Chapter 12: Lessons in Marketing Strategies during Recession from High-Speed Management to Sun Tzu's *Art of War*

Alexander, R. S. (1965). *Marketing Definitions.* Chicago: American Marketing Association.

Marketing News (March 1, 1985). AMA board approves new marketing definition, 1.

Aukstakalnis, S., and Blatner, D. (1992). *Silicon Mirage.* Berkeley: Peachpit Press.

Clancy, K. J., and Shulman, R. S. (1991). *The Marketing Revolution: A Radical Manifesto for Dominating the Marketplace.* New York: Harper.

Cushman, D. P., and King, S. S. (1993). Visions of order: High-speed management in the private sector of the global marketplace. In *Organizational Communication and Management,* ed. A. Kozminski and D. P. Cushman. Albany: State University of New York Press.

Cushman, D. P. and King, S. S. (1995). *Communication and High-Speed Management.* Albany, N.Y.: State University of New York Press.

Donnelley Marketing. (1992) *Fourteenth Annual Survey of Promotional Practices.* Stamford, Conn.: Donnelley Marketing.

Dumaine, B. (February 22, 1993). The new non-manager managers, *Fortune,* 80–84.

Farquhar, P. H. (1990). Managing brand equity, *Journal of Advertising Research* 30/4.

Fitzgerald, J. (February 15, 1988) Integrated communications, 18.

Fraker, S. (February 13, 1984). High-speed management for the high tech age, *Fortune,* 34–60.

Gardner, M. P. and Shuman, P. J. (1987). Sponsorship: An important component of the promotions mix, *Journal of Advertising,* 16:11–17.

Griffith, S. B. (1963). *Sun Tzu: The Art of War.* London: Oxford University Press.

Ju, Y. A., and Cushman, D. P. (1993). Revolutionizing management and managing revolution: Toward a more refined theory of high-speed management, working paper, August.

Kendrick, J. (March 1992). Benchmarking survey builds case for looking to others for TQM models, *Quality,* 1.

Khoo, K. H. (1992). *Sun Tzu & Management.* Selangor Darul Ehsan, Malaysia: Pelanduk Publications.

King, S. S. and Cushman, D. P. (1994) *High-speed management and organizational communication: Cushman, King and Associates.* Paper presented at the Inter-University Center Conference on Organizational Communication, Sydney, January 10–12.

Kleiner, A. (January 16, 1989). The public relations coup, *Adweek's Marketing Week,* 20–23.

Kotler, P. (December 1993). Kotler on segmentation, *Marketing,* 24–26.

Levitt, T. (1962). *Innovation in Marketing.* New York: McGraw-Hill.

Martin, E. F., Jr., Cheng, Y. M., Wilson, G. B., and Tsui, Y. W. (June 1993). *Advertising Images among Hong Kong Chinese: A Preliminary Study of Individual Modernity and Western Orientation.* Paper presented at Asian Mass Communication Information Centre Conference on Communication, Technology, and Development: Alternatives for Asia, Kuala Lumpur.

Moore, H. F., and Canfield, B. R. (1977). *Public Relations: Principles, Cases, and Problems* (7th ed.). Homewood, Ill.: Richard D. Irwin.

Ohmae, K. (1985) *Triad Power: The Coming Shape of Global Competition.* New York: Free Press.

———. (Spring 1987). The triad world view, *The Journal of Business Strategy* pp. 8–19.

———. (1990). *The Borderless World.* New York: Harper.

Peters, T. and Waterman, R. H. (1982). *In Search of Excellence.* New York: Harper and Row.

Peterson, C. and Toop, A. (1994). *Sales Promotion in Postmodern Marketing.* Hampshire: Gower Publishing Limited.

Port, O., Cary, J., Kelley, K., and Forest, S. (November 30, 1992). Quality, *Business Week* 66–72.

Quelch, J. A., and Cannon-Bonventre, K. (November–December, 1993). Better marketing at the point-of-purchase, *Harvard Business Review,* 162–169.

Rapp, S., and Collins, T. (1990). *The Great Marketing Turnaround.* Englewood Cliffs: Prentice Hall.

Russell, E., Adams, A., and Boundy, B. (Winter 1986) High-technology test marketing Campbell Soup Company, *The Journal of Consumer Marketing* 3(1):71–80.

Sadler, A. L. (1944). *Three Military Classics of China.* Sydney: Australasian Medical Publishing Co.

Wong, S. Y., and Whiteley, A. M. (1991). Marketing management. In *Management Case Studies in Hong Kong,* ed. S. F. Y. Tang and A. M. Whiteley. Hong Kong: Longman Group (Far East) Ltd., 161–184.

Chapter 13: Lessons in Managing Government Competitiveness

Cullen, R. B. (1995). Public sector performance and private sector management. In *Communicating Organizational Change: A Management Perspective,* Cushman, D. and King, S. Albany: State University of New York Press, 147–159.

Ohmae, K. (1994). *The Borderless World: Power and Strategy in the Interlinked Economy.* London: HarperCollins, x–xi.

Osborne, D., and Gaebler, T. (1993). *Reinventing Government: How the Entrepreneurial Spirit Is Transforming the Public Sector.* Harmondsworth, Middlesex-England: Penguin Books, 331.

Peters, T. (1993). *Liberation Management: Necessary Disorganization for the Nanosecond Nineties.* London: Pan Books Ltd., 760.

World Economic Forum (1994). *The World Competitiveness Report 1994.* 14th ed. Geneva, Switzerland: The World Economic Forum.

Chapter 14: Lessons in Government Communication Strategies of Best Practices in Australia

The Allan Consulting Group (1994). *Successful Reform: A Review of the Implementation of Australia's National Training Reforms.* Report to the Australian National Training Authority, Melbourne.

Argyris, C., and Schon, D. (1978). *Organizational Learning: A Theory of Action Perspective.* Reading, Mass.: Addison Wesley.

The Australian Financial Review (June 8, 1989). The de unionisation of Australia, 14.

———. (March 1, 1995). Unions: Kelty's last stand.

Australian Manufacturing Council (1994). *Leading the Way: A Study of Best Manufacturing Practices in Australia and New Zealand.* Melbourne: AMC.

Australian Manufacturing Council and Pappas, Carter, Evans and Koop (1990). *The Global Challenge.* Melbourne: Australian Manufacturing Council.

Curtain, R. (1988) Skill formation in manufacturing: Obstacles and opportunities, *Human Resource Management Australia,* 26:7–21.

Curtain, R., Gough, R., and Rimmer, M. (1992). *Progress at the Workplace: Workplace Reform and Award Restructuring.* A report to the Department of Industrial Relations from the National Key Centre in Industrial Relations, AGPS, Canberra, ACT.

Deery, S. (1990). Productivity, organisational change and the management of employee relations, *Asia Pacific Human Resource Management,* 28:5–15.

Department of Industrial Relations (1993). *Interim Evaluation of the Australian Best Practice Demonstration Program.* Australian Government Printing Service, Canberra, ACT.

Drago, R., and Wooden, M. (1989). Trade Unions and workplace efficiency in Australia: Some preliminary results. Paper presented to AIRAANZ Conference.

Dunphy, D., and Stace, D. (1990). *Under New Management: Australian Organisations in Transition.* Sydney: McGraw Hill.

Ferguson, M. (1994). Enterprise bargaining as a means to workplace reform. In Proceedings from Best Practice: Achieving success, conference, Sydney, 37–41.

Hilmer, F. G. (1990). *Work in Competitive Enterprises: New Games, New Rules.* Angus and Robertson, Australia.

Industry Task Force on Leadership and Management Skills (1994). Economy depends on management skills, *Leadership Australia's Business Challenge,* 5.

Ivanoff, P., and Prentice, E. (1994). International best practice in management development: An Australian perspective. Paper presented at ASTD International Conference, California.

Johnston, R. (1993) Communication via competence: A communication perspective of training reform in Australia. Paper presented at International Conference of Centre for Workplace Communication, Sydney.

Lansbury, R. D., and Spillane, R. (1991). *Organisational Behaviour: The Australian Context.* Melbourne: Longmans Cheshire.

Limerick, D., and Cunnington, B. (1993). *Under New Management: A Blueprint for Networks and Strategic Alliances.* NSW, Australia: Business and Professional Publishing.

Marchington, M. (1992). *The Practice of Joint Consultation in Australia: A Preliminary Analysis of the AWIRS Data.* ACIRRT working paper 21, Sydney.

Senge, P. (1993). *The Fifth Discipline: The Art and Practice of the Learning Organisation.* Sydney: Random House.

Sloan, J. (1994). A memorable year: A review of Australian industrial relations in 1993, *Asia Pacific Journal of Human Resources,* 32/2.

Warburton, R. F. (1994). Meeting the challenge of international best practice. In *Proceedings from Best Practice Achieving Success Conference.* Sydney.

Webber, T. (1994). Organizational communication characteristics of enterprises seeking best practice. Unpublished master's project, University of Technology, Sydney, NSW.

Weick, K. E. (1979). Cognitive processes in organisations. In *Research in Organisation,* vol. 1, ed. B. Straw. JAI Press, 41–74.

Contributors

Ron Cullen is CEO of Performance Management Solutions, a consulting firm based in Melbourne, Australia. The consultancy specializes in evaluating and improving the performance of public-sector organizations and other organizations with complex service missions. Dr. Cullen served as the director of finance for Australian Telecommunications, head of a public service agency in Victoria, and head of the Higher Education Coordination Agency in Victoria. He holds a Ph.D. in organization theory from the University of Melbourne and has been involved as a consultant or manager in many public-sector change projects. He has published a number of articles on public administration and has led a number of government-sponsored reviews of programs and agencies. He is involved presently in authoring a book on public-sector management with Donald Cushman.

Donald P. Cushman is professor of communication at the State University of New York at Albany and holds a Ph.D. in communication from the University of Wisconsin. He has served as a consultant for government and private corporations in Australia, Bolivia, Canada, Germany, Great Britain, Japan, Korea, Mexico, and Yugoslavia. Cushman has written over 60 journal articles and 10 books. His latest book, coauthored with S. S. King, is *Communication and High-Speed Management* (State University of New York Press, 1995).

Artur Czynczyk is Human Relations director for ABB Europe and the former director of the Asea, Brown, and Boveri Management Development and Training Center in Warsaw, Poland. He is currently pursuing a Ph.D. from the University of Warsaw School of Management.

Randall Harrison, after graduating from the University of Wisconsin with a degree in economics, spent a decade as a professional communicator (wire services reporter, cartoonist, business magazine editor, TV newsman). He then returned to Michigan State

University where he earned a Ph.D. and became a full professor. He also taught at the University of California, Stanford, and the University of San Francisco. He is a former research psychologist and adjunct professor of communication at the University of California Medical Center in San Francisco. He still teaches two courses for the University of California Center for Media and Independent Learning (available on America Online). He is the author of six books, including *Beyond Words* (Prentice-Hall, 1974) and *The Cartoon: Communication to the Quick* (Sage, 1981). When not traveling, he and his wife, Betty, divide their time between San Francisco and Gold Run, California.

Robyn Johnston (M.A. Dip.ED.) is a lecturer in Adult Education at the University of Technology, Sydney, Australia. She is interested particularly in organizational communication and human resource development practice in Australian organizations at a time of significant microeconomic reform and organizational change. She has been involved actively with the Australian Institute of Training and Development and regularly serves as a consultant to Australian industry and organizations.

Sarah Sanderson King is professor of communication at Central Connecticut State University. She was chair of the Department of Communication at Central Connecticut State University, chair of the Division of Communication Arts at Marist College, and chair of the Department of Communication at the University of Hawaii. She has served as fellow or research associate at the University of Chicago, Ohio State University, Harvard University, and the East-West Center in Honolulu. She was a Fulbright Scholar to Yugoslavia and coedited with Donald Cushman *Political Communication: Engineering Visions of Order in the Socialist World* (State University of New York Press).

Andrzej K. Kozminski is professor of management and director of the International Post-Graduate Management Center at the University of Warsaw. He is also on a regular basis a visiting professor at the University of California-Los Angeles Anderson Graduate School of Management. He has written over 250 scholarly articles in six languages and several books, including his latest, *Catching Up: Organizational and Management Change in the Ex-Socialist Bloc* (State University of New York Press, 1993). He is an active consultant and serves as president of a private training company, the International Business School in Warsaw, Poland.

S. Robert Lichter is codirector of the Center for Media and Public Affairs and an adjunct professor of government at Georgetown

University. He previously taught political science at Princeton and George Washington Universities and holds a Ph.D. in government from Harvard. His latest book is *Good Intentions Make Bad News: Why Americans Hate Campaign Journalism* (Rowman and Littlefield, 1996).

Robert MacDougall is a graduate student at State University of New York-Albany, working toward a joint Ph.D. in Sociology and Philosophy. He has published articles in the rhetoric of science with Bronco Kovacic and Donald Cushman.

Ernest F. Martin, Jr., is head of the Department of Communication studies at Hong Kong Baptist University. He received his Ph.D. from the University of Missouri-Columbia in 1971. He previously held positions at Syracuse University, University of Kansas, and Iowa State University. Industry positions included vice-president/general manager of KDNL-TV (Preview), director of research with Cox Broadcasting, senior research project director with Frank Magid Associates, and director of research and marketing for KPLR-TV. Publications include *Professional Interviewing*.

Susanne Morris is deputy director at the Management Training and Development Institute in Washington, D.C. She manages and leads many of the institute's activities, including its research projects for public- and private-sector clients. She has taught public policy and directed the Master's Program in Public Policy and Administration at Michigan State University for a number of years. Prior to her work at Michigan State, she was a policy analyst for the legislatures of the states of Michigan and California. She has been a Foreign Service Officer with the U.S. Information Agency.

Krzysztof Obloj is associate professor of management, School of Management, University of Warsaw, and director of the MBA program at the International Business School, Warsaw. He has been conducting research in the fields of strategic and international management, and has lectured at universities in the United States, France, Israel, Norway, and Denmark. He was a visiting Fulbright professor in 1995 and 1996 at the University of Illinois-Champaign. He serves as consultant to Polish companies and foreign corporations investing in Poland. He is an author or coauthor of over 60 journal articles and four books. His latest book, *Winning* (State University of New York Press, 1994), was co-authored with Donald Cushman.

Bill Quirke has worked internationally over the last fourteen years on issues related to communication and the management of change. He trained with TBA Resource, Inc., in New York and worked with it across Europe and North America. He has worked with some of the organizations that have pioneered change programs—Apple Computers, British Airways—and with public-sector organizations introducing change—British Navy, Social Services, and Customs and Excise. He is the author of three books, including *Communicating Change* (McGraw Hill, 1995).

Giuseppe Raimondi is communication manager and vice-president at IPR-Immuno Pharmacology Research, an Italian firm specializing in high-tech diagnostic kits. He received his M.A. from the State University of New York-Albany in 1993. He received his undergraduate degree in contemporary history from the University of Catania, Italy, in 1989. He worked previously as a copywriter for a number of Italian advertising agencies.

Ted J. Smith III is an associate professor in mass communications at Virginia Commonwealth University. A specialist in media analysis and criticism, public opinion, and propaganda, and organizational decision making, he is the author or editor of five books, including *The Vanishing Economy: Television Coverage of Economic Affairs, 1982–1987*. He lives in Richmond, Virginia, with his wife, Rosemary.

Index